beyond belief · By Liam Fay

Liam Fay was born in 1965. He attended Saint Michael's Christian Brothers School, in Trim, County Meath, but was educated elsewhere. His series of *Hot Press* articles exploring the underbelly of religious devotion in Ireland won him an ESB National Media Award in 1996. Unlike all other authors, he does not divide his time between London and Cape Cod. His confirmation name is Oliver.

HOT
PRESS

books

First published in 1997 by Hot Press Books,
13 Trinity St., Dublin 2.

British Library Cataloguing in Publication Data
is available for this book.

ISBN No: 0 9524947 5 2

Design by Paula Nolan, Hot Press
Lead Photographer: Michael J. Quinn
Cover Photograph: Deirdre O'Callaghan
Cover Design: Niall McCormack

Printed by Colour Books,
Baldoyle Industrial Estate, Dublin 13.

Liam Fay

Acknowledgements

I have no intention of taking all the credit for this book. Others aided and abetted its creation and they too deserve to share in the afterglow of publication. Especially if there is any chance that this might entail an eternal char grilling amid the savage flames of Hell. If I go, they go.

All of the pieces that appear in this collection first reared their ugly heads in *Hot Press*. Since 1988, I have been proud to serve as *Hot Press* Theological Correspondent In Chief, a title more commonly abbreviated by my colleagues to Big Drunk Lad From Meath.

I am deeply indebted to editor Niall Stokes for the patient encouragement and latitude which he has shown me over the years. I am even more deeply indebted to Mairin Sheehy for signing the expenses cheques.

Photographer Michael J. Quinn (a.k.a. Mickey The Lens) accompanied me on most of the odysseys recounted herein. A fine companion and a magnificent snapper, Mick did the driving and plotted the course for our trips, always ensuring that, no matter where we were headed, we passed through Moyvalley *en route* so that we could stop for a hearty fried breakfast at Mother Hubbard's.

Much appreciation is also due to Cathal Dawson, Deirdre O'Callaghan and Brendan Duffy, valiant photographers whose excellent work further helps to prove that I haven't been making this whole thing up.

Jackie Hayden offered suggestions and advice as only he can. Pat Montague gave me the guided tour to Donegal. The assistance of Damian Corless in pinning down Jesus Of Coolock was indispensable, as was the emergency computer surgery repeatedly performed by Emmett O'Reilly. On innumerable occasions, meanwhile, Mette Borgstrom demonstrated that she is a woman of supernatural organisational skills. Maureen Buggy and Niamh O'Reilly also provided vital support behind the scenes.

In the *Hot Press* production department, I am grateful to all those who typeset, proofread, subbed, headlined, captioned and generally improved these pieces. I am particularly beholden to Paula Nolan for her design genius and labour beyond the call of duty, and to Niall McCormack for the cover design.

A special word of thanks goes to my spiritual advisors, Declan Lynch and Liam Mackey, for their honesty, inspired counsel and capacity to make me laugh until the tears run down my legs.

Finally, I would like to salute the tragically departed Bill Graham, whose approving chuckles were the most eloquent and flattering reviews an aspiring Theological Correspondent could ever have hoped for.

CONTENTS

To Anne.

With love and thanks for keeping the faith.

"We must respect the other fellow's religion, but only in
the sense and to the extent that we respect his theory
that his wife is beautiful and his children smart."

H.L. Mencken

"Eternal suffering awaits anyone who questions God's
infinite love. That's the message, right?"

Bill Hicks

INTRODUCTION

2,000 years ago, Jesus Christ came
down to Earth, to a region of the Ancient Middle East known as Palestine,
where He dwelt among us in the form of a man. In January, 1990, Jesus
Christ returned to Earth, this time to the Foxhill area of Coolock, on
Dublin's northside, where He dwelt among us in the form of a doorman.

In the beginning was the Word, and the Word was God. In Bethlehem,
the Word was made Flesh. In a curious parallel, in Coolock, the Word was
made Teak. The face of the Son of God materialised in a 5in. x 3in. pat-
terned ring on the top left hand corner of a bedroom door in a semi-
detached house.

To the untrained eye, the simulacrum could easily have been mistaken

1

for an unexceptional knot of the type routinely found on wooden artefacts such as planks, chairs, hurleys, crucifixes, even Thai bum beads.
Fortunately, the owners of the house, the Molloys, were people of vision
and faith, capable of seeing through outward superficialities to the unvar-
nished truth below.

It was the Molloys' young daughter who was the first to prise open this
intriguing door of perception. One morning while preparing for school,
she informed her parents that Our Lord was alive and well, and hanging
out in her bedroom door.

At first, Mrs. Molloy was somewhat dubious. A regular mass-goer, she
casually accepted that the body and blood of Jesus could be converted
into a disc of pitta bread and a mug of *vin ordinaire,* but, instinctively,
she drew the line at transubstantiation into a fixture and fitting. The very
idea seemed a bit silly.

Still, Mrs. Molloy was reluctant to dismiss her daughter's assertion. For
several days, she scrutinised the bedroom door. She closed it, unclosed it,
closed it again, and stared and stared and stared. On January 12th, the
countenance of Christ eventually became visible to her. Ten days later,
Our Lady herself turned up on the front of a built-in wardrobe in the
same room.

Reports about the appearance of Jesus of Coolock spread rapidly. The
news that God the Son had been joined in joinery by the Virgin Mary suggested that this was indeed a singular marvel, the ultimate Mother and
child reunion. The story made the front page of the *Evening Press.* Its significance was debated on the national airwaves.

The number of callers to the Molloy home soon became unmanage-
able. Restricted visiting hours had to be initiated in order to contain
demand. Over a few short weeks, more than 900 pilgrims presented
themselves at the household and asked to be shown the door.

I am proud to say that I was among that 900. For me, the encounter

with the Jamb of God was a watershed moment. It affected me profoundly and became the inspiration for the personal quest that unites the pieces
in this collection.

The experience helped me to realise that there is more to religion than
novenas, vigils, floggings, invasions, wars, executions, misogyny, homo-
phobia, rape, incest, slavery, extortion, paedophilia and Dana. It helped
me to realise that religion can be fun . . .

I was greeted on arrival by Mrs. Molloy, who led me upstairs in reverent silence. When we reached the landing, she stood aside and motioned
me in the appropriate direction with a wave of her outstretched arm. Out
of respect for the Messiah in the woodwork, the bedroom door He occupied was left open at all times, the obvious conclusion being that Jesus of
Coolock was very fond of ajar. The likeness of Christ appeared on both
sides of the door, just as, say, a wood-knot might. Mrs. Molloy related
how this inexplicable bilocation had been interpreted by some as a
reminder to humanity that the Almighty is eternally ubiquitous. It struck
me that a more literal reading would be that the Almighty is eternally two-
faced.

Inside the bedroom, a pair of middle-aged, alabaster-haired women
and a dapper, bearded gentleman huddled in murmured prayer. In a
moist whisper, Mrs. Molloy explained that she didn't like to leave the
Saviour alone in His room for very long and that she and a select few
neighbours were endeavouring to keep Him company whenever possible.

But the Saviour was never really alone in that room. Not with Holy
Mary, the Mother of God, serenely peering out from the built-in wardrobe
further along the wall.

To the unbeliever no more than a couple of long, naturally-occurring
lines running down the walnut veneer, the Virgin was, once you looked

hard enough, every bit as real as her son. Nobody had noticed Mary until January 22nd, when a guest pointed out her veiled figure to Mrs. Molloy. (One can easily imagine how the guest might have phrased such a discovery too: "That's Our Lord in the door, is it, Missus? Yeah, and there's the Virgin Mary herself in the wardrobe!")

On the bed in the centre of the room lay an A-4 sized writing pad, inscribed with the names of the witnessing faithful and their accounts of what they had seen, under a ruled column, subtly headed WHAT I HAVE SEEN. By far the most common entry read, "Our Lord and Our Lady." However, other sightings were also recorded, among them "Padre Pio," "God the Father" and "A woman carrying a child in her arms." Convincing proof, if such proof were needed, that everyone sees God in his or her uniquely individual and indeed singular way.

One of the two visiting matriarchs regaled me with her own particular spin on the phenomenon. It was, self-evidently, an anti-abortion statement. Directing my gaze to a small cashew nut shape within the image, she described how, "It's just as if Christ is holding a little foetus in His arms, as if He's protecting it." (The disembodied face which, to rational observers, wasn't even a face had suddenly sprouted arms, presumably from just below the ears it didn't have.)

The foetus/cashew nut silhouette was slightly less distinct on the other side of the door but Mrs. Molloy breathlessly interceded to gladden all present by assuring us it was becoming clearer with each passing day. "It must be a message," she added.

Try as you might, you cannot make stuff like this up. After agreeing to hail a couple of Marys and to glory some bes with the bedroom assembly, I took my leave of the Molloy home. I remember walking away from the Foxhill estate with a spring in my step, singing hymns not merely aloud but at the top of my voice. This was especially surprising given that I didn't know the words to any hymns.

What I did know was that, at long last, I had chanced upon my journalistic vocation. I was going to become a theological correspondent, specialising not only in celestial intervention through hard-grained furnishings but in all manner of quirks, knots and splotches in the interior decor of the religious life to be found in its abundance in contemporary Ireland.

My short sojourn *chez* Molloy had convinced me that patrolling the outer precincts of Pioustown was going to be the job of my dreams. It was a classic case of love at first apparition.

Fortunately, my editor at *Hot Press,* Niall Stokes, is an enlightened citizen, keenly aware that it is not so much God as His followers who move in mysterious ways. Stokes gave me the space, the time, the freedom, the encouragement and the motivation to travel around the country accomplishing my mission (what he actually said was, "Get out! And don't come back until you can deliver copy that doesn't read like it was written in the snow by a three-year-old with a stick," but it amounted to the same thing).

Sell 'em hope, ship 'em shit. This is the catchphrase of the American television infomercial industry. It is also the (usually) unspoken creed of hawkers of retail religion everywhere.

Too many people who write about religion make the error of taking the subject at its own valuation of itself. They treat it as though it were a science and not the minor branch of stage conjuring it really is. They obfuscate its meaninglessness with florid, impenetrable language, language that frequently includes terms such as *obfuscate.*

During my stint at the chaliceface, I have tried to concentrate on the devotees and the modern day visionaries who fall between the slats of doctrine and dogma, and on the uncharted twilight zone where the hope and the shit collide. I was originally going to call this book *When Hope And Shit Collide* but I think that may already be an Alice Taylor title.

Occasionally, over the years, my mind has wandered back to the Molloy family and to their bedroom door and the way it might look at you. I will certainly never forget the parting conversation I had with the bearded gent who had become one of Jesus of Coolock's daily companions.

With a monsoon of fervour brimming in his eyes, this remarkably earnest fellow told me about a longtime atheist of his acquaintance who had returned to the Christian fold as a direct result of his coming face to face with Christ, in the Molloys' bedroom door.

"It gave him something to latch on to," he declared.

• January, 1997.

PRIEST FOR A DAY

It was an under collar operation. The mission? To experience the true fate of our Fathers by impersonating a Catholic clergyman on the streets of Dublin.

Nobody can reasonably expect too many moments like this in the course of a single lifetime. Here I am, on a summer afternoon, standing on a footpath in Saint Stephen's Green, and Des Hanafin, *the* Des Hanafin, is paying me major respect. He's hanging on my every word. Nodding deferentially at whatever I say. Staring adoringly into my eyes. If I'm not careful, he may drop to his knees and beseech my blessing.

"Yes, Father, all we can do is our best," says Des, the discernible humility in his voice suggesting that, try as he might, he could never do quite as much as me.

"Oh now, Mr. Hanafin, you have done much, much more than anybody could justifiably expect of one man, certainly one lay man," I reassure him, unable to resist that little *lay man* dig. His face brightens and his puppy dog eyes brim with pride. The temptation to pat him on the head is immense.

"What order are you with yourself, Father," asks Des, not in an accusatory way. He really wants to get to know me. Perhaps we might eventually become friends.

I mutter some gibberish about my being part of an on-the-ground, ground level, groundwork, groundbreaking, outreach, community project. I then beg leave to impose on the great man. "I'm sure you're very busy, Mr. Hanafin, but would you ever pose for a photograph with me?" I plead. "For my scrapbook."

"Certainly, Father," he replies, tucking in his gigantic belly a yard or two. He's keen to look good in the scrapbook.

By this point, I must admit, I was babbling like a drunk at a student party. But, boy, I wished they could see me now, all my fellow men of the cloth, my boyz in the priesthood.

Here was Des Hanafin, the Grand Dragon of the Ku SPUC Klan, and he was falling over himself to demonstrate the high regard in which he held me. Sure, we are both on the same side but Des knows his place. I am an officer in God's army. He's merely a member of the civil defence.

"Thanks very much, Father," says Des, giving my arm an affectionate, little, united-we-stand squeeze before he trudges off into the heathen throng, his very being sanctified by our encounter. "God bless you, Father."

In many ways, preparation for spending a day as a priest has been going on all my life. Most of us are so subliminally familiar with this strange species in our midst that we can almost mimic their every gesture, act and intonation without thinking about it.

The difficult bit was getting my hands on the necessary threads. Most costume hire outlets are quite reluctant to rent out priests' uniforms on the grounds that they are too often used by fraudsters who operate scams to swindle money from the old, the sick and the vulnerable. These scams are strictly governed by copyright control. It is only *bona fide* priests who are lawfully permitted to operate them.

Eventually, with the assistance of a fancy dress store called Clown Around, I got the cloth that I was soon to become a man of. Cursed with a congenital inability to use a washing machine, I dress in black most days anyway so all I needed was a soutane and a collar. The instant I put these garments on, I underwent a dramatic and profound personality transformation.

I began steepling my fingers at every available opportunity. I sprouted a smirk so oily that I probably qualified for membership of OPEC. I started referring to every woman under the age of 55 as "my child." And, for reasons that I still don't understand, I involuntarily acquired a Kerry accent.

Psychologically and physically, I was ready, but I knew that some of the more subtle nuances cannot be so instinctively replicated. There is a certain aura which surrounds priests, that is to say, a *perfume.* I remember it from my childhood, which was the last time I was within regular sniffing distance of these guys, but it's hard to describe. A sort of combination of camphor, Sunlight soap, Brylcream, disinfectant and some special *eau de sky pilot,* the secret ingredients for which are obviously kept under lock and key in The Vatican. To find out exactly what it is, one has to receive the sacrament of Holy Odours.

Within an hour of getting all gussied up in my canonicals, however, I did develop that faint scent of sweat that is as synonymous with the priesthood as daily mass, Audi 80s and making inappropriate suggestions to altar boys.

It's no wonder the clergy are always giving out. They're sweating their nuts off underneath that rigout. By comparison to the discomfort of everyday clerical garb, Jesus Christ's infamously excruciating crown of thorns was a light fedora worn at a jaunty angle.

You might think that it takes a certain amount of bottle to spend an entire day walking around Dublin in the guise of a priest, and you'd be right. The specific bottle I chose held a litre of Cork Dry Gin.

Most of the time, nobody pays a strolling priest a second glance. Not even, as I was to discover, if he's strolling around the shopfloor of a

Knickerbox lingerie store, taking an inordinately close interest in the merchandise. If he's swilling from a large flagon of hooch, however, he's suddenly a traffic stopper.

On Grafton Street, a German tourist asked if he could photograph me. An Irish bloke requested a blessing and, more enthusiastically, a swig. In Saint Stephen's Green, a party of Americans camcordered me but they took the precaution of staying a safe distance away, just in case. Imagine their delight though; here was a mad Irish priest guzzling gin in the open air *before noon* – and they had the evidence. The video will probably end up on *60 Minutes* as part of a report on the evils of racial stereotyping.

Outside White Friar's Street church, the reception was more frosty. Two old ladies walked by. When they saw me with bottle in hand, well, in mouth actually, they both made the sign of the cross with a fervour which suggested that they had just seen Beelzebub himself. An elderly man stood for a moment and gave me a pitying look that had no pity in it whatsoever. "Can't a man even have a drink in peace," I protested, and shuffled off.

I was beginning to get more than a little disheartened. It was well into the day and I'd still seen no sign of the perk that was supposed to come with this job, *to wit:* the babes.

Like most priests, the only celibacy I know is the one who sang the theme song from *Goldfinger*. Apologists for the Catholic Church have long fostered the notion that there are droves of women out there who are hell-bent on seducing us clergymen and luring us away from our sacred vows of chastity. I was dying to meet one of these collar groupies. A sexy siren who fancied a nice piece of surplice. A fox who could ring my chasuble. A bit of a church *goer,* if you catch my drift.

But, alas and alack, it was not to be. The nearest I came to a carnal riot was when a decrepit neighbour showed me her legs. She'd been badly bitten by a dog and she wanted me to pray that the wound would heal quickly.

At one point, while photographer Cathal Dawson was taking snaps of me on O'Connell Street, he was approached by a middle-aged Dublin woman. "Oh, is that Father Buckley?" she asked him. "I've seen him on the television."

Keen to exploit the situation, Dawson confirmed that, yes, I was indeed Fr. Pat Buckley, the rebel priest now based in Larne. In order to find out if this made me a demon or an angel in the woman's eyes, he tested the water. "He's a bit strange, isn't he, this Father Buckley?" said Dawson tentatively.

"Ah yeah," countered the woman, "but he's from up the North you know."

It was time for a spot of shopping. I glided into the Hayes, Conyngham & Robinson pharmacy on Grafton Street with a suitably portentous rustle of my skirts to herald my arrival.

"Can I help you, Father?" asked the young blonde lady behind the counter.

"I hope so, my child," I replied, clasping my hands demurely on the cupola of my stomach in a gesture of butter-wouldn't-melt-in-my-briefs piety I had learned from watching Bishop Eamon Casey on television. "I'm looking for some condoms."

The look on the woman's face was a picture-dictionary definition of the term *Gobsmacked*. She immediately began to back away from me but her sense of professionalism, and the fact that there is not really that much backing away space behind a HCR counter, forced her to stop.

"Here you are, Faa . . . , here you are," she stuttered, indicating with a limp hand the pyramid display of johnnies to her left.

I was enjoying this. Too often, the staff in some of these snooty city centre chemists seem to get a kick out of intimidating their more timid customers, and not only when it comes to purchasing willy wear.

"Now, tell me, my child, what's the difference between ribbed and fetherlites," I enquired contemplatively, like a man well used to wrestling with the complexities of moral choice.

"Eh, eh, maximum sensitivity," answered the assistant in a barely audible croak. As she uttered these words, her face contorted in a fleeting grimace of distaste as though she had just used one of the most disgusting word formulations possible in the English language, like *suppurating scrofula sores,* say, or *Progressive Democrats.*

11

With a decisive smack of my palms, I gleefully announced that I'd chance the fetherlites because "I like the picture of the lassie on the box." Despite the half dozen coats of make-up on her face, it was clear that the chemistatrix was blushing.

While ringing the purchase into the cash register, however, she underwent yet another visible mood change. Her lower lip started quivering furiously and she erupted into a hacking, barking fit of coughs. She was obviously trying her best to stifle a laugh. "Ho, ho, ho," I chuckled along, the way priests often do.

But then, that's the power of the clergy for you. In the scant three minutes it had taken to complete the simple transaction, my request to buy a packet of sheaths had sent this woman on an emotional rollercoaster ride, from shock to fear to disgust to embarrassment and, then, amusement.

As I took my leave of HCR, she experienced yet another rush of feeling, this time, cockiness born of sudden, dizzy relief.

"Bye now, Father," she chirruped, rippling her fingers in a little pantomime wave. "I hope they're the right size."

Throughout the day, people kept asking me to bless them. It got to the point where I thought *they* were taking the piss.

It seems that if a priest so much as winks at some people, they'll touch him for a rub of his relic, so to speak. There was the small, squat, head-scarfed woman outside Trinity College, the young guy selling *The Big Issues* on O'Connell Street, the cider-head with the eye-patch in the Green, and up to a half dozen others. Being an amicable kind of padre, I obliged every time.

The bit of arm waving was always going to be easy enough. It was summoning up some convincing verbiage that I expected to cause the problems. Curiously though, whenever I was called upon to bestow a benediction, the term *Dominus Vobiscum* spontaneously leapt to my lips.

As I probably should have predicted, the fact that I haven't a bull's notion what comes after *Dominus Vobiscum* didn't seem to matter to those I was blessing. I just gibbered and they gratefully bowed their heads in silent worship.

By lethargic late afternoon, when my *Dominus Vobiscum* began to dissolve into a half-hearted *Dominuzzzz Vobizzzz*, the proprietors of the bowed heads still didn't look askance. I threw in the term *Domino's Pizza* a few times and nobody even noticed.

One of the most disconcerting phenomena I had to get used to during my day as a priest was the ludicrously obsequious politeness shown me by shopkeepers, particularly male shopkeepers.

"Oh thank you very much indeed," burbled one grinning old geezer, his face aglow with an expression of appreciation and admiration. It was as if I'd given him the orgasm of his life *and* next week's winning Lotto numbers, not just the 22 pence to which he is legally entitled for a packet of Wrigley's Extra Sugarfree Gum.

The guys selling newspapers on the streets were even worse. Most days, these *Evening Heggald* vendors frighten the blue bejaysus out of me. On those rare occasions when I summon up the courage to meekly approach one of them and ask if I could trouble him to allow me to purchase a newspaper, the response is usually a scowl and a look in the eyes which suggests that a gob of spit is imminent. Today, however, I was a V.I.P.

"The blessings of God on you, Father," beamed a pavement newsagent who I pass almost every afternoon of the week, an individual who normally exudes all the warmth of the galvanised kiosk in which he plys his trade. "The country would be lost without the priests." And this after I had bought a copy of *H & E* magazine.

At about 4.30, I popped into a little sweetshop on Dame Street for a cold soft drink. Having pondered for a moment whether it was Cidona or Sprite that was the more in keeping with the tenor of the current pontificate, I eventually settled for the traditionalist purity of a bottle of Ballygowan. I paid the young man at the cash desk. He handed me my change and smiled. "It's a thirsty old day, Father," he chirped with a kindly nod.

Steadily holding his gaze, I framed my features into a bouquet of gentleness and affection, and said, "Go fuck yourself!"

Around 9pm, I decided it was time to serve the Lord in a more clois-
tered, more meditative environment, namely the snug of my favourite
licensed premises.

I was tired and footsore. The collar was strangling me so ferociously
that I had developed the crimson, gouty complexion of a bishop. I had
muttered D*ominuzzzz Vobizzzz* so often that the words had started to
lose all meaning.

After my third pint, it dawned on me that, at any stage during the day,
I could have swept into a church of my choosing, plonked myself inside a
confessional booth and complete strangers would've come in and told me
in intimate detail about their every sinful notion and deed. I thought
about this for a moment – and then shuddered at the thought.

Another realisation occurred. I had wasted an opportunity to fulfil a
lifelong ambition. Had I tried hard enough, I could've travelled out to
Howth and celebrated mass in Gaybo's local house of prayer. Then, when
the man himself arrived at the rails for communion, I would have gotten
to proclaim the immortal words, "Here is your host, Gay Byrne!" Perhaps,
next time.

Did I take pleasure from my day as a priest? Yes. Getting to swan
around town in a dress was a liberating and uplifting experience. The
respect and deference I was paid by everyone from drunks to cops to Des
Hanafin was almost exhilarating. I also enjoyed the gin enormously.

Still, when midnight came, it was with considerable relief that I abandoned the Church. I defrocked myself with a raucous yelp and flung my
vestments across the room.

I was now, officially, a spoiled priest, and was determined to act like
one.

THE HEAVY METAL PRIEST

Meet the hard rockin' Tridentine cleric who keeps holy
the Black Sabbath day.

"I am the Jim Morrison of the Catholic Church," boasted Fran Heaton the first time I met him.

We were in his dressing room in O'Shea's Hotel, Bray, moments before he was due onstage. Wearing a leather jacket, black strides so skintight you could see the contours of his veins, gleaming white cowboy boots, a sequin-speckled neck-halter and a rash of silver studs, he was kneeling before a full-length mirror, a microphone stand held aloft above his head. He wasn't posing, aerobicising or bull-working his biceps. He was praying.

"Dear God," he implored, eyes trained Heavenward. "I ask that You watch over our gig tonight, and grant us the grace to do our jobs well. Thank You for the little bit of talent that You've given me and help me to use it wisely. May those who hear us come closer to You through enjoyment of our music. I ask this through Christ our Lord. Amen."

His spiritual communion completed, Fran leapt to his feet. A motion

15

study in energy and turbulence, he tossed the mike stand in the air like it was a majorette's baton.

"Other musicians do a sound-check before a show," he said with what could only be described a Devilish grin. "I do a God-check! Tonight, we're going to use rock to crucify Satan, not Jesus."

It was the summer of 1991. Fran Heaton was slaying audiences in the spirit and in the aisles with a metal covers combo called White Rose. Fran's act was essentially a tribute to his two great heroes, Ozzy Osbourne and Jesus Christ.

As well as being a hard rockin' mutha, Fran Heaton is a Tridentine Catholic priest.

Bray, you don't need me to tell you, is not exactly Los Angeles. On the night of a White Rose gig, however, the seafront could easily have been mistaken for Sunset Strip itself. It was like a leather, denim and hair festival had come to town.

The word had spread that White Rose were an outfit who knew how to kick ass, and that's exactly the kind of skilled labour that's conspicuously lacking in a place like Bray.

Inside O'Shea's ballroom, there was a family-outing feel to the proceedings. Kids, mammies and daddies, even grannies, mingled freely with the hardened, not to say congealed, metal-heads. "Father Fran is great," I overhead one old lady opine. "He's a lovely man. He reminds me of Saint Francis of Assisi."

Back in those days, a White Rose audience was a broad church. It had its own ritual and etiquette. The older folk sat at the back where the noise was only a dull rumble. Those with younger ears clotted together near the stagefront, the vapour rising from their hunched backs supplanting the need for a house smoke machine. The children flitted between both groups, unsure where the real fun was.

At full pelt, the show was loud enough to raise your cranial lid. White Rose were highly proficient manufacturers of the full metal racket. Songs by Whitesnake, Free, Van Halen, Dave Lee Roth, Poison and others were conscientiously facsimiled; every nut, bolt and rivet in place. But the indisputable star was Fr. Fran.

He's a big man, with a prizefighter's chest, built to the same structural plans as Meatloaf or the central bank. Yet I could see that he was a rocker from his toes to his nose. He bounded around the stage with remarkable agility, his arms windmilling furiously, his bubble-butt waddling only inches above the deck.

Throwing back his bottle-blonde mane, Fr. Fran neighed like a stallion, and rotated his groin in a manner which suggested that that is not where the resemblance ends.

The bulge in Fr. Fran's crotch was indeed impressive and the focus of many eyes among the O'Shea's faithful. Dave Lee Roth had only recently admitted that his famous groin protuberance was, in reality, a plastic falsie. I assumed, however, that a man of the cloth would not seek to deceive his public in such a devious fashion.

Fr. Fran is a master of every trick in the bible of HM fantasy. From the vampirish make-up to the werewolf grimace, he's got the full repertoire of strut and stomp, scowl and howl. "I learned everything I know from Ozzy Osbourne," he told me later.

Never mind that, in 1991, Ozzy was already a walking sandwich-board for the geriatric nursing service. To Fr. Fran, he was God, or, at least, a god. "Ozzy is *it*," he enthused. "I actually met him in person a few years ago. I went backstage after his '86 show in the SFX and I found him to be a warm-hearted creature. He's just an ordinary guy getting up there to sing rock songs. There's nothing at all Satanic about him."

There was more to Fr. Fran's performance than mere mimicry. The instant he vaulted from the wings, you knew that this was no ordinary hairy, horny metal Devil. "Hello Bray," he roared as the band sliced into Osbourne's 'Shot In The Dark'. "I love you people. God bless you all."

Fr. Fran kissed the foot of his mother-of-pearl crucifix after he finished each song. Throughout the gig, he never missed an opportunity to invoke the blessings of The Almighty, Christ, the Holy Ghost, the Virgin Mary *et al* on his monster mosh.

Almost every Metal standard covered was invested with a unique Christian slant. This often necessitated a complete inversion of the original lyrics. For example, the White Rose version of the Free classic went: *"All right now/Jesus, it's all right now."*

Their interpretation of Dave Lee Roth's interpretation of The Kinks' 'You Really Got Me' featured the couplets: *"God, you really got me goin'/You got me so I* do *know what I'm doin'/God, you really got me now/You got me so I* can *sleep at night."*

During the chorus of Brian Adams' 'Somebody Like You', Fr. Fran repeatedly pointed to the ceiling suggesting, I believe, that the 'somebody' in question was, in fact, Our Heavenly Father.

The highlight of the show for me came when the band did Poison's 'Every Rose Has Its Thorn'. As the number reached its cigarette-lighter-in-the-air climax, Fr. Fran produced a bunch of white roses from a plastic shopping bag, and started distributing them from the stage.

"That's a little present for the lassies," he announced sombrely. "Now, I have some advice for the laddies. I hope that all you laddies show proper respect to your lassies. The lassies can be weaker than the laddies. They're stronger in other ways but you have to show proper respect for each other. God bless you all.

"But enough of that, we're at a concert, not in a church. Let us rock! Yeurgggggggh!"

✚ ✚ ✚ ✚ ✚ ✚ ✚

In Church terms, Fr. Fran Heaton has always been a marginalised man, a fringe figure on the fringes of the tiniest fringe groups.

Born in Newry, Co. Down, in 1949, Francis Gerard Heaton was one of three children procreated by William and Philomena Heaton. William, a Protestant from Warrenpoint, converted to Roman Catholicism in order to marry Philomena. When Fran was four, the entire family moved to Dublin.

He describes his upbringing as "staunchly Catholic but not bigoted." After he left school, he drifted from one McJob to another, variously punching the clock as a truck driver, a sales rep, a cash and carry shelf-stacker, a labourer with a light engineering firm, and even a military policeman in Cathal Brugha barracks.

Throughout the '70s, he grew disillusioned with post-Vatican II Catholicism. He particularly lamented the loss of the Latin mass, with its pomp, circumstance and "Heavenly music."

Gradually, Fran found himself increasingly drawn to the arch-traditionalist stance adopted by the French schismatic, Archbishop Marcel Lefebvre. Around 1979, he became friendly with an Irish priest from a similar-but-different breakaway fold of Tridentine clerics, The Order Of The Mother Of God (a fold so small that it's best categorised as a crease), whose founder was the South Vietnamese archbishop, Peter Martin Kno Din Tuk.

In early 1980, at the venerable old age of 31, Fran began the five year initiation procedure of Holy Orders. In keeping with the traditionalist ethos of his community, his induction followed the old-fashioned, pre-Vatican II route, advancing through the minor orders of Porter, Lector, Exorcist and Acolyte, and subsequently the major orders of Subdeacon, Deacon and Priest (these 'steps to the priesthood' were revised by the Holy See in 1971 and are now deemed canonically unlawful).

"It wasn't a bolt-out-of-the-sky vocation," Fran insisted. "It was more a practical thing. I wanted to help the poor in the inner city areas and elsewhere, and I loved the Latin mass. I felt I could operate without treading on the toes of mainstream Catholics."

On March 19th, 1985, the feast of Saint Joseph, Fran was one of four men ordained by The Order Of The Mother Of God in an oratory in Birr, County Offaly. Among those officiating at the ceremony was Most Reverend Bishop Michael Cox, a distinguished prelate of whom more can be read elsewhere in these pages.

"The ordination is valid but unlawful as far as Rome is concerned," argued Fr. Fran. "Under the supernatural law, it is valid. The Vatican would say I don't represent the Catholic Church, I don't belong to them. By joining the confraternity of the Mother Of God, I automatically incurred suspension *ad venus* from Rome – that's Latin for 'You're suspended'. In other words, I'm not in their union. The Church classes me as a Yellow Pack priest.

"I'm an outsider, a rebel. But I've never become so estranged from the Church that I wanted to leave. In fact, I'd be very close to the current Pope on most issues, except the Tridentine mass. I am very inclined towards John Paul and I have made representation to Rome about a possible reconciliation."

For all intents and most purposes, however, Fran was living the life of a conventional priest. He dressed like a priest (when not performing), he was celibate, he recited his daily office and regularly visited people in hospital and prisons as an unofficial chaplain.

In his dressing room after the show in O'Shea's, Fr. Fran and I chatted for a couple of hours, primarily about music. He had a huge record collection, which included comprehensive sets of albums by Black Sabbath, Deep Purple, Thin Lizzy, Van Halen and Aerosmith. He was also an avid collector of *Kerrang* and *Metal Hammer*, those precious gospels of the Good News.

Clearly, he saw no contradiction in being a Heavy Metal frontman and a priest, a priest who espouses extremely traditionalist values at that.

"Lots of priests sing rock'n'roll but they probably wouldn't be as energetic as me," he grinned. "Other singing priests would wear tweed trousers and white shirts but I don't see much difference between that and black leather and studs. There's nothing wrong with Heavy Metal as long as it's not sexually abusive to women or a glorification of Satanism. All that stuff is just silly.

"Some priests have attacked me but I've really gotten very little flak from the Catholic Church. Most priests disapprove publicly but then mutter under their breath, 'Go for it and enjoy yourself, it's only rock 'n' roll'. Not in so many words of course, but similar words."

The Jim Morrison of the Catholic Church resolutely rejected the suggestion that sex and drugs are an integral part of rock 'n' roll. "Certainly not with me," he claimed. "I don't drink. The only drug I take is an odd Woodbine. I'm celibate. People like Jim Morrison were about more than just sex and drugs. A lot of the things he said make a lot of sense, especially about war and individuality. The same goes with Ozzy. 'War Pigs' is a very Christian, anti-violence song. Obviously, I don't identify with everything about Ozzy and Jim.

"I love the world and other people. I have lots of girlfriends, women who I can talk to, but without the sexual aspect. I adore women. They're probably my greatest influence and inspiration."

Did White Rose attract groupies, I wondered?

"Very rarely," Fr. Fran maintained. "Lots of girls come up to me when the gig is finished and we shake hands or hug. Then, I say, 'Goodbye, I hope you enjoyed the show'. That's it. There's no question of sleeping with any woman or anything like that. The other guys in the band are very stable too. They're a great bunch of lads. Very decent, good Christians and great rockers. We can cope with it."

Five years later, in May of 1996, I tracked down Fr. Fran again. From the minute we renewed our acquaintance, it was obvious that he still adopted a refreshingly relaxed attitude to matters of title and ecclesiastical officialdom.

Our initial contact was on the telephone. I enquired if he was still a priest. "Not as much as I used to be," he declared.

We agreed to hook up in Dublin's Ormond Multi-Media Centre, where Fr. Fran was rehearsing with his latest band, Riff Raff. White Rose never did make the big time the way Fran had hoped they would. Fortunately, the verb *to quit* has no place in the Heaton creed. Repeatedly during the previous half decade, he had picked himself up, dusted himself down and tried again.

He fronted two bands in particular, Time Machine and Archangel, for whom he had also expected great things. Both acts enjoyed reasonable popularity, especially in biker circles, but personality disputes and *les différences musicale* eventually forced Fran to withdraw his services.

Fr. Fran Heaton speaks a great deal about the infernal fires of Hell. The instant I entered the Ormond Centre, I knew exactly what he was talking about. On a sweltering summer afternoon, the stygian murk of a rehearsal booth in the bowels of this cavernous building is about as close as anyone should hope to get to the flames of Hades. Inhale deeply and you could breathe the foul stench of the damned, or perhaps it was just the ripe odour of commingling sweat, socks and cigarettes.

A monument of black leather, PVC, chunky chains and silver studs, plinthed by an enormous pair of bulky biker boots, Fr. Fran had certainly not softened his image since we had last come face to face.

As I slipped in unobtrusively, his head was bowed reverently in a

21

moment of silent prayer. His three new concelebrants – guitarist Frank Isaacs, bassist Darren Clarke, and drummer Dec Clark – were exuding an air of solemn anticipation, clearly preparing themselves to celebrate the sacred mysteries by calling to mind their sins.

Fran blessed himself with a twitch of his leather-cuffed wrist, like he was sprinkling salt over a dinner plate, and then raised his voice to the Lord in that much-loved responsorial psalm, 'War Pigs' by Black Sabbath.

Fr. Fran's hair was a lot longer, and a crustier shade of grey-speckled blonde than in his White Rose days. On civvy street, it's a mane which can look like a cock of musty, mildewed hay that's been left too long in the shade of a damp barn. Come showtime, however, he always ensures that it's transformed into a golden halo of silken splendour. "Thank God for the gift of mousse," said Fr. Fran with a smoke-frayed chortle.

A fundamentalist in doctrinal matters, Fran's musical convictions also tend towards the orthodox. He is a great believer in the time-honoured values of classic rock. While still a devout apostle of Ozzy Osbourne, Fran had developed a more daring vocal style in recent years. He didn't simply "do Ozzy" anymore. He endeavoured to emulate Whitesnake's David Coverdale and Deep Purple-era Ian Gillan as well.

"I'm not Ozzy Osbourne," asserted Fr. Fran candidly, "but I admire the guy. Ian Gillan may be a better singer but, as a mass communicator with a sense of humour, there's nobody who can come near Ozzy Osbourne. As a singer though, I've been trying to grow and get more adventurous.

"I was singing in The Sportsman's Inn in Timolin one night, and didn't I let a scream out of me. It was incredible. I really enjoyed the scream and I held it. Gillan's record for holding that note was 15 seconds, I held it for about nine. I went home and dug out the *Deep Purple In Rock* LP – a great record, Ian Gillan at his best. I started listening to it every day, and I practised and practised to be able to sustain the scream.

"I love Whitesnake. David Coverdale is a major role model of mine. I have various influences: Iron Maiden, Van Halen, Aerosmith and very much Phil Lynott of Thin Lizzy, God rest him. What I'm interested in singing is not Heavy Metal stuff like Metallica, it's more the melodic rock, a combination of Gillan and Coverdale."

Fran Heaton had turned 47 a month earlier. The process of pushing forward his musical frontiers had been complemented by an expansion of his physical borders. His chin appeared to have been playing doubles or quits, and losing heavily. His bare upper arms undulated with more wobble and bounce than a *Baywatch* rescue scene. Winch him down into a field and he could *be* Castle Donnington.

However, the Heaton holler was still a sonic marvel guaranteed to leave one awe, dumb and thunder struck. A deep sandpaper growl that makes Napalm Death's frontman sound like an alarmed castrato one minute, a laser-guided missile hitting notes of armpit-igniting altitude the next.

For Fran, expertise in the art of precision roaring and shouting is not only a valuable musical asset, it is also a spiritual laxative, an outward sign of inward Christian grace. Call it the sacrament of Extreme Ructions.

"I cry a lot," admitted Fr. Fran, as the parching heat of the rehearsal room beaded on his forehead. "When I think about the various troubles in the world, I can get very upset. Something like the Hizbollah, they depress me wholly. There's nothing else to do but sit down and cry. But I find that screaming can be a great release. It's very good for you, very therapeutic.

"I often practise my scales while I'm in the car. I have a little 1985 Peugeot 104 with a tape deck and I just scream along with Gillan when I'm driving. It releases adrenaline and can be very relaxing. In itself, it's a sort of religious experience. After a good scream, I get out of the car and I feel cleansed, a new man."

A tireless money-maker for charity, Fr. Fran is a regular sight in shopping centres all over Dublin, flogging bingo cards and shaking a collection bucket for cancer research, asthma relief, The Irish Wheelchair Association, the ISPCC, you name it.

Nevertheless, Fran has made no secret of the fact that keeping his own body and soul together has been a constant and immense struggle.

As a freelance priest who receives no income from any order or community, Fran survives on social welfare and has been driven into cabaret just to keep himself in food, clothes and copies of *Kerrang* and *Metal*

Hammer.

"I often go to a venue where a band I know is playing and get up and plod out a few songs of a commercial nature," he affirmed. "Every Sunday night, in a venue called Catherine's in Kildare, I get up with the band and sing 'Achy Breaky Heart', 'Living Next Door To Alice', Joe Dolan's 'Sweet Little Rock 'n' Roller', stuff by Queen and The Bee Gees, that kind of thing. It's not the sort of material that Ozzy would approve of but I have a pop side too. It's not a big money thing, just a few bob, and I enjoy it."

In the autumn of 1995, Fr. Fran's life was routed by tragedy. His mother, Philomena ("We called her Phyllis like Phil Lynott's mum"), suffered a massive heart attack and died.

"We were extremely close in the spiritual sense as well as in the motherly sense," mourned Fran. "We were the best of mates, the best of friends. I have accepted her death now but, oh God, I spent many, many lonely times. I have great friends though. But the true friend I have is the poor divil on the cross. I love that man *so* much. The Rosary saved me, even though I thought it wasn't going to help me at the time. I'm a great believer in the Rosary."

Devotion to the blessed beads was now central to the *modus operandi* of Fran's rock 'n' roll career. "I pray for my enemies," he averred. "I don't think I have any enemies but I pray for any I might have. As a musician, I've been ripped off in the past. Those that ripped me off, I love them moreso and good luck to them, but I don't think it will happen again. I hold no bitterness against band managers. I just pray for them.

"I like to see everybody succeeding, be it Daniel O'Donnell, Joe Dolan, The Corrs. Anything that's Irish I love to see succeed. I pray for them all, all the Irish acts coming up and the established acts. I pray for Boyzone and The Cranberries. Van Morrison, I pray for him every night. If it's within my power to help them along, I do. Part of my Rosary is always set aside for my brothers and sisters in the music business."

I asked Fran if he recited the Rosary daily?

"No," he replied, "mainly in the evening."

Leading Riff Raff through their paces in the Ormond Centre, Fr. Fran radiated a palpable sense of confident excitement. At last, he believed, he had found a band with the instrumental bite to match his astonishing bark. His self-assurance had been further boosted by his recent starring role in a feature film. "I'm back with a vengeance, please God," he proclaimed.

The motion picture is entitled *On The Front Line With The G-Force,* a small-budget, independently-financed movie set in contemporary Dublin in which Fr. Fran plays the elusive villain, renegade cop Hawk Miller. The project was written and produced by journalist and film-maker Tom Prenderville whose past screen credits included a rockumentary about The Oakridge Boys, a slew of rock videos and a full-length feature for the American network, HBO, called *The Insurance Man.*

"The plot of *The G-Force* concerns four existential policemen," explained Tom Prenderville. "They lose their jobs with a top secret police unit through incompetence. They enter into a permanent state of denial, convinced it's only a hitch, and refuse to vacate headquarters, give back their patrol cars or hand back their guns. They become squatters in their own police unit.

"They're out to nail the biggest villain in the country, Hawk Miller. The problem is that, if they catch this guy, the scandal could destroy them. If somebody else catches him, the scandal could be worse because the guy they're looking for was once a member of their unit. He knows where the bodies are buried.

"The film contains a strong satirical element. It says a lot about the lawless and disorder mob who are so much on the rise in this country. If people go and see it, they'll either hate it or love it. We're not going to write the posters until we've done our test screenings. If people laugh at it, it's a comedy. If they don't, it's a thriller."

Fr. Fran first met Cecil B. DePrenderville in 1994, at a Battle of the Bands competition in the Arthur Conan Doyle pub, in Phibsboro. "I was singing with Archangel and we won that night," recalled the cleric, punching the air in commemoration of the victory. "My stage persona really impressed Tom. My first reaction when he told me about the film was, 'Me, an actor? No way!'. But I discovered that I had a little bit of talent for acting. I had to develop a Kerry accent for the part which was difficult. I play a baddie but with a gentle nature – a loveable hooligan, a bit like myself."

Everyone involved in the shoot was brimful of praise for Fr. Fran's performance. "Fran is an outrageous man, in a good sense," maintained Prenderville. "He did a fine job, and will definitely be back in the follow-up, which I think will be even better. He doesn't have to act. He was wondering what way he should play the part, I said, 'The best thing you can do is play yourself'. If Father Fran plays himself forever, I don't think he'll ever be short of work."

The cherry on the cake for Fran was that Riff Raff recorded the theme song for *On The Front Line With G-Force*. The number was written by axeman Frank Isaac, an old friend of Fran's and a musical journeyman of some repute who has played with such luminaries as Orphanage (Thin Lizzy in chrysalis) and The Spyder Simpson Band.

"Riff Raff is about the best thing that's ever come my way," chirped Fr. Fran. "Even though we do a lot of covers, original material is our top priority. Frank is Ireland's Stevie Vai and a prolific songwriter. I've written the lyrics for about ten to 15 songs which I hope to get down with Riff Raff. I have the ideas and, please God, Frank will write the music.

"One song relates back to Germany during the war, and is about Jews travelling on a train through a concentration camp – it's called 'Never Let It Happen Again'. It's more of an album track, a serious album track. I have a song about the life and times of John Dillinger, 'The Ballad Of Johnny D'. There are other slow songs of a Bon Jovi nature related to peace, and one particular song where I have a go at the fat cats in Rome, the extravagance of the bigwigs in the Vatican.

"With Riff Raff, I hope to give the music business my full whack. As soon as we get a record contract, we'll be flying. On the back of the film, and the songs, we're seriously looking at America, and maybe the Eastern bloc."

Fr. Fran no longer yearns, as once he did, to be recognised by popular Catholicism. He has broken away from all societies and fellowships. Free from the constraints of any brand of disciple discipline, he is proud to stand alone. Fran the Man, priest without portfolio.

"I'm solo mio," he beamed. "I'll never deny the fact that I am a priest, but I do my own thing. If I was a mainstream priest, I'd lose all my friends. I certainly wouldn't be dressed in leathers, or singing like Ian Gillan. I certainly wouldn't have long hair.

"I don't encroach on Rome. I never interfere on their turf. I don't have a church building. I don't recruit others to my way of thinking. In relation to Rome, I fully accept the Holy Father as the legitimate Vicar of Christ on Earth. I'm not saying the English mass is the wrong mass, it's a valid mass. But The Tridentine mass is valid too."

Fr. Fran has many friends among the conventional clergy who keep him well stocked with fresh supplies of chalices, chasubles, cassocks and assorted liturgical knick knacks. Once a month, he says a low Latin mass at his home in Whitehall. It is attended only by himself and a friend who acts as altar boy.

"It's a votive mass," emphasised Fr. Fran. "It's a mass for people's intentions. I don't receive a stipend. Apart from that, I go to the English *novis orum* mass in a local church to receive Holy Communion. But I think the Latin mass in its pure state is the most beautiful thing this side of Heaven."

Fr. Fran's parish is the stage, his congregation the kids who just wanna rock. "I like to project the word of God through my music," he affirmed. "It's a love message, not in relationship with man-and-woman love but in participation with the audience and making them feel that they're going to have a good time and a good laugh and be rid of all their problems and traumas and depression for two hours. I want people to have lots of fun.

"Without preaching, I also send out my very simple message: Don't do drugs, hard drugs or soft drugs; don't get involved with Satanic masses or black death metal albums; love Christ; love your parents and love your family. It couldn't be simpler."

Fran appears utterly sincere in his desire to lead by example. He still doesn't booze and claims no need for artificial euphorics. Even amidst the din and dander of a live show, his choice of stimulants has a cosy simplicity. Fr. Fran never goes onstage these days without a tray carrying a pot of tea, a mug, and a plate of Chocolate Goldgrain. "I demand that everybody has a good time and has a good laugh at me, especially when I'm supping my tea and my few biscuits," he said.

Much of his flock is drawn from among a most despised and misunderstood denomination. In the same way that Jesus dug the company of fishermen, Fr. Fran likes to hang out with motorcycle fiends. "I like biker people," he professed. "I love their wild, happy, non-offensive way of going on. And, boy, can they drink. I've played many gigs for bikers but I've never seen an incident or a fight. A lot of them talk to me about different bits and pieces of a personal nature, be it family or relationships or problems with the drink. I make time for them. I share with them."

Cheek by jowl with his ministry of pastoral care lies Fr. Fran's crusade against Satanism. His mission to reclaim hard rock from "the forces of darkness" continues.

"Satan is delighted with Deuicide and Slayer and their like," he insisted. "'Deuicide' in Latin means 'kill Christ'. Glen Barton, the bass player and lead singer with Deuicide, hopes to help open the seven gates of Hell when the battle comes with the Antichrist. They encourage cruelty to animals and drug-taking, and a philosophy of do-what-you-want. All that Devil-worshipping black metal is just silly, very immature. But it's playing with fire. Black masses are extremely dangerous. If the proper rite is enforced, you can find yourself in a lot of serious trouble. I want to bring the young people back to Whitesnake, Deep Purple, and the old traditional rock bands."

To Fr. Fran's absolute horror, a small Devil's spawn of Satanists began attending White Rose shows in the wake of my 1991 *Hot Press* feature which had obviously alerted them to the existence of the hellzapoppin' clergyman. "They got the wrong idea," he proclaimed indignantly. "They were just youngsters but committed Satanists. They specialised in slagging off the Holy Mother. I had a chat with them, and got to know them. I'm glad to say that one of them has now gone back to mass.

"I'm often approached by young lads with black death metal influences. I've spoken to them and said, 'Forget about all that Deuicide and Slayer shit, and listen to Ozzy, listen to his lyrics'. There is a great anti-war message and a love message in Ozzy's lyrics.

"The bat thing was a mistake. He didn't know it was alive when he took the head of it. He suffered for it. It bit him before he killed it. He regretted that. He repented, and said how stupid it was. He's reformed now and back with his wife, Sharon, and his family. They go tour with him. Ozzy's a good influence."

There are only so many times that one can listen to pacifist sentiments as expressed through the scorching bars of 'War Pigs' without being overcome by an urge to cheer on militarist regimes everywhere and to hip hip hurrah the accomplishments of murderous tyrants.

However, with Fr. Fran on the premises, an interminable afternoon of Sabbath bloody Sabbath was at least occasionally relieved by bouts of stimulating debate on the serious issues facing the modern Church. "There isn't enough metal on TV," propounded the head-banging theologian. "I'd love to see more Whitesnake, be it old stuff or new material. 2FM on Sunday evenings is not too bad but they play too much thrash metal, Napalm Death, Sepultura, auld stuff like that."

Phonecalls to Fr. Fran's home nowadays are often answered by a young woman who identifies herself as Anne Marie. It would be natural to assume therefore that Fran, like so many of his clerical peers, had taken himself a wife, but it would also be thoroughly wrong. In the teeth of current Church trends, Fr. Fran remains obdurately loyal to his priestly vow of celibacy.

"Anne Marie does a bit of book work for me, takes messages, does some cooking, and that kind of thing," he stated. "She and her little son come to visit me regularly. She was actually a Mormon at one stage and she asked me to help get her back into the Catholic faith. Even at that, she attends the English mass. I didn't try to entice her into my own way of thinking. I'm not into the numbers game.

"I'm celibate but I love women. My mum taught me respect. I've great respect for women and I treat them on an equal par. I have lots of girlfriends, mainly from the biker battalions. We get a lot of women in our audiences. At the end of the night, we come down and we chat to them and ask them how their mums and dads are, how their bikes are going and so forth. I'm very close to the girls in The Black Widows motorcycle club. We talk a lot and I get the usual hugs from them. But that's allowed, isn't it? It's mild."

Fr. Fran admitted that he was shocked and saddened by the disclosures about the family life of his brother in holy showbiz, Fr. Michael Cleary. "Mick was one my heroes," he avowed dolefully. "Poor Mick. He was in a difficult situation. I'm not in the judgmental business. It happened. I pray for the man a lot and, the poor divil, he suffered, so let it rest. He was up against Rome and the poor divil was probably scared shitless to divulge anything like that while he was alive.

"The whole Mick Cleary thing made me think about my own life. I'm glad to say that I'm very optimistic about the world that God gave us. I love life. Okay, I'm not David Coverdale and I'm a big fat lump. I'm bigger than Ozzy now – he lost four stone. Having said that, when I get out on the stage, I come alive. That's when my spirituality comes out.

"I'm not pious. I'm just a happy headcase. All I want is peace and a drug-free country. Jesus would love our concerts. He was a revolutionary and a rebel Himself. He'd be tolerant of me. He'd probably turn around and say, 'Keep it going, Fran, and good on ya for discouraging kids from doing drugs'."

Fr. Fran Heaton knows that, at the mention of his name, there are many who are as likely to make the sign of the winding finger at the temple as the sign of the cross. He is oblivious to such derision but longs for an opportunity to attempt a single, grand gesture that would convince sceptics of what he calls his "spiritual authenticity." The Northern Ireland peace process, he has concluded, provides the ultimate platform for such a gesture.

"My folks on my father's side come from a mixed bag, Orange Order and Patrick Pearse, if you know what I mean," he explained earnestly. "I'm a dolly mixture. I want to extend a lot of love and the hand of friendship to the people of Northern Ireland, both Loyalist and Nationalist. Let them not hesitate to call me if they want me to do a concert on the

Shankill or the Falls Road if it would, in any way, enhance the peace process.

"I love the Loyalist people dearly, no matter what happened in the past, as brothers and sisters in Christ. I've always wanted to say how much I love them, even the hardest of them, because I know that there's good there. David Ervine, Billy Hutchinson, Gary McMichael, I love them all. Gerry Adams, Mitchell McLoughlin, I love them too and want to extend all the peace I have in my heart to them as peacemakers. Music, fun and love, that's what brings people together."

KNOCK! KNOCK!

County Mayo's famed Marian shrine attracts
1,500,000 pilgrims every year. It's Catholic Ireland's
answer to Disneyland. A real Mickey Mouse operation.

By the time we arrived, I was so hungry I could've eaten a nun's arse through a convent gate. If they preferred, the restaurateurs of Knock could, of course, describe such a dish more reverentially (lightly braised fillet of Ursuline rump served on sizzling filigree wrought-iron, perhaps) but this is precisely the sort of devotional delicacy they should be offering on their menus. Especially if they expect to have any hope of satisfying the needs of the discerning 21st century pilgrim.

Unfortunately, imagination isn't a strong suit in Knock. The Mayo shrine's sole concession to religious theme park cuisine is a string of seedy snack bars purveying chips which look like they've been withering in the pan since the 1932 Eucharistic Congress.

Knock is a bizarre and distasteful place, its nose at once sanctimonious-ly high in the air and greedily deep in the greasy till. Its stock in trade is a treacly, catchpenny concoction of superstition and tinsel, trumpery and schmaltz, all served up in gluttonous heapfuls and doled out like manure off a shiny shovel.

If its administrators ever decide they need a logo, an emblem which embodies the true spirit of Knock, they could do no better than the face of Tammy Faye Bakker, the lachrymose and extravagantly gaudy wife of the discredited American televangelist, Jim Bakker.

There is an enduring image of Tammy Faye's puss at the time of her husband's disgrace: a knickerbocker glory of rouge, tears, fake beauty spots and false eyelashes. That's Knock in a Kodak moment.

The shrine craves respectability. It heralds itself as a sacred tabernacle of spiritual ecstasy, miracle cures, and everlasting life. That's what's so nefarious about Knock. It makes a covenant with the gullible, the naive, the ill and the infirm and then makes a vicious pantomime of them.

My day in Knock began badly and went steadily downhill. Having dri-ven directly from Dublin, photographer Mick Quinn and I were so fam-ished that we allowed our defences to drop the moment we disembarked. Not a good idea in this neighbourhood.

We entered a dark and dank premises where the house policy is that cans of cola are best served dusty, warm and by a scrofulous old man with a complexion last seen among the dancers in the *Thriller* video. I asked for Pepsi but his hearing was obviously on the blink. What he gave me was dyspepsia.

The sandwich I purchased was a case for Mulder and Scully. The two slices of bread, the hamlike-substance between them, and the cellophane wrapper had sweatily fused to form a single slab of unearthly matter. It is not difficult to understand how visits to Knock have become occasions for fasting and abstinence.

In the sagacious words of the *Knock Pilgrim's Guide 1996*, "Pilgrimages should be made in a spirit of fervent prayer, self-denial and recollection." That was me to a tee, provided you left out the fervent prayer, the self-denial and the, eh, oh, what was it?, yeah, the recollection.

✚ ✚ ✚ ✚ ✚ ✚ ✚

Elvis Presley *is* dead. He was murdered by a group of CIA assassins who wanted to create a network of loonies who believed that he was still alive. The CIA plan was that people who think that Elvis is still alive would make Kennedy conspiracy aficionados, some of whom suggest that Lee Harvey Oswald acted on behalf of the CIA, look like crackpots too.

Too far-fetched, eh? Okay, if you don't buy that yarn, try this one. At approximately 8pm, on August, 21st, 1879, 15 inhabitants of the tiny village of Knock, County Mayo, witnessed an apparition at the gable end of their local church. They saw the Virgin Mary, her hands raised in benediction, flanked by assorted angels, as well as Saint Joseph, and Saint John the Evangelist dressed as a bishop. Beside them, a little to the right, was an altar with a cross and a lamb upon it.

This tableau was mobile and seemed to float about 18 inches above the ground. Despite the heavy rain which was falling that evening, the figures were shrouded in radiant white light. None of them spoke but they remained visible to the 15 spectators for two hours. . . . .

When it comes to apparitions, believing is seeing. It may not be the way we do things here on planet Earth, but the foregoing story is taken as fact by a huge proportion of the citizens of this country.

Between May and October every year, Knock is visited by over 1.5 million people, of whom 85% are either from the Republic or from Northern Ireland. Crunch those numbers and tell me again that we live in a rational age.

"Knock is the single biggest attraction in Ireland," insists the Assistant Manager of Knock shrine, Pat Lavelle, a former civil engineer. "The National Museum gets about one million visitors annually. Dublin Zoo comes second with about 400,000. Knock gets more visitors than the combined numbers who go to see the two largest quoted attractions in the country."

The administrative statistics tell us that the overwhelming majority of those who come to Knock are 55 years old and over, with a two to one ratio of women to men. Some of the pilgrims appear so inhumanly

34

ancient and frail that they may well have come to Knock not to pray for longer life but expressly to remind God that they are *still* here, and getting impatient for that call to the eternal reward.

Pat Lavelle's boss is Monsignor Dominick Grealy, the Parish Priest and Administrator of Knock. Monsignor Grealy and his two curates oversee an almost incessant programme of services and ceremonies every day of the week during pilgrimage season.

They are assisted in this by regular battalions of visiting priests who choose to vacation in Knock every year because of their special infatuation with 'Our' Lady, a coinage which, incidentally, I find extremely presumptuous. I don't know about you but I want no hand, act or part of the woman. To me, she will always be Their Lady.

Monsignor Grealy is the successor to the much mythologised Monsignor James Horan. Horan, originally from nearby Partry, was the real miracle of Knock. The wily priest with the Russian hat and the really *bad* comb-over was a consummate showbiz pro. Thanks to his determination and uncanny knack for self-promotion, he achieved his dream of turning a two bit curiosity into what Knockians can today claim in their brochures as "the foremost Marian shrine in Europe after Lourdes and Fatima."

Knock is now featured in Bord Failte literature, and even has its own stand at Holiday World. There are shrine offices (tour operators) in both Dublin and Limerick.

Horan's greatest coup was in securing a visit by His Head Honchoness, Pope John Paul, who said mass in Knock before a crowd of 450,000 on September 30th, 1979. Later, during the '80s, Horan and his shrine doggedly survived the boom in competing mystically meandering masonry.

Body-popping statues were becoming commonplace but Horan managed to maintain Knock's market share with a combination of hype and hard neck. He is also the man responsible for Knock International Airport, which was declared open in 1986.

Mick and I visited this legendary landmark, ten miles away from the shrine. It has to be said that Knock International Airport is only marginally bigger than the flag which reads 'Knock International Airport' on the terminal building. While we were there, we saw nothing touchdown but two blackbirds, and even they had trouble trying to avoid each other on the runway.

Cleverly disguised as a stretch of concrete and a warehouse amid some thistles and heather on the brow of a hill, the airport would make an excellent location if NASA ever did decide to stage a hoax landing on Mars, like their fictional counterparts did in the movie, *Capricorn One*. The place is so eerily quiet that you can literally hear the handful of people who work there talk to each other while you're parked a half mile away.

The airport's champions insist, however, that it has become an essential element in the infrastructure of the west of Ireland. James Horan's original scheme was that the airport would encourage charter companies to bring groups of foreign pilgrims to Knock, and that is already happening. As of 1996, there are five charters a year from America, and this number is set to grow rapidly over the coming decade.

In what may have been a stunt designed to damage the reputation of a competing shrine as a place of well-being and health-enhancement, Monsignor Horan dropped dead during a visit to Lourdes in 1986. If he could have pulled it off, I'm sure he would liked to have popped a rivet in Fatima as well.

Unfortunately, some things were beyond even him.

Money doesn't grow on trees in Knock. It springs forth from the ground in abundant, lucrative fountains. The Mafia may think they're clever, what with their numbers games, drug rings and protection shakedowns. But they've missed out on one of the juiciest scams of all time. It's called the holy water racket.

Holy water from Knock is much revered, by holy water buffs everywhere. At the perimeter of the shrine's processional square, there are 18 holy water taps which are activated by pressing a stone disc. It couldn't be easier if you were holidaying in Bedrock.

In an ingenious ploy by the Knock authorities, the holy water is proffered free of charge, so you can take as much as you like. The catch is that you need something to put it in, unless you want to end up with a holy puddle on the backseat of your car.

Now, you could simply pour it into any old receptacle. But then, it would look just like regular water, and someone like me might accidentally use it to dissolve a tab of Solpadeine.

This dilemma is known, to all good confidence tricksters, as the "sweet spot" of the sting. The hapless pilgrim, salivating at the thought of the holy ocean that is just within grasp, dashes to the souvenir stalls.

His or her sole intention is to purchase a few items from the Knock holy water bottle range, ideally with the words KNOCK HOLY WATER BOTTLE inscribed on them, so that even the sodality smartypants will be denied an opportunity to question its authenticity. No matter how firm the resolve, however, the moment a single foot is placed on memento soil, the trap is sprung. Within seconds, the poor sucker will be forking out fistfuls of hard-earned cash for the kind of useless shoddy dross that is fit only for giving as presents to in-laws.

For decades now, esteemed theologians have argued and debated about the Knock apparition, its relevance and meaning. Opinons differ about how the imagery and structure should be interpreted. Why were the BVM's hands held the way they were? What was the significance of St. Joseph's participation? Why John the Evangelist rather than any of the other apostles?

I haven't the faintest idea, naturally enough. But I do know what the appearance of the lamb on the altar means. It's there to symbolise the sacrificial fleecing of the generations of pilgrims to come.

Two things I learned in Knock: *Uisce Coisricthe* is the Irish for holy water, and the local term for "shabby old crap" is *Irish Craft Shop*. The souvenir market is a half-acre tract of tarmac directly across the road from the shrine grounds. It is the site of a dozen cluttered kiosks, each one the shape and little more than the size of an upturned raspberry punnet. As a commercial spectacle, it has all the atmosphere of an Arabic souk, only without the colour, the charm or the energy.

The first assault on the senses is the head-spinning variety of bottles, pots, jars, vessels and, of course, fonts on display. It's as if the entire history of human existence in this region has been one long quest for containers. If the wheel had been invented in Knock, the idea would never have progressed beyond the drawing board. Its capacity for holy water is too small.

By far, the best sellers in the world of holy water conveyance are the hollow plastic figurines of the Virgin with blue screwcap crowns. Some of these are of incredible and microscopic detail. Peer closely enough at the moulded faces and you can see eyebrows, lips, dimples, even smiles. If the technology to check were available, one would not be surprised to find that, beneath the folds of the intricately sculpted robes, Mary's privates come complete with appropriately intact plastic hymens.

Then, there are the death accessories. All of the souvenir booths are fronted by elaborate arrays of Knock wreaths, Knock 'In Loving Memory' vases, Knock tombstone plaques as well as, the latest innovation, all-weather Knock grave ornaments (you just can't stand in the way of progress, can you?).

The hard sell which accompanies these items is loathsome in the extreme. The difference between tourists and pilgrims is that pilgrims are expected to return with gifts for their dead friends too. Knock knick knacks may be only slightly more tawdry versions of the religious objects available elsewhere but the point is that they have the imprimatur of *being* Knock knick knacks.

The shrine authorities get their slice of the pilgrim pie by running the caravan park, a folk museum and a religious bookshop. Dipping their toes only thus far into the entrepreneurial waters, they can plead commercial squeamishness and appeal for charity as well, which is precisely what they do.

"If you come to Knock and go to mass, there's never a collection taken up," Pat Lavelle avers. "We're totally dependent on people making voluntary donations. People in this day and age are so fed up with collections, they appreciate that when they come here to Knock it's left entirely up to themselves if they want to make a donation. Generally, they're very generous, on average. Lots of people come here and leave nothing at all. But others make substantial donations."

Officially, the shrine management keep the souvenir market at arms-length. However, with the gymnastic powers of reasoning for which

Catholic panjandrums the world over are admired, they also insist that the two operations go hand in hand.

"If you go to Lourdes or Fatima or any of the shrines in Italy or France, you'll always see the souvenir shops," asserts Pat Lavelle. "They're just part and parcel of these shrines. The Church have no involvement in the shops here at all. We'd hope that the people in the shops would use their discretion, and not do anything too tacky but we wouldn't get involved.

"There are some things that are very unsavoury, I suppose, but we'd leave it to the shop owners themselves because they're parishioners, all of them. In a way, they're dependent on the shrine for a livelihood. Be it shops, restaurants or bars, we would hope they would give a good service to the pilgrims who deserve a good service."

My copy of *Roget's Thesaurus* lists merely 47 synonyms for the word *rubbish*. Dr. Roget obviously never visited Knock. Early in the day, I had chuckled knowingly at a man selling pink sticks of Knock rock ("4 for £1"). By late afternoon, I sought that man out and begged his forgiveness on bended knee. Compared to the debris and refuse being hawked by some of his fellow retailers, his was produce of undeniable quality and distinction.

Among the gimcrack goods for which there is no expression in *Roget's Thesaurus* are the following: Padre Pio kitchen magnets, Sacred Heart of Jesus tape measures, Lamb of God keyrings, Connemara marble rosary beads, Connemara marble rosary bracelets, Padre Pio plates, Blessed Virgin Mary cigarette lighters, Jesus Christ colouring books, and, naturally, Jesus Christ crayons. For the busy believer with only limited living space, there is a combination luminous grotto, holy water bottle and money box, a snip for £4.99.

There are statues of the Virgin selling at prices ranging from 99p to £199. The Bible tells us that Mary was a Jewish girl from the 'burbs of Nazareth. Yet, without exception, the images and representations available in Knock seem to depict her as a pale Ban Garda from the Midlands, all swanked up for the Rose of Tralee finals. This, I believe, is taking Vatican II a little too far.

In one shop, I spotted a Padre Pio clock. Much to my disappointment, its hands did not have the stigmata. Padre Pio himself, however, seemed happy, a melon-slice smile of contentment on his face. Where he was positioned, he appeared to be gazing up the skirts of a dozen Irish Colleen dolls.

There are t-shirts bearing such inspiring religious invocations as "Guinness Is Good For You" and "Ooh Aah Cantona." There are leprechauns and shillelaghs, *lots* of leprechauns and shillelaghs.

There are also a plethora of arms dealers in Knock. Admittedly, the weapons are toys but the warmongering glee with which they are marketed is unmistakable.

Is this the message of Knock? And lo, the Mother of God did appear and say, "Sell plastic swords, blaster squirters, squirt blasters, double dart gun sets, Dirty Harry magnums and potato guns in my name!"

The most unusual bazaar in the souvenir market is an emporium called Irish Heritage Tapes which specialises in cassette recordings, many of their sleeves bleached almost beyond recognition by years of exposure to sunlight. Among the Irish Heritage artists most prominently featured are KC & The Sunshine Band, Sheena Easton and Dollar.

As if the vendibles were not cause enough for jaw-dropping, one is also confronted by the vendors. Browsers are constantly assailed by proprietors and assistants who come out from behind their counters and subject them to the remorseless interrogation which many Irish people seem to think is friendliness.

At one stall, I was having a private dilemma, the kind of thing that pilgrims often have during these periods of retreat and reflection, I imagine: Would I buy the joke brandy glass which looked half full but was actually empty? Or would I be better off spending the same amount on a cute, little, white mechanical mouse (with a tail that twirls around) *and* a pen with a tombola of tiny bingo balls on top which would assist me in choosing my Lotto numbers?

While wrestling with this quandary, I found myself being bombarded with relentless demands for personal information by a plump, middle-aged guy in a sombrero and Batman cape (a clever souvenir merchant always models his own stock).

I think I may have gotten stuck for a moment on the confirmation name of the boy I used to sit behind in Maths class and I definitely stumbled over the PAYE number of the undertaker who buried my great-grandmother, but otherwise I sailed through the exam with flying colours. Given space to think again, I opted for the mouse (with a tail that twirls around) and the pen.

The fact that I was carrying a notebook and, now, proudly making notations with my Lotto pen aroused the interest of the owner of another kiosk. Reluctant to repeat my biography, I decided to head him off at the pass,

"Yes, I'm from Dublin. Yes, I am single. Yes, I am tall. And no, I don't think Mayo will do well in this year's football championship," I quipped icily.

"And where do you work in Dublin?" he persisted, oblivious to my sharpness of manner.

"In the Revenue Commissioners office," I retorted.

A glacial silence descended. My inquisitor looked at me like I was the holder of a quasi-judicial position who had just called for the decriminalisation of heroin. He turned away, mumbling something in Irish.

I was asked no further questions by the tat tycoons.

Before Their Lady dropped by, the village of Knock was just another desolate pebble amidst the mossy pile of rubble that is County Mayo. The marvel of the 1879 apparition is not only that the BVM and friends visited the locale but rather that, having had an initial look around, they were still prepared to stay for two hours.

Today, the shrine grounds are a magnificent sight, replete with ornately paved pathways, kaleidoscopic flowerbeds and more carefully cultivated hedging than you'd find in a Bishop Brendan Comiskey press statement. Each shrub and bush looks like it has been individually styled by David Marshall. The lawns are so gloriously lush, verdant and alive with nature's luxuriant fertility that they have to be artificial.

The supernatural exaltation of Knock has had an ironic consequence. Whipped into shape as a place of pilgrimage, it is now a perfect example of the triumph of resourceful, creative humanity over God's chaotic wilderness. It is a votive offering before the altar of Readymix and Moss Peat.

The Knock real estate, owned outright by the Catholic Church Ltd, comprises 85 acres of grounds and three enormous car parks; a total of 100 acres. It may be regarded as outdated elsewhere but the Irish clergy are still staunchly faithful to their vow of property.

Of the 55 full-time staff employed by the shrine authorities, the majority are involved in the year-round maintenance of the hallowed grounds. Knock has its own private nursery, and grows its own bedding plants. A fleet of tractors continually zip around the precinct, carrying, I like to think, crews of emergency para-gardeners poised to tackle any horticultural crises which may arise.

Since the centenary of the apparition, an extraordinary environmental transformation has occurred. The once barren soil of Knock has become so bountifully fecund that it can now sustain an infinity of blooms and vegetation. As I strolled by the profusion of glistening tulips on the banks of the irrigation canals which were installed in 1979, I found myself utterly convinced that this incredible phenomenon can be genuinely explained only as a sign from God.

The centrepiece of the shrine grounds is the processional square, a vast concrete plaza which cleverly takes its name from the procession it hosts every afternoon. At 2.15pm every day, a parade of pilgrims recites the Rosary and walks around in circles several times after a man wheeling a statue of the Virgin in a sort of rickshaw thing. I'm sorry if that sounds a bit sarcastic but that's what they do.

Spiritually rejuvenated by the procession, and perhaps a little dizzy, the pilgrims return to the Shrine Chapel for the blessing of pious objects. I didn't want to be a party pooper so I tagged along. While my fellow worshippers held up rosaries, medals, holy water fonts and sacred pictures, I hoisted my cute, little, white mechanical mouse (with a tail that twirls around) in one hand and my Lotto pen in the other.

One of Knock's proudest boasts is a building buried partly underground, like a nuclear shelter. It's called the Church of Reconciliation. Opened in 1991, in response to public demand, this is an absolution multiplex with facilities for up to 60 priests to hear confessions at the same time.

The practise of going to confession has, apparently, declined sharply in Ireland as a whole. But pilgrims to Knock seem unable to stop themselves from dropping to their knees and singing like canaries.

On Sundays, during high season, the shrine's repenthouse suites are invariably jam-packed for a continuous eight hours, all five dozen clerics furiously doling out the penance at full throttle. Some of these assembly-line disciplinarians have gotten so quick and efficient they could give the girls who advertise in the back pages of *In Dublin* a run for their money.

The Basilica Of Our Lady Of Knock Queen Of Ireland was built for the Pope's visit in 1979. Its title alone is one of the most imposing structures in the country. 20,000 people regularly crowd into the basilica for mass. The same 20,000 regularly look up dictionaries and thesauruses to discover what the difference is between a cathedral and a basilica. None of them ever find out.

The wide ambulatory which encircles the basilica is supported by 39 stone pillars. The first four pillars on either side of the entrance are made from Mayo stone. Each of the remaining pillars represents one of the other 31 counties and is constructed from stone indigenous to that county. Fascinating, eh?

In my experience, there is a limit to how often you can be dazzled by the sight of a giant church. It's the awe of diminishing returns. The first time you encounter one, you stand back, take in the full dimensions of the spectacle, and gasp a humbled, reverential 'Wow!'. The second time you encounter one, you stand back, take in the full dimensions of the spectacle, and gasp a humbled, reverential 'Wow, let's eat!'.

Helpfully, maps and You-Are-Here guides dot the processional square, but there is at least one major flaw to the shrine's layout. The Gents toilet is not immediately visible no matter what direction you happen to be coming from. After an excruciating half hour of leg-hopping, I eventually found it, tucked away down a ramp beside the Blessed Sacrament Chapel, about 50 yards away from the Mná lavatory.

Nor was I the only gent to be caught short. At various times during the day, I spotted several septuagenarian pilgrims giving up the chase, and relieving themselves behind the same convenient expanse of evergreen foliage. It was obviously a Fír tree.

By definition, most of the people who worship at Knock are daytrippers. Even those who come for nocturnal devotions tend to hop on a bus and return home the morning after the vigil before.

This poses a self-perpetuating problem. Without a sufficient number of overnight visitors to make them viable, decent-sized hotels have not developed, which means that it is difficult to attract a sufficient number of overnight visitors.

Therefore, wallets, sorry, pilgrims are regularly leaving Knock before they've undergone a thorough cleansing. And, fat wallets, sorry, Americans are merely making fleeting stops on the way to their four-posters and mini-bars in Galway and Westport.

"The accommodation situation in Knock is something we're trying to address at the moment," maintains Pat Lavelle. "With people coming from overseas, if they can't be accommodated in Knock, they're a little bit disappointed. B and B's are fine for families, but we need a big hotel for large groups. We'd be delighted if someone came in and opened a 200 bedroom, three-star hotel. A hotel between here and the airport would serve both needs. We ourselves have plans for a large three-star guesthouse, with special access for the handicapped and disabled, and that will improve things. But, even now, the standard of B and B here is very good."

I was about to put this proposition to the test. Recklessly, I had decided to stay over for the late show, an all-night vigil organised by The Apostolate Of Our Lady Of Fatima (a fraternity who turned out to be a diverse group of believers drawn together by their belief that the enigmatic Third Secret is "Never wear clothes that match!").

Mick Quinn, a man with an acute sense of when enough is enough, decided to drive back to Dublin that evening and to leave me to it. Before he departed, he offered some reassuring words of encouragement. "Ha, ha, ha," he said, as he slammed his foot on the accelerator and screeched away in a hail of gravel.

The B and B I selected was exemplary in every way. Except for the trifling detail that its proprietors somehow managed to confuse their Bed with their Breakfast. The morning meal they served had all the flavour and aroma of a mattress while the mattress they supplied was a mixed grille of loose springs, broken lattice and miscellaneous pikestaffs.

The landlady ran, worked in or was helping out in one of the inevitable souvenir shops nearby. In order to show me to my room, she had to take a break from whatever it was she was doing in the store, probably applying price tags to the exotic new line of merchandise she had fished out of her vacuum cleaner bag only an hour before.

"You don't have anyone in with you," she said handing me the key, in what I took to be a casual query about my travelling arrangements.

"That's right," I replied, "I'm on my own."

"No," she corrected me, "I mean, you *don't* have anyone in with you!"

The woman was down the stairs and out the door before I realised that I had just been afforded a stern warning and a morality lecture. It took an hour or two before I understood that, given the age, attitude and appearance of most of my fellow pilgrims, I had also been afforded a terrific insult.

My room was a double in the sense that that is what I was being charged for, but also in the more literal sense that it occupied the same volume of space as two pub measures of spirits.

For the added satisfaction of the zealous pilgrim, the bed was decked out with four pillows, each one as fluffy and as comfortable to rest your weary head upon as a communion host.

Everything about the accommodation reeked of austerity, which is why some people come here, I suppose. Nevertheless, if you felt that you were still being too decadently pampered, you could mortify your sinful flesh with a bracing, purifying shower in the bathroom, located a bracing, purifying 600-yard walk away from your bedroom.

A set of towels fashioned from roofing felt were thoughtfully provided. One vigorous rub and it's bye bye unsightly body hair, even in those places where you're supposed to have unsightly body hair.

It took 700 years but morning finally dawned. Breakfast consisted of rashers so transparently thin they could have been sliced from the body of a living pig without waking it. As for the alleged sausages, you'd taste more pork if you kissed a cop's helmet.

I was joined at the table by three bespectacled nuns, which really aided my digestion. They, however, were too pre-occupied to pay any attention to me. They were planning a heist.

When the landlady had served everyone and left the dining room, their scheme swung into action. First, one nun produced an empty ketchup bottle from beneath the table and proceeded to fill it with milk from the jug.

Simultaneously, one of her accomplices grabbed a fistful of sugar sachets, both brown and white, from the bowl and stuffed them up her sleeve while the third cohort seized a substantial quantity of homemade brown bread wrapped in a napkin.

When they caught me staring, the ringleader smiled diffidently and said, "We're on a pilgrimage."

The relationship between institutional Catholicism and the supernatural realm is comparable to the relationship between Sinn Féin and the Provisional IRA. The clergy are the Shinners, desperate to be seen as responsible, reasonable, wholesome participants in the real world. With a nod and a wink, however, they make it clear that they are aligned with unseen, mysterious elements, whose power is unpredictable and awesome.

Angels, saints and the rest of the Heavenly host are guerrilla insurgents, who claim the right to strike at will. They explain themselves to mere mortals by allowing the Church to "speak authoritatively" on their behalf. They may not be an armed wing but it is claimed that many of them have winged-arms.

There is a profoundly malevolent side to all this. Out of the side of its mouth, the public face of this movement will mutter about miracles and divine intercession. They don't want to make too much of a song and dance about such marvels, because they don't want to undermine their credibility. Instead, there's more nodding, more winking.

In Knock, they talk a lot about a woman from Athlone called Marion Cullen who claims that, in 1990, she was miraculously cured of multiple sclerosis while visiting the shrine. Ms. Cullen is adamant that she did not undergo remission or suffer a misdiagnosis. The word that both she and the Knock authorities use constantly is "miracle."

Her case has been recorded and is being monitored by what is referred to, deadpan, as The Knock Medical Centre.

"Marion is in great health to this day," proclaims Pat Lavelle. "The Church will start to investigate the claim of a miracle after seven years has elapsed, that's the rule. Marion comes back to Knock frequently and is greatly loved by a lot of people here. Everybody wants to talk to her."

It boils down to faith and trust. You either believe and trust in Knock, or you've had a ham sandwich there. The descendants of people whom the Mother of God chose as her special emissaries to humankind are today propagating the eternal truths of rock candy and Made In Thailand gewgaws. Now, *that's* irony.

"We get people coming here who have the most serious problems imaginable," says Pat Lavelle. "Those problems might be financial, marriage, drugs, drink and all that. We have people here praying for their partners, their mothers, praying for their sons or daughters who are dying. We also get a large number of the terminally ill, people with only a couple of weeks to live.

"They all come here and they have tremendous faith in Knock. There aren't miracles every day but there are occasions when people get their problems solved. Everybody believes that they might be next."

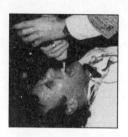

BAD FRIDAY

*Jesus took the easy way out. He died on Good Friday.
The rest of us have to live through it.*

With a groaning thud, Good Friday falls once a year, every year. It just lies there, motionless and moribund, for 24 dreary hours, refusing to get up and leave until Easter Saturday rides out of the sunrise to save us.

Good Friday is the most boring day on the calendar. Everybody knows this. It is such a gala jubilee of tedium that it makes Ascension Thursday feel like a week-long fact-finding trip to Sodom and Gomorrah, on an MEP's expense account.

Obviously, for Christians throughout the world, Easter is an important festival and the mystery of the season merits special reflection by each and every one of us: How *do* confectionery companies get away with charging such outlandish prices for brittle pseudo-eggs made from a sliver of chocolate?

For those of us who pledge allegiance to neither the Judeo-Christian nor the Rowntree-Mackintosh tradition, however, Good Friday is nothing but an Olympic-standard yawnathon.

True, it is a Bank Holiday, a break from the trials and tribulations of having to earn one's daily Butterkrust. But, it is also a day on which we are all prohibited, by law, from enjoying ourselves. Bars and restaurants close, cinemas and theatres darken, shops are shuttered up.

Down here in the free state, we quite justifiably laugh at the intolerant prudery of Northern Unionists until we do ourselves serious intestinal injury. We gloat about the fact that they refrain from playing cards on the Sabbath. We snigger that it is against their religion to have sex standing up in case God thinks that they're dancing.

Yet the pot *qua* kettle inconsistency seems lost on Catholics whose own Church decrees that, on Good Fridays, the entire population of the Republic, faithful, infidel and heathen alike, is permitted all the social mobility of a cage of lab rats.

When Unionists (damn their priggish, bowler hatted souls!) insist upon the closure of public parks in Catholic areas on Sundays, they're bigots. When the Irish constitution asserts that on an arbitrary Friday in April, I am to be denied the right to see the latest Hulk Hogan movie on the big screen, as it was meant to be seen, it is a legitimate expression of majority rule.

Like Line Dancing, Michael McDowell and Waterford, Good Friday is an idea whose time has long passed. It should be abolished forthwith.

The Christian churches are very upfront about Good Friday. They do not, to coin a phrase, pull their Pontius. Jesus Christ, they tell us, was the Son of God and He died on the cross to save the world. If you accept such a thesis, then it's clearly right and proper that you should starve, flagellate and immolate yourself on Good Friday (it's worth remembering though that while the modern Church smiles on penitential rites, the use of whips, nipple-clamps and rectal delectals is very much a matter for the conscience of the individual believer).

The problem is that if you view the very concept of a God Jnr. as preposterous, and the story of Him being nailed to the cross as mere *hammer* horror, a work of cruci-fiction if you will, you are still compelled to live in a state of privation and self-denial on this particular day every year.

In Ireland, the observance of Good Friday is enforced by the might and majesty of the State. This is religious persecution. It is also a violation of human freedom, a flouting of European Community fair trade legislation and a right pain in the arse.

For me, the day always starts the traditional way. I do the stations, several times. But there's never anything worth watching on TV on Good Friday, on any channel, so I invariably wind up flinging the remote control into the goldfish bowl, and storming out of the house.

But you can't even indulge in a refreshing spot of storming out on Good Friday because, the moment you encounter the fresh air, you realise that you were better off inside. Everywhere is shut. The idea, presumably, is that with nowhere to go and nothing to do, the thoughts of the faithful will inevitably turn upwards, to their Heavenly father. Consequently, they will all then hit the prayer mats with a collective thump of adoration. This is a dubious proposition.

It is an incontestable fact that whenever there's nothing to do and nowhere to go, the thoughts of everybody, especially the faithful, inevitably turn *downwards,* to their private parts, and to the myriad ways that these versatile organs can be used to while away the empty hours.

I doubt very much if an afternoon of wrist-cracking self abuse is quite what The Vatican have in mind for their flock on Good Friday, but that's precisely what they drive them to every year.

Drink, of course, is the time-honoured way of keeping the minds of the young and the old away from their genitalia but the Good Friday Police also seal off that particular avenue of escape.

Since the dawn of time, gentlemen, please, we Irish have used alcohol to help boost our frail self-confidence, to fortify our morale, to palliate our inherent melancholia and to get us in the mood for farting games. The Good Friday pub shutdown is an assault on a nation's natural habitat.

Without a thought for the environmental consequences, a wanton stampede of lounge lizards, barflies and stool pigeons is released into the wild.

Even the crucified Messiah, we should remember, was allowed to wet His whistle while tacked to the woodwork on the first Good Friday, albeit with a slurp of sour vinegar from a centurion's sponge. How ironic then that modern day vendors of sour vinegar are not permitted to open for business on what should be their commemorative day. But no, nightclubs have to close their doors on Good Friday too.

House parties are an option, though not a very realistic one. A virulent strain of cabin fever stalks the land on Good Friday. Anyone who has had the foresight to stock up on trays of Tuborg and tubes of Pringles (now in yummy Cheezums!) is unlikely to feel like splitting his or her rations with every hungry dog and divil on the estate.

This is the true spirit of Good Friday. Those who have, hoard, and get helplessly, hopelessly drunk while those who haven't can go pigstick nutty on red diesel cocktails for all anyone else cares.

It is one of the great ironies of Good Friday therefore that the licensing laws have conspired to make the drinking of alcohol during these hellish 24 hours virtually the sole prerogative of citizens who have not yet reached the legal age for the drinking of alcohol.

You can see them in the parks and greenbelts. Sullen knots of youths with numb, unfocused glares, honouring the passion of Christ by getting crucified on Scrumpy Jack and bottles of Liebfraumilch so noxiously acidic that the Saviour Himself couldn't turn them in the wine. A couple of flagons of that stuff and *you'd* start calling yourself the King of the Jews.

There's another thing about Good Friday. It is one of the bloodiest periods of the year. Statistics that I have carefully collated from the top of my head prove conclusively that more acts of mindless violence are committed on this day than on any other occasion, with the possible exception of Christmas.

It stands to even a Christian's power of reason. Shut down every amenity in the country for a whole day, force the population to get liquored up on stockpiled take-outs and glamorise the fun that can be had with a mallet, a fistful of Hiltis and a hippie's limbs and you've got yourself a gourmet recipe for serious trouble.

Under such conditions, it is axiomatic that large swathes of the citizenry are going to engage in vigorous bouts of fisticuffs, not to mention footicuffs, loaficuffs and, in some cases, even deadly-weaponicuffs.

Sunday is the Lord's day, and He can keep it. All the Virgin Mary had to do was make one lousy assumption and she gets a special feast on August 15th. And, while not everyone agrees that the tradition of subjecting decent country folk to a day trying on blazers and slacks in Clery's is a particularly immaculate conception, December 8th is still an important date in the religious diary.

My point is that Christians are welcome to have all the holy days of obligation that they feel the need for, but they've got to stop dragging the rest of us down with them.

There is no good reason why pubs, clubs, cinemas, shops and arcades should ever close for a full day. A very bad reason to do so is because it's Good Friday.

Anyway, if God so loved the world, how come He pulled this crucifixion stunt on a payday? Why didn't He ensure that His eldest lad made the ultimate sacrifice on a Monday, a Tuesday or a Wednesday? Fasting and total abstinence are a helluva lot easier when you're broke.

Father, forgive them, for they know bloody well what they do.

THE EXORCIST

Most Reverend Bishop Michael Cox lives alone in a derelict textile mill in the wilds of County Offaly. Nevertheless, the Tridentine prelate may well be the most powerful clergyman in the country.

I n historical terms, Cree, County Offaly is a hotbed of insignificance. For hundreds of years, its lush, verdant fields, abundant hedgerows and imposing, gnarled oak trees have provided the backdrop to zip, zilch, zero and absolutely nothing whatsoever.

It's the townland which laid the golden goose-egg, the kind of locale that wouldn't merit a favourable mention anywhere other than the annual prospectus of the FBI's Witness Relocation Programme.

Since July 1995, however, this Yawnopolis of bucolic anonymity has become the unlikely Episcopal seat of Bishop Michael Cox, one of the country's most remarkable religious outlaws. The only consecrated Latin

Tridentine prelate in the 32 counties, Bishop Michael's diocese is spiritual rather than geographic, but his ecclesiastical presence has conferred upon the area an aura of considerable curiosity, to put it mildly. To put it less mildly: these days, Cree makes Twin Peaks seem like Crinkly Bottom.

Five miles outside Birr, on the main road to Roscrea, there's a cross-roads known as The Black Bull. A right turn will take you to Shinrone, the Sun City of the Midlands. Left, up a desolate, hilly, dirt track, lies Saint Colman's Church, Cree – Bishop Michael's palace and cathedral.

It's 11.30am, but everywhere is shrouded in bluish dusk as photographer Mick Quinn and I arrive at the appointed place. Our instructions had been clear: we were to bypass what Bishop Michael called "the Vatican II Roman Catholic English mass church," and stop only when we came to the spanking new, papal gilt-tipped wrought-iron gates of Saint Colman's.

Bishop Michael is understandably proud of his new gates. They were one of his first and most lavish expenses when he took over the property. Unfortunately, given the disrepair and squalor which lurks behind them, the gates have all the charm of a set of gleaming gold cufflinks on the sleeves of a destitute beggar.

Built in 1844 by the Church of Ireland, Saint Colman's belongs to the great Protestant tradition of Big Shed Architecture. Four walls and a roof with neither spire nor pinnacles, the building design is so dull and unimaginative it could get its own chatshow on RTE. The elegant effect is enhanced by the mudslide which laps at its foundations. As Mick and I wade our way in, each of our shoe-prints is immediately engulfed with a slurry of water and muck.

The doorway to Saint Colman's is a pointed arch, the wooden door itself strapped and hinged, apparently in preparation for some sort of siege warfare. The porch is yet another fantasia of austerity, surrealistically enlivened by the storage of a chainsaw, four spare wheels, and Bishop Michael's modest collection of Catholic statues (among them a small alabaster Jesus that bears a disturbing facial resemblance to Brendan Keeley).

Inside the main body of the church, it takes several seconds for my eyes to readjust to the pit-like gloom. The room feels vast and frosty, its bare stone walls plastered by coatings of grime and filth, so that their original grey is now black. My immediate impression is that the whole hovel is barely held together by rot, crows' nests and the great sooty hammocks of cobweb which dangle from the recessed arches.

The centrepiece of the ceiling is an immense gaping hole through which roars a whistling, pounding gale, its sound as chilling as its breeze. The draught follows visitors around the place like a bad reputation, impossible to shake off.

Saint Colman's was an active house of COI worship until about 20 years ago. Then, it was bought by a local businessman and converted into a textile mill. In the late '80s, the factory ceased operation. The premises has been derelict ever since, but most of the floorspace is still occupied by mammoth looms and weaving contraptions.

In the glacial dark, it's easy to feel that these huge machines have taken root through the floorboards and are slowly freezing into one giant, immovable hunk of solid metal. However, their owner has promised to remove them on a piecemeal basis over the coming months.

Suddenly, a bronchial cough jerks my attention towards a balcony halfway up the huge lancet window at the gable end. A short, plump figure rises from the murk in silhouette. "Good morning, gentlemen," declares a hoarse but soft voice. "I am Most Reverend Bishop Michael Cox. You'll have to forgive the state of the place, I'm afraid, but you are welcome to my home."

Paunchy, jowly, his cheeks darkly pinkened by a heart condition, Bishop Michael looks considerably older than his 50 years. He moves slowly and deliberately, as though perpetually carrying a brimming cup. While he may be about as popular as pork in a kosher butchers with the Catholic panjandrums, he makes no apologies to anyone for his beliefs or his actions.

He luxuriates in Episcopal pomp: the vestments, the silver ring, the reverential jargon. Yet he is also at pains to stress that he is essentially a very humble man. To his mind, there is no contradiction between the two states.

As his cats (Tiger and The Roadrunner) scramble about his feet, and his brawny dogs (Goldie and Brandy) sumo wrestle with each other, Bishop Michael gets straight down to business. From the get-go, conversation flows out of him like steam off a boiling pot. "I live like a monk," he tells me, citing Saint Francis of Assisi as his chief role model. "I want you to know that before we go any further."

Most mornings, he rises at 5.30am. He then celebrates a Latin mass, attended only by his pets and the congregation of looms. Depending on what his *Romana Missala* decrees is appropriate for the day, Bishop Michael may also sing his own high mass, his tenor voice resounding unheard by other human beings in the icy dawn.

His Grace's favourite hymn is the 'Kyrie Eleison', a rambling, discordant drone to these ears, the lyrics of which, I've always presumed, translate as *"Lord, have mercy and forgive us our trespasses against all known laws of coherent melody."* Nevertheless, as Bishop Michael treats me to a few bars, he manages to endow the caterwaul with at least some semblance of tunefulness.

His musical talent is prodigious. A champion button-accordionist in his youth, he is also a fine singer and an accomplished uilleann piper, and is the Leinster representative of Na Piobairí Uilleann. Prohibited from smoking and drinking for medical reasons, Bishop Michael says that his only real form of amusement is his music. He plans to give music lessons (free of charge) at Saint Colman's when it is eventually renovated, and would also like to host a folk festival in and around the church at some future date.

Such schemes seem impossibly grandiose at the moment. Bishop Michael's living conditions are pathetically primitive. He sleeps, eats and says mass on a 4ft by 8ft makeshift loft which was erected during Saint Colman's factory days, as a kitchenette in which tea could be brewed away from the dust and din of the machinery.

The backrests of five rickety wooden chairs form the perimeter 'wall' between this three-sided garret and a 14 foot drop. Against the window, there's a sheet-draped table which masquerades as an altar, incongruously heavy with gold chalices, candles and a monstrance.

Two ancient, decaying gas heaters squat morosely in one corner, radiating drowsy warmth and a suffocating, torpid odour, like a pair of old and moulting sheep dogs. Friends and supporters have helped install some stopgap electric wiring and a telephone, but the veneer of relative comfort afforded by this, and the TV and video, is thoroughly undermined by the fog of damp steam which rises from all of Bishop Michael's vestments and clothes.

His Lordship sleeps in a cell the size of a toilet cubicle, a ratty, smelly chickencoop with scarcely enough room to swing a Catholic. A plastic sack serves as a 'door' separating the boudoir from the rest of his quarters. Above his bed hangs a crucifix and rosary beads, beneath it sits the basin that constitutes Bishop Cox's bathroom. Hidden away is the small chemical lavatory which he empties in a neighbour's house every morning.

Mindful of his isolation and vulnerability, the bishop keeps a .22 rifle by his pillow. "I love people and I couldn't even harm a fly," he affirms. "But God says that we have a duty to nourish and protect our bodies. The shotgun is fully licensed and I'd use it if I had to, as a last resort. I'd aim for the legs."

Bishop Michael's penthouse can only be reached via two flights of hazardously narrow steps which form an ascent so mercilessly steep it belongs in one of the Nazarene's parables about how difficult it is for the rich to enter Heaven. Unsteady on his feet at the best of times, there have been days when the bishop has been unable to clamber down from the loft for fear that he would not be able to make it back up again.

The landing is little bigger than a playing card. It acts as a combination pantry, attic, closet and medicine cabinet. Decontamination requisites such as mops, buckets, shovels, bottles of Domestos, Dettol and Jeyes Fluid, and a tube of Bob Martin's flea powder, are stacked alongside a small bundle of jumpers, a heart-shaped shaving mirror, assorted tubs of pills and the peeling, leprous suitcase which stores Bishop Michael's precious uilleann pipes.

Apart from a drum of salt, some teabags, cartons of milk and a tiny jar of instant coffee, the most conspicuous eatables are a half dozen cans of C&D catfood. An empty box festooned with pictures of the Winterwarm All-Night Electric Blanket bears witness to a solitary splash of frivolous luxury. It's all a far and plaintive cry from the opulent extravagance

57

favoured by Michael Cox's Episcopal *confrères* in the Vatican II branch of Catholicism.

"I'm a very humble man," attests Bishop Michael. "I don't agree with the materialism of the other bishops. Our Lord Jesus Christ was born in a stable at Bethlehem. He lived in a humble little cottage in Nazareth. He didn't go in for luxuries. He walked the roads with His disciples. They didn't have motor cars. I feel that example should by shown, by the priests and bishops. But the bishops in this country are too fond of the luxury.

"There's an awful lot of unemployment and when an unemployed person sees a priest going around in a big new car and living in a luxury palace, it doesn't do much for the faith. Parish priests seem to have one big house, and I emphasise *big* house, and the curates have another one between them. Why not the parish priest and the curates share the one house? If they were to live in surroundings like this, they would be more in tune with Christ and the true meaning of Christianity. I live this way because this is the way it has evolved for me. I have no regrets.

"We must keep in tune with the example of Christ. He was a humble man. He humbled himself. He was born in a stable and allowed Himself to die on a cross for our failings. It's a long way away from BMWs and palaces. How many bishops were born in a stable? How many priests were born in a stable?"

It's a bad time for the Most Reverend Bishop Michael Cox. The 20th century, that is. Spiritually, he is a man from another age.

"All Catholics were Tridentine until 1965 when they brought in Vatican II," he says, pronouncing that last phrase with a grimace of sour distaste, as if he had just discovered some mouse poop in the altar wine. "Tridentine means that we adhere to the laws set down by the Council of Trent (1545-1563). There's a document called *Quo Primum Temera* which was issued by His Holiness Saint Pious IV at the conclusion of the sacred Council of Trent. What that basically says is that all which is contained in the *Romana Missala,* the original missal, cannot be added to or taken from or changed in any way.

58

"Anyone who would change it, he decreed, would bring the wrath of Almighty God and His holy apostles down upon themselves and the whole world. The Latin Tridentine mass, and the old catechism that went with it, was to be permanent, to remain until the end of time."

Bishop Michael was born in Mitchelstown, County Cork, on March 2nd, 1945. His father was from Birr, County Offaly, but was a member of the defence forces so he and his young family were forced to move around the country quite a bit. Nevertheless, Michael received the bulk of his education from the Christian Brothers in Birr.

In his mid-teens, Michael decided to follow in the footsteps of his old man (not to mention his beloved Saint Francis) and become a soldier. He spent a total of ten years in the army, working as a sparks (a communications technician) with the Signal Corps, primarily in the air traffic control tower at the Baldonnell airstrip. He was medically discharged in 1973 for not reaching "the standard of army physical fitness."

In the meantime, Michael had gotten married. But the union was not a happy one. The marriage was never consummated, and, within a few months of the wedding ceremony, his wife, Bridie, absconded with another man.

"I'm still legally married but my marriage was annulled by the Roman Catholic Church," explains Bishop Michael. "She was only a short time with me. His Holiness Pope Paul VI decreed that my marriage was not valid. She never intended to enter into a real and lasting marriage with me and I had every grounds in the book, every grounds in the book. It became abundantly clear that it wasn't a valid marriage. Shortly after the marriage, she went away with a certain person and she's been with him all the time since."

It took four and a half years but Michael Cox eventually received his annulment (his case, incidentally, was handled by Doctor William Walsh, now Bishop of Killaloe). Always a devout Catholic, Michael says that he found himself relying more and more heavily upon his faith throughout this difficult period.

After completing an ANCO course, he secured a job with an engineering plant in Shannon, and later worked in Germany for two years. Incurably homesick, he returned to Offaly. Now in his early 30s, he set up a TV repair business in the village of Crinkle. A year later, he felt "an overwhelming calling by God."

"I got the calling very strong," reflects Bishop Michael. "I just couldn't resist the calling. It's difficult to put into words. I always had it in me for the priesthood, always. I knew it wasn't a calling to the Vatican II church. It had to be the old Latin mass because I was always of that nature. I never actually changed over to Vatican II.

"Like a number of other Irish people who were thinking along similar lines, I travelled to Palma De Troya in Spain where we had heard there was a community of Tridentine priests. All it took was the price of the flight. But we didn't agree with the way the Palmarians were doing things. They were ordaining kids, very young boys, and then making them bishops a few days later. So, a few of us went to another community in Switzerland, in Bourge San Pierre, and that's where I became a priest."

To fully appreciate Bishop Michael's story, we must remember that the late '70s was a time of considerable upheaval in the Church. Dissent among arch-traditionalists, which had been slowly fomenting since the Second Vatican Council, in 1965, finally spilled over into outright mutiny.

At the forefront of what was to become the breakaway Tridentine sect was the French archbishop, Marcel Lefebvre, and his Order Of Saint Pius X. However, there were other renegades too. To cut a very long and very convoluted story short, Michael Cox became part of a group which founded its own community, The Order Of The Mother Of God. On May 1st, 1978, Michael was ordained by five legitimate Roman Catholic bishops whose "apostolic succession" (ecclesiastical validity) was guaranteed by a rebel South Vietnamese archbishop called Peter Martin Kno Din Tuk. Four years later, on April 27th, 1982, Michael was consecrated bishop within The Order Of The Mother Of God.

The attitude of the conventional Catholic hierarchy towards Tridentines (both brands, Lefebvre and Kno Din Tuk) is that they are sipping from a cocktail comprising a concentrated solution of most grievous error and 100% proof Devil spawn. The Tridentines, meanwhile, regard Vatican II Catholics as the "un-lawful" ones, "the violators of the sacred Council of Trent." It's the Crips versus the Bloods, only with more hostility.

"When Vatican II came about, they threw the statues out of the churches," fumes Bishop Michael. "They ripped out the altar rails. They got some of the altars and split them down the middle and brought the table part forward. Take Birr chapel, for example. I remember when they got these chainsaw yokes and they sawed down the marble. They were beautiful altars, and they ruined them.

"The priest should face the East, the Holy Land, when he's saying his mass. In the old Latin mass, the priest brought the people with him to Christ. That's why the priest had his back to the people. They worshipped together and faced the same way, towards Christ in the East. Now, you have the priest facing the other way. They interfered with the mass, and that's unforgivable.

"To me, Vatican II is a watered-down version of Catholicism. In the olden days, you had the Latin mass and devotions and you had a catechism that spelled out the dos and the don'ts. It was straightforward. The Vatican II Church had no catechism until recently. I shudder to think what the youngsters have been taught. It's all wrong."

South Offaly, in general, and greater Cree, in particular, are regions populated with far more Protestants than are strictly necessary. It has always been thus. Until relatively recently, for instance, Birr used to be known as Parsonstown.

In virtually every second homestead, one can see tangible evidence of the traditional Protestant values; hard work, frugality, self-reliance and enormous deposit accounts. Double-barrelled names abound, and every one of them is loaded.

Before he moved to Cree, Bishop Michael lived in a house he owned at Coolderry, in nearby Brosna. It was a comfortable residence but, without a church in which he could celebrate the Latin mass, His Lordship could never really call it home. When Saint Colman's was placed on the market by its proprietors (the Guinness Group Pension Fund), the bishop immediately sold the Coolderry premises, and bought the Church Of Ireland building. It cost him £8,000.

"I signed the deeds on July 12th last year," he says, and begins to chuckle heartily. "There's a headline for you now: 'Tridentine Bishop

Signs For Church Of Ireland Building On Orangeman's Day!' I'm not without a bit of humour, Liam. I have a sense of humour in spite of it all."

His dreams for Saint Colman's are nothing if not audacious. As well as a fully refurbished Tridentine church, he sees it becoming a community and drop-in centre, and a night school offering free classes in everything from music to languages. With only an invalidity pension of £66 per week as income, and a modest shares account with Birr Credit Union as collateral, Bishop Michael has his work cut out. To make up the obvious cash shortfall, he intends approaching the National Lottery, FAS, Offaly County Council and, perhaps, even some of his wealthy neighbours, Catholic *and* Protestant.

"I'm a very shrewd man," Bishop Michael proclaims. "My intellect is very sharp. You're talking to an educated man here, and I say that in all humility. I am a qualified radio telegraphy communications technician with a knowledge of mechanical and machine engineering. I'm capable of making uilleann pipes. I have great knowledge in religious matters. I'm not going to go around boasting. I don't get a swelled head. I know that a lot of people share my views. They may attend the Vatican II church but they share my views. They just go along with things for an easy life."

While he's "a great admirer of Protestants," Bishop Michael is certainly not one of those lily-livered trendies who would blur the boundaries between Protestantism and the one true faith.

"I have no objection to people praying together in my church but, remember this, if a non-Catholic enters a Catholic church, they do not believe in the Blessed Sacrament, the true presence," he states sternly. "Catholics who go into the Roman Catholic church genuflect before the Blessed Sacrament. Non-Catholics do not believe in Transubstantiation. For someone to enter a Catholic church and not to genuflect is wrong.

"I get on splendid with Church of Ireland people. I'm surrounded by them here and they welcome me. I love them. I'm very fond of them. I'm not patronising, I actually like them. Even the Protestant Reverend in Birr, Canon Archdeacon Keegan. We salute each other when we meet on the road. We should all worship in accordance with our informed conscience. By all means, let us pray. But we must not enter into heresy.

"I believe that the Catholic faith is the one, true, holy and apostolic faith. One fold and one shepherd. For everybody to become one, they would all have to become Catholics."

Bishop Michael does not take every article of Romespun wisdom at face value. Having experienced the trauma of a broken marriage at first hand, he was sympathetic to the Yes lobby during the divorce referendum (though, as a prelate, he felt "professionally obliged" to vote No). Conceivably, he may even obtain a divorce himself, to formally enshrine his annulment in state law.

"I could, but I don't think I will," he ventures. "What's the point? We've been parted since 1972. On the other hand, it might stop some of those who would like to say that I'm not a valid bishop because I'm still married in the eyes of the law."

His Grace has no problem with the idea of married priests. He argues that there is "no theological reason why they shouldn't wed." Bishop Michael is also prepared to concede that, in the past at least, many of his fellow religious were little more than hoodlums in clerical collars.

"When I was a child, the Christian Brothers were brutal," he asserts. "They were violent men. I was beaten badly, and I was a good little kid. I was a small, chubby, little fella with a big bunch of curls and a big smile like a Cheshire cat. A happy-go-lucky little fella. But what they done to me was wrong. They beat me black and blue. They beat religion into me. That was wrong. Jesus Christ never beat a child."

A lesser man might have been turned off religion for life by such savagery, but not Bishop Michael Cox. "The method they used was wrong," he acknowledges. "But the religion itself was correct. They were very wrong. They beat children, and the nuns the same. There was no need for it. If I wasn't a bishop, I'd use stronger language and say that the Brothers were a shower of you-know-whats. But I have to be diplomatic, because of my position.

"I'm not here to knock any religious but I'm here to tell the truth. There was people badly beaten. I saw it myself. I heard Gay Byrne glorifying them the other day: 'Thank God for the Christian Brothers, there'd be no education in the country without them'. Why didn't he go a step further and admit that they beat people black and blue? Corporal punishment is removed from the schools now, thanks be to God. I detest violence. I am a man of God. I am a man of peace. I love people and God. I love the trees and the flowers. I love God's creation. Violence has no part in my life."

Bishop Michael has been perturbed by the flood of sexual scandals which has deluged the Catholic Church in recent times. Would he be prepared to argue that they too have their roots in the apostasy of Vatican II?

"To me, Vatican II Catholics are lapsed Catholics," he replies. "That's all I'll say. I condemn anyone who would abuse a child. Those who are found guilty are wrong. It's a terrible betrayal of trust. Me, I will pray for both perpetrator and victim, in my Rosary and in my mass. It's very sad for the victim and the families but also for the immortal soul of the priest that would commit such things.

"But these are matters for the Vatican II hierarchy. I shouldn't even be commenting on Vatican II. I don't step on their toes. They don't interfere with me, believe it or not, and I don't interfere with them. We live and let live. They respect my conscience and I respect theirs. We all have to answer to God. Each individual has to answer to God, from the Pope down."

In January, 1992, Bishop Michael Cox briefly attained widespread notoriety when he performed an exorcism on the RTE studios in Donnybrook. The casting out of evil spirits is yet another hallowed rite which he believes the Vatican II Church has foolishly neglected during the past three decades. When it became apparent to him that diabolical demons were running amok inside our national broadcasting service, he felt duty-bound to take his holy water and crucifix to the gates of Montrose.

"It was Gerry Ryan who was the final straw," maintains Bishop Michael, more in sorrow than in anger. "Strange though it may seem, I actually like that guy. I actually like Gerry but I get annoyed sometimes at what he does say on the radio. Before I did the exorcism, Gerry was describing certain biological actions of an unpleasant nature. I'd rather not say exactly what. He was saying things that he shouldn't be saying. Also, the *Nighthawks* programme was jeering Mother Teresa at the time. A few other things *Nighthawks* were doing upset me too. Another radio programme, *Scrap Saturday,* was making a complete jeer and skit of His Holiness Pope John Paul 11 and his statements on natural contraception.

"There was a combination of things that were going on at the time which were very distasteful. I phoned RTE and I wrote to them, but I didn't get a satisfactory reaction. So, I went up and did the exorcism. I asked God to subdue Satan and to send His holy legions, His archangels and saints, to surround RTE. I wanted those working in RTE to be freed of all Satanic influence and to have time to think about what it is they're doing. In other words, to allow them to cop themselves on."

The bishop believes that the RTE exorcism was a successful exercise and that it had a purifying impact on the station, at least temporarily. "I'd say its effects were felt for a good while afterwards," he contends. "It's a matter of public record that a strike came about soon afterwards." A dead beat. "And that Gerry Ryan got sick for three days."

In 1994, Gay Byrne displeased Bishop Michael when he featured an irreverent student debate about the love life of Eamon Casey on *The Late Late Show*. Enraged, the Tridentine prelate spoke publicly of divine retribution and appeared to summon down dire fulminations upon Byrne's head. In September 1995, as we now know, the TV idol was seriously incapacitated by a grave, though unspecified, illness.

So, was Bishop Michael responsible for almost ensuring that Gay Byrne was himself the late, late? And, if so, could he be arrested and charged with G.B.H.?

"If a priest invokes divine penance upon somebody, it is not a curse," the bishop avers. "To curse somebody is to say, 'That you may go to Hell' or 'That you my break your leg'. But for a priest to chastise someone, to put them on warning, is a very different thing. They then have a choice: 'Either you apologise and straighten yourself out, or the wrath of Almighty God will befall you'. That's not a curse, that's an invocation of the power of Christ.

"I said that Gay Byrne would become ill, quite ill, if he did not apologise to Bishop Casey and to his family and friends. Those young people who came on made a complete skit, mockery and laugh of Bishop Casey. There was no need for it. The poor misfortunate man is after having enough problems. He admitted what he did, he apologised and went to confession and was given absolution. When a Catholic, Christian person is given valid absolution, that's the end of it as far as the Church is concerned.

"Gay Byrne chose not to apologise and ended up in hospital as a result, and that's all I'll say. I didn't set out to harm Gay Byrne. It was in Gay Byrne's own hands. I left it in his hands to apologise and behave himself. He chose not to. Gay Byrne can do an awful lot of good. Why dabble in this kind of stuff? Does he not realise that human beings can be hurt? And that his own immortal soul can be endangered?"

Though compelled to carry out acts of spiritual laundering, wherever necessary, His Grace is nevertheless extremely wary about tackling Beelzebub in face-to-face combat too often. The Devil, after all, can hardly be expected to play fair. Shortly after the RTE exorcism, for instance, Bishop Michael was standing on a scaffold (and, ironically, holding a spirit level) at his erstwhile home in Coolderry when he inexplicably fell to the ground shattering his right leg. So serious were his injuries that he was confined to a wheelchair for several weeks. He is convinced that the accident was a Satanic machination.

"An exorcism is not designed to injure, it's designed to help," he argues. "If anyone gets injured it's the poor old priest, God love him. Any clergyman will tell you that an exorcism is a very serious matter. You're taking on you-know-who. Satan, *(makes the sign of the cross)* and God bless us and save us after using that name, *will* have a go at the person who's having a go at him. Usually, in my case, it happens after the ceremony. It takes an awful lot out of me. I do be drained out for weeks afterwards. And the temptations that are sent can be cruel, wicked. All sorts of temptations, working on one's human flesh. Any weaknesses a person has are cruelly exploited.

"It's hard to explain but barriers also appear to prevent one's good work for Christ. An old trick of the Devil is to try and get you angry so he will incite people to try and cause annoyance. I have to be careful because I'll tell you something, Liam, he's had a right go at me. Even since I've been here in Cree, this church we're sitting in has seen some fierce spiritual battles. I get down on my knees and pray and I go over to the shrine of Our Lady of Clonfert regularly to meditate and pray for strength."

At the moment, Bishop Michael is steeling himself, spiritually and physically, for another bruising confrontation with the powers of darkness. One of these days he plans to exorcise Leinster House.

"There's a cluster of politicians up there and, in my opinion, they're completely un-Godly," he charges. "I watch the *Oireachtas Report* on the television. I watch all the debates in the Dáil and the Senate. And I've come to the conclusion that they're not at all mindful of Christ up there.

"There are some individuals who are worse than others. I was not one bit pleased with Proinsias De Rossa's comments during the divorce referendum, for example. There was no need for him to call bishops 'liars'. And there was no need for Alan Dukes to call a bishop a 'bastard', as he did some years ago. I mean no disrespect to you by using the word 'bastard', Liam. I'm using the word 'bastard' not as a curse or as an offence to God. I'm simply quoting. He did call a bishop a 'bastard'. That was unprofessional, un-Christian and it was certainly not gentlemanly.

"To attack any clergyman in such a manner is plain wrong. The bishops do not have to take that kind of abuse. I certainly am not going to take it lying down."

✛ ✛ ✛ ✛ ✛ ✛ ✛

Almost immediately after his ordination as a priest, Bishop Michael was miraculously bestowed with two extraordinary faculties: the gift of Divine Revelation and the gift of Divine Healing.

In mere-mortal-speak, Divine Revelation means that when God communicates with Bishop Michael, he dials direct.

"I don't actually hear His voice," the bishop insists, reassuringly. "It's more like a light bulb suddenly going on in a room. It's an awareness of something that was not there previously. It can happen at any time, but it happens to me mostly during the holy sacrifice of my mass and also when I go to Our Lady of Clonfert to meditate. I can tell you that it has been revealed to me through Divine Revelation that I should talk to you today and go public to the young people, telling them what it is I'm about."

Divine Healing is self-explanatory. Several times every week, Bishop Michael takes to the highways and byways in his red 1982 Ford Escort (the engine of which pleads and whines for the Last Rites in every gear above second) and visits the sick with what he calls his "Divine Healing Kit."

There are many people in south Offaly and beyond who are passionate believers in Bishop Michael's powers of spiritual sustenance and physical restoration. They have great respect for the old Cox succour.

"I use nothing but holy oils, candles, holy water, some crucifixes and the might, majesty and dominion of Almighty God," he discloses. "I put on my purple stole, and recite the Credo. I also do the laying on of hands, and the blowing of my breath in the sign of the cross over the unwell person. There's always at least one other person there. I insist on that to keep things right and proper. At the end of the ceremony, I put a candle in the centre of the room with a crucifix, and ask all present to join hands and pray. Then, I conclude with the shaking of the holy water and application of the holy oils.

"Several people have actually been cured of serious illness. The latest is a 27-year-old nurse from Moate. She contracted transverse mellitus, a condition of the lower spine. She was paralysed from the waist down. Her mammy contacted me and I said I would help. When she was allowed home from hospital for a weekend, I did three Divine Healings on her. Lo and behold, she's fine now.

"Those who haven't been healed fully have felt better in themselves and a great sense of peace, as a result of my Divine Healing. If their condition doesn't get any better, it doesn't get any worse. It arrests the illness."

As he speaks, His Lordship is abruptly interrupted by what he says is an attack of severe heartburn. A glass of milk helps bring some relief, but the phrase, *'Physician, heal thyself'*, crosses my mind.

"I can eat nothing only salads and salad rolls," he relates. "I can't eat fries. I'm very restricted in my diet. I purchase salad rolls in Birr every day. I may look stout but that's because of my medication. Unfortunately, Divine Healing does not work on oneself. I have a horrible stomach problem. May I show you? I'm not being disrespectful, Liam. Seeing is believing. I hope you don't mind."

Bishop Michael clutches the front of his jumper and soutane, and hoists them to chest level to reveal his belly. Above his navel, there is a six inch square embossment of gruesome weals and scars, grisly mementoes from a litany of surgical incisions.

"I've had several stomach operations," he groans with a wince, pulling his clothes back down. "But that's only part of it. I suffer from the following: I have a hiatus hernia. I have three small duodenal ulcers and I suffer from abdominal spasm. I have angina. When I was living in Dublin, I woke up one morning and I was trembling from head to foot. My mother had passed away. I was admitted to hospital and put into the heart unit. They told me that I was suffering from bereavement and burnout. I was completely stressed out, and I still get panic attacks.

"I also have an injured spine. My left hip is a problem too, the socket doesn't work correctly. I smashed my right leg after the exorcism in RTE. I had to have six screws, six pins and a bone graft put in."

Such afflictions are, he muses, the will of God. But there have been other torments too, so many in fact that the bishop might be forgiven for believing that they emanate from a more sinister source.

"In the mid-'80s, I was involved in a whiplash," he states. "A fella ran into the back of my car. I got a chipped bone in my neck. On the ridge road in Banagher, on April 4th, 1994, I was in a head-on collision with an articulated truck. The scaphoid bone in my wrist was broken. My arm, shoulder and ribs were injured. The scaphoid is the little bone that allows you to operate your wrist and, even though it's repaired now, I get terrible trouble with my left hand, especially in winter.

"Soon afterwards, I went into a local hotel while my arm was in a sling. As I was sitting down on the toilet, the toilet seat went one way and I went the other. I wrenched my back, aggravating the already existing problems with my spine. On April 24th last, a man ran into the little Fiat I had at the time. He made bits of it, writ it off completely. I got another whiplash between my shoulder blades. I'm suffering quite a lot from that."

Bishop Michael currently has three cases for damages (relating to the two most recent car crashes, and the hotel toilet-seat incident) pending before the courts. "It's a case of having to," he warrants. "Whatever money I get will be put to good use. It won't be spent on personal luxury, I can assure you. I could do with a decent car though. The one I have is hard to start in the mornings."

It's not yet 3pm and already nightfall appears to be closing in on the Cree horizon. Inside Saint Colman's too, the mood has turned darker. Bishop Michael Cox is talking about the imminence of what he calls, "the A-pop-a-lips."

"I believe we are in the beginning of the last times on Earth," he propounds. "Based on my own observation of what has happened since 1965, since Vatican II, I believe these are the last days. People have gone away from Christ in a way that they haven't before. The kids are not being taught properly. The catechism was kicked out of the school 30 years ago. In the old days, you knew where you stood. Since Vatican II, the best that people can hope for is a watered-down version of the truth.

"Morality is gone out the window. Satan seems to have got a grip on the world. Look at abortion, homosexuality, crime, massive unemployment. Machinery and technology and computers are taking over the whole world. People don't seem to have the belief in Christ that they should. We're living in another Sodom and Gomorrah. Even in Catholic Ireland.

"There's disasters happening all over the world. This is part of the Apopalips. There will be plagues and wars. Look at AIDS. Oh Lord, I pity any poor crater that has AIDS. I feel for those people. No matter what they got up to, I'll pray for them. If they've done something wrong, they shouldn't have been doing it but that's beside the point. I don't know when the end will come. But, I'll tell you one thing, the poor old Earth hasn't that long more to go. We'll see it in our lifetimes. Almighty God has begun to issue his Last Judgement."

All is not lost just yet, however. As Mick and I prepare to take our leave, Bishop Michael Cox calls me back and says that there is a special prayer, the prayer to Saint Michael, which used to be recited at the end of the Latin mass, and he believes that it can counteract even the Devil's most nefarious plots.

With discernible emotion in his eyes, Bishop Michael asks me to publish it in its entirety.

"Saint Michael the Archangel, defend us in the time of conflict.
Be our safeguard against the wickedness and snares of the Devil.
May God rebuke him, we humbly pray.
And endow our Prince of the Heavenly hosts.
By the power of Almighty God, cast into Hell Satan
And with him all the evil spirits who wander through this world for
the ruination of our mortal souls."

II

Nine months after the foregoing piece was published, I returned to Cree and found that all had changed, changed utterly.

The progress wrought in the condition of Saint Colman's Church was remarkable. Chaos had given way to scrubbed order. The miracle was evident the moment I arrived. Water gurgled in gutters, drainpipes and gullies, no longer splashing down the walls. The choppy waves of mud which had dashed against the church's plinth had been quelled by a pathway of gravel from the gates to the front door.

As His Lordship led me through the newly-varnished doorway, my nostrils were treated to a refreshing air-bath of cement dust and paint fumes. The once grotty interior was now suffused with a sense of decontaminated freshness, the kind of sweet sensation that one feels whenever a politician leaves the room.

The textile-mill apparatus was long gone. The cobwebs had been dislodged. The walls were patched and plastered. The ceiling was completely repaired. The floor had been stripped and scoured. Oblong buckets of white emulsion tiered in one corner bore testimony to the thorough paint job underway.

The precarious balcony which had constituted the bishop's home had been demolished. His altar was reassembled on solid ground, at the foot of the lancet window, atop a 20ft square expanse of crimson carpet.

Bishop Cox's much-derided dream of Saint Colman's becoming the country's first Tridentine cathedral was now several steps closer to reality. "The power of Almighty God knows no bounds," he declared. "I'm trusting totally in Christ. It's working wonders."

That Bishop Michael Cox had so dramatically transfigured Saint Colman's was astonishing. That he had done so on his meagre budget numbed even one's faculty for astonishment. In fact, most of the renovation work had been carried out for free, either by well-wishers who support Bishop Cox's Tridentine stance or as appreciative gestures by people who feel they have been helped by the bishop's faith healing.

In the wake of the original *Hot Press* story, Bishop Michael hit the national headlines. Extracts from our interview appeared on the front page of the *Irish Mirror,* and in a variety of other newspapers, national and international. The bishop himself was invited to go on RTE Radio 1 with Joe Duffy, for what turned out to be an exceptionally entertaining programme, during which His Lordship even treated listeners to a few tunes on his button accordion.

At every opportunity, Bishop Cox spoke about his Divine Healing gifts. Within weeks, his humble abode in Cree was inundated with appeals for help from the ailing and infirm. "I have treated about 1,000 people since the *Hot Press* article," he told me. "Most of them have been cured. People have come in here quite lame and have walked out the door. I say that in all humility. You know me, Liam, I am a humble man. I wonder at the power of God, and I never stop thanking Him and talking to Him.

"They came from all over. I'd come out in the morning and there'd be another car outside with someone waiting to see me. Where necessary, I travelled to the homes of people too ill to leave their beds. Otherwise, I asked them to try and come here. I've been to Kilkenny, all over the east and as far away as Clifden. I refused nobody, never turned anybody down. Cannot and will not."

Prepared to treat both humans and animals, Bishop Cox had notable success with horses. Word soon spread throughout the Kildare equestrian community in particular that the bishop had "magic hands." One afternoon during the summer, he returned home to find a queue of cars draw-ing horseboxes outside the gates of Saint Colman's. Some owners made the pilgrimage to have the bishop simply bless their horses.

Bishop Cox never charged a single penny for his services. He merely suggested that satisfied customers might like to make "a donation" to his church repairs fund. It turned out to be an inspired strategy. The response was flabbergasting.

The first sign that his luck had changed came when a local "admirer" (the bishop's word) sold him a 25ft Rio Vista mobile home for £800. "I'm told it's worth between £2,500 and £3,000," he gloated. "My conditions are a lot better since I moved into it. It has everything in it. Very cosy."

Electric power was supplied courtesy of another true believer. "I treat-ed a nurse from Roscrea with shingles," recounted Bishop Cox. "She was very bad with her legs and her stomach lining and her eyes and then her hands broke out. She suffered from terrible shingles. The doctors were doing no good. After a few visits to me, she started to get better. She was completely and totally cured over a short period of time.

"She was so impressed with my work that she sent her husband over to wire the church, in thanksgiving. He also rigged up the electrics from the church to the caravan."

Water and sewage facilities soon followed. A friend of the woman with the shingles travelled to Cree seeking relief for a painful foot affliction. When he started to believe that the Divine Healing was having an effect, he had his brother and another man ("a Methodist man," specifies the bishop) sink a well behind the church. A further group of pleased clients clubbed together and installed a septic tank on the grounds.

A brand new chalice, paten, monstrance and ciborium were purchased for the Saint Colman's altar by a woman who felt that Bishop Cox had restored her "balance." "She found it hard to stay standing," he elaborat-ed. "It was a middle-ear thing. She was cured instantly. She was very pleased."

A series of financial thanksgiving contributions allowed the bishop to put his temperamental Ford Escort out of its misery, and to substitute it with a 1986 Ford Escort diesel van.

The bubble had to burst, however. So busy did Bishop Cox become that he eventually suffered a physical breakdown. Already far from healthy, he had been over-exerting himself to the point of virtual burnout. When we renewed our acquaintance, he had only recently emerged from a period of convalescence in Tullamore General.

The sojourn in hospital inspired His Lordship to launch the most ambitious endeavour of his ecclesiastical career: The Bishop Michael Cox Healing and Confessions Service, a unique 24 hour telephone hotline offering absolution, redemption and Divine Healing, and all for only the price of a premium rate phonecall. The power of Almighty God knows no bounds, *or* area dialling codes.

Bishop Michael Cox is an acutely logical man. At his daily solitary mass in Saint Colman's, he would pray for the recuperation of people who lived far away and had asked him to do so. Some of these people claim to have recovered as a result, without ever having met the bishop in person. If his Divine Healing ability was effective over such long and scattered distances, he reasoned, it would surely be at least doubly effective if directed down a phoneline.

"God is in the Heavens," proclaimed Bishop Cox. "We pray to Him and He hears us, even though we assume He's a fair distance away, if we were to think of it in space terms. He is present with us all the time. He gave us the wonderful gift of communication with Him. Using the phone is another way of doing things. It's being done for the greater glory of God. Jesus Christ Himself would approve."

Before Telecom Eireann agreed to sanction his phoneline, they asked to see documentary evidence of Michael Cox's credentials as a bishop. After numerous entreaties, a letter of validation was forthcoming from a senior bishop in the Irish Catholic (Vatican II) hierarchy. Bishop Cox prefers not to publicly name that bishop, but his testimonial was sufficient to satisfy Telecom's concerns.

From the hotline, Bishop Cox hopes to earn most of the estimated £80,000 required to advance work on Saint Colman's to the stage where the general public could be safely invited to mass beneath its eaves. The number of The Bishop Michael Cox Healing and Confessions Service is 1570 122 940. The service costs the caller £1 per minute, 25 pence from which goes directly to the bishop. When you get through to the main number, you hear an introductory script telling you about the line. You are then offered a menu of choices.

There are five line options in all: 1) an interview with the bishop; 2) an excerpt from a Latin Tridentine mass celebrated in Saint Colman's; 3) the healing service; 4) a facility by which callers can leave special intentions for which they would like the bishop to pray; and 5), the confessions service.

Bishop Cox is not personally on hand to take the calls; that would be too much to expect from even a man of his abilities. All of the material you hear is pre-recorded but the bishop does listen in (via a confidential PIN code) to the special intentions and the litanies of sins several times every day.

Inevitably, it's been the proffering of the sacrament of reconciliation over the blower that has caused the biggest ruckus. Thanks to Bishop Michael, the Irish can now let our fingers do the confessing. Dial a pizza, then dial a 'bsolution. You don't even get any penance. All you have to do is leave your message after the atonement.

"On the confession line, I invite callers to say a little prayer before they make their confessions and ask that they remain anonymous," explained Bishop Cox. "When I was making the recording of the absolution, my motive and intention was, in union with Christ, to forgive those who would phone in. It will aid those who find it difficult to speak to a priest. It is completely within my understanding of God's power as given to His apostolic ministers.

"Obviously, because it's a tape, I won't be giving out penance to the callers. The absolution is more important. A Roman Catholic, be they Vatican I or Vatican II, will know themselves that they will have to do a certain amount of penance. I kinda leave it up to themselves. If they're truly sorry for their sins, they'll know, from their childhood, that they will have to say a number of prayers or do an act of kindness."

Bishop Michael Cox may have medical trouble with his spine but there is nothing wrong with his backbone. He is convinced that his resolve to live and practice as a Tridentine bishop constitutes a provocative challenge to the Irish Roman Catholic establishment in a manner both extremely profound and, erm, very profound.

While he talked about the setting up of his phoneline, it was obvious that he relished the prospect of another contentious religious storm breaking above his head. Indeed, he had hired his own PR advisor from the Dublin-based company, Promodirect, to ensure that there was such a storm.

As the interview wound up, Bishop Cox winked a conspiratorial wink and mimed a mixing gesture. *Stirring it,* I believe, is the expression.

"There will be healing miracles over this line," he predicted. "Many people will be very interested in what I am saying about the need for a return to traditional Catholicism. Others will be very interested in the idea of going to confession over the telephone, a service that, to my knowledge, has never been offered anywhere else in the world.

"There will be a theological debate, of a very interesting nature. There will be debates all over the place. I would welcome that. If anybody wants to debate publicly with me, I am happy to do so. I am prepared to go on radio and television."

AS HAPPY AS HARE

They are reviled on the streets. They pray from dawn
to dusk. They shun drink, drugs, gambling, sport, television, rock music and recreational sex. And yet, they
claim to live their lives in a state of permanent ecstasy. Enter the alternative universe of the Hare
Krishnas.

You hear a *hari-nama* before you see
it. A *hari-nama* is the Sanskrit term for the congregational street chanting
that is the global trademark of the Hare Krishna movement.

Most afternoons, when numbers permit, a crew of up to a dozen
Krishnas set off from their Dublin ashram, at 6 South William Street, and
dance a meandering circuit through the clogged arteries of the metropolis.

Today, there are only three females among the parade of devotees, as followers of Krishna like to be called. It is a principle of their faith that women must cover every inch of their bodies so as not to arouse lust, so the girls are safety-wrapped in vividly variegated saris, and headscarves of bright cotton.

The guys could be runners-up in a Bruce Willis lookalike pageant. Most of them are flashing lascivious expanses of bare stubble-scalp. They're wearing Indian robes or *dhotis,* some in saffron, some in white. This being breezy Dublin rather than balmy Delhi, the *dhotis* are augmented by thermal longjohns from Dunnes Stores. Krishna devotees may share little else with mainstream Irish religion but they are great believers in Saint Bernard.

The Krishnas use an array of exotic instruments, such as Bengali *mridanga* drums and *kartalas* hand cymbals, to create their unique sound. As music, it ranks alongside the din one would hear emanating from the kitchen of a busy restaurant. It's the cacophony of plates crashing to the floor, knives being sharpened, soapy water spluttering down a plughole. Up close, a *hari-nama* is extremely noisy. The racket shudders the bones, jars the teeth and makes eyeballs tremble in their sockets.

Essentially, the devotees have one tune which they ingeniously rehash under several guises. Their repertoire is also hidebound by the fact that on special occasions, such as the Appearance Day of a great devotee, the Krishnas must sing any hymns which that devotee may have written.

Many of these ditties date from 16th or 17th century India, and they leave you in no doubt about it either. You don't have to be tone deaf to be a Hare Krishna, but it helps.

The Hare Krishnas are a gentle, affectionate, inoffensive bunch. They are, therefore, despised by society at large. As I spend an afternoon traipsing after them, up and down the thoroughfares and footpaths of city centre Dublin, I am repeatedly stunned by the force of the dread and abhorrence which these impractically mild-mannered folk manage to churn up in their wake.

If you are one of the race-proud zealots who still espouse the self-delusional myth that the Irish are a tolerant, friendly, easygoing people who live and let live, I have a suggestion for you: Take a walk down Grafton Street sometime in the sandals of a Hare Krishna.

You might be doing nothing more provocative than offering pieces of *halavah* (a scrumptious confectionery made by the Krishnas from grains, butter and raisins) to a passing citizen but this gesture alone might be sufficient encouragement for that citizen to recommend, with the legendary Dublin warmth, that your best bet now would be to take that sweet and shove it up your hole, so it would.

If your duty is the distribution of books about Krishna, you automatically graduate to being a target for physical violence. There are gangs of young men, habitués of the Grafton Street area in particular, whose idea of high jinx is running up behind an unsuspecting devotee and courageously shouldering him to the ground. For maximum merriment, they favour doing this at least four or five times in a single day.

The motto of the Hare Krishnas is, "Be more humble than the straw on the street." They tend not to hit back or even express distress when they are knocked over. "Everyone tramples on us," says one battered and bruised devotee. "We don't think that we deserve any respect because we're pretty insignificant."

As this afternoon's procession turns off Dame Street onto College Green, the devotees are barracked by two slack-jawed youths in peak-backwards baseball caps and shell suits. "Talk English, will ya, for Jaysus' sake," they oink in unison, this pair of incisive wits who look like they couldn't sustain a fluent discussion about the weather without the services of a dialogue coach. "We talk English in this fuckin' country!"

At the bottom of Grafton Street, the Krishnas attract the attention of a mangy mutt, and his pet dog. These two creatures are so closely related, in a Darwinian sense, that when the four-legged beast licks its balls, the two-legged one wears the expression of delight. With a hiss and a wrist movement, the biped goads the quadruped to harass the Hares. Instinctive animal-lovers that they are, the devotees merely yelp back playfully at the barking hound and involve it in their jaunty cavalcade.

Disappointed by his failure to wreak any canine terror, the dog-owner clearly decides to shout something, but has to struggle for a moment in order to come up with the *mot juste*. At last, he finds it. "Cunts," he roars.

"Ye're a shower of cunts. Cunts!!"

Outside McDonald's, the troupe is cautiously joined by a vagrant. Rheumy-eyed, virtually toothless and decidedly doddery, the man would pass for 60 if his abundance of jet black hair did not assert his comparative youth. His skin is as sooty, as tattered and as wizened as his donkey jacket. The side of the poor bastard's head is adorned with a hideously inflamed abscess, the colour and shape of a small sea urchin.

Moving with the studied helplessness of the chronically drunk, he slowly insinuates himself into position at the tail end of the Krishna conga. A few moments later, he starts to chant Hare Krishna, and with such phlegmy fervour that one could be forgiven for assuming he's been doing it all his life.

The Hare Krishnas have many friends among the city's homeless and hobo population. On Wednesday and Saturday evenings, between 6 and 8, the devotees operate a mobile soup kitchen on the northside of the Ha'penny Bridge, on the plaza in front of the Dublin Woollen Mills. They serve rice, vegetables, dal, chapati, poppadoms, chutney and tea to the destitute, the dipsos and the just plain hungry. No questions asked and no converts sought.

"The homeless guys really appreciate it," a devotee called Sharma will tell me later. "They know it's not just ordinary food. You can see that on their faces while they're eating."

Nothing draws a crowd quite like a *hari-nama*. Shop assistants emerge from doorways. Buskers hold their fire. School outings stop dead in their tracks. Some onlookers simply enjoy the spectacle but a sizeable minority feel the need to heckle, point and snigger. They are obviously atheists. No Christian, I'm sure, would have the gall to sneer at the absurdity of another creed.

Suddenly, a short, fat, middle-aged woman in an oilskin raincoat bursts out from amidst the throng. She yanks the hapless bum by the arm, and drags him away from the devotees. While he attempts to regain his equilibrium and his dignity, the plump dowager proceeds to harangue him for fraternising with the Hares.

"Stay away from those people," she implores, with a passion that amounts to *venom*. "Have nothing to do with them. They'll brainwash you. They're not Christians. They're filthy, dirty heathens."

Hare Krishnas have a strange effect on matriarchal types. On the streets, it is noticeably they who recoil most furiously when offered the basket of *halavah* by the devotees. These women obviously view the way-out clothes, the queer hairstyles and the foreign jargon of this weird cult with extreme repugnance. And yet, if a member of their own devout tribe were to announce that the face of the Blessed Virgin Mary had miraculously appeared to her on a pop tart, they would be the first to declare their pride and spiritual rapture. Curious, innit?

The truth is that Hare Krishnas lead lives of such harsh asceticism that they make even the most self-flagellatory Catholics seem like wanton voluptuaries. These people could give Matt Talbot lessons in how to beat yourself up for the Almighty.

The Hare Krishna doctrine belongs to the ancient tradition of Vaishnava Hinduism. It was founded by Lord Chaitanya Mahāprabhu, a 16th century re-incarnation of Krishna, who taught that by chanting the name of Krishna, the one true God, and by studying his works and devoting ourselves to his service, we could free ourselves from life's biggest inconvenience: death.

The Hare Krishna bible is the *Bhagavad-gita,* an extensive extract from the *Mahabharata,* ancient India's most famous epic poem which is itself about eight times the combined length of the *Iliad* and *Odyssey.* The *Bhagavad-gita* comprises a dialogue between Lord Krishna and his disciple Arjuana.

Its language is Sanskrit, an archaic sacred tongue derived from Old Persian. Sanskrit is used in Hinduism much as Latin is deployed in Catholicism, as an ecclesiastical *lingua franca,* designed to stupefy and intimidate the masses.

For Hare Krishnas, their famous mantra is more than simply an act of devotion. It is "a transcendental vibration, the highest undertaking of philosophical life." Without chanting, we are just "academic spiritualists, chewing on the crackers of dry speculation."

The words 'Hare' and 'Krishna' are themselves divine. The medium is the message and vice, as they say, versa. Recitation of the mantra is the only hope that humans have of liberating themselves from bad karma. Happiness in this life is an illusion, *maya*.

Hare Krishnas deny the truth of Darwinian evolution. Nature, they believe, is a manifestation of Krishna, and animals, especially cows, are revered. It follows that beef barons, butchers and burger vendors are gatherers of exceptionally bad karma.

To Krishnas, the Earth is just one of many planets on which we must pass time before our consciousness has been sufficiently purified to allow us return to the Godhead. Frequent reincarnation is another basic tenet of Krishna dogma so it would appear that our consciousnesses are in no hurry back. It's just as well, therefore, that the Godhead is infinitely patient. 4,320 of our years constitute a single one of his days.

According to the *Bhagavad-gita,* we are currently living in the Age of Kali-yuga, "the age of quarrel and hypocrisy." As you will have noticed, it is a time of "descent into darkness." The Age will last a total of 432,000 years (a mere 100 days on the Godhead calendar), having begun 5,000 years ago (late yesterday afternoon, for the Godhead), when Krishna appeared in India.

To be a devotee of Krishna, one must turn one's back on all forms of "sense-gratification." At the heart of their faith lies the rejection of what the man who brought Hare Krishna to the West, Srila Prabhupäda (pronounced Shreela Prab-ou-pad), called "the four pillars of sinful life": intoxication, meat-eating, illicit sex and gambling. Each of these categories is defined in the broadest manner possible.

Devotees abstain from alcohol, narcotics, cigarettes, chocolate, coffee and tea. They are strict vegetarians who shun all fish and egg dishes too. The prohibition on gambling extends to non-monetary wagering of even the most innocuous kind.

Sex is permitted solely within marriage and, even then, only for the procreation of children. Divorce, abortion, contraception and homosexuality are regarded as deeply wicked. Masturbation is also frowned upon. 90% of Hare Krishnas get married at one point or another, but until they do they are expected to practise both celibacy and chastity.

Women and men live side by side in South William Street, but they may as well reside on different continents for all the contact they have with each other. They sleep in separate dormitories, eat at opposite ends of the dining room, and generally treat members of the contrary gender with an indifference that would not be out of place in the most desolate of rural Ireland's Bachelortowns and Spinstervilles.

The president of the Dublin Hare Krishna temple is a 25-year-old from Birmingham who used to be called Mark, but today glories in the name of Mahotsäha, which is Sanskrit for "great enthusiasm." For simplicity's sake, he introduces himself to outsiders as Mo.

In the late '80s, Mo shared a flat with the aforementioned Sharma. Sharma sang with a rock band then, and Mo helped out as a sound engineer. "We were very into music, especially George Harrison and The Beatles," Mo asserts. "George Harrison's lyrics were all about karma and reincarnation and philosophy, very strong stuff for pop music. We were very attracted to all that and began to read up on it. We then started to hang around Hare Krishna temples in London a lot."

About five years ago, Mo and Sharma both became devotees. Their fervour and energy quickly impressed their elders in London and, last year, they were chosen to spearhead the rebuilding of the Dublin Hare Krishna community.

As a child, Mo visited his grandparents in Ireland regularly. His estranged father now lives here but Mo claims no particular desire to rekindle their relationship. Prabhupäda is, he insists, his spiritual father, and that's all the family he requires.

Mo is effusive in his excitement about practising Krishna consciousness in this country – a society which he pays the ultimate compliment of describing as "very Indian." In the Hare Krishna world, things Indian are accorded special honour.

"I remember my grandparents churning their own butter," he recalls. "They had no electricity. No water, just a well. That's how people live in India. It is our ideal to live a simple, self-sufficient life. Ireland is a few years behind Germany, America and England. People are more simple and not so lost in material reverence. Prabhupäda's philosophy was,

'Simple living and high thinking'. Out of all the countries I've been in, Ireland is the most similar to India, though India is a little warmer.

"From our viewpoint, the fact that divorce has been illegal in Ireland is, morally, very good. It shows there are moral standards here. Now, unfortunately, they've pushed it, and divorce is legal *(sigh)*. I know Dublin is becoming a more happening place for material things but it's still backward enough, in a good sense, to be conducive for us."

The entrance to the South William Street ashram is the door next to the Harvest Wholefood Shop. Just before Christmas '95, the Hare Krishnas signed a three year lease for the uppermost two storeys of the building, which were formerly used as a youth hostel.

The intervening months have been dedicated to refurbishment. The top floor is now divided into segregated sleeping areas, complete with two separate shower cubicles each, for the boys and for the girls. Believing the comfort afforded by a bed to be a form of the dreaded sense gratification, the devotees get their shut-eye in sleeping bags which are unrolled randomly on a carpet mat.

The temple room, on the lower floor, is the ashram's largest and most consistently frequented chamber. With its whitewashed walls, bleached ceiling and expanse of pale mauve floorboards, the ambience is serene and soothing, but there's something curiously sterile and child-proof about the setting. It feels like a cross between a sanatorium, a gymnasium and a crèche.

At one end of the temple room hangs a heavy velvet curtain behind which there's a narrow stage. This is used during the Sunday festivals when the public are invited in to watch concerts and instructional dramas, and to enjoy a vegetarian feast. Microphones, amps and speakers stand mutely in a corner, awaiting their chance to hiss and crackle for Krishna.

The Dublin ashram cannot yet afford to have its own deities: shiny resin statues of Krishna and his consort Radha, in any of their many incarnations. The community lacks both the cash and the personnel necessary for such sacrosanct monuments. Like the names of Krishna, a statue of

Krishna is regarded as "none different" from Krishna himself. It is not simply a representation of Krishna, it *is* Krishna.

In lieu of the real thing, the Dublin fellowship has transformed one of the temple room's walls into a two-dimensional shrine, featuring devotional portraits of Krishna, and the six *goswami* (saints), devotional paintings of scenes from the *Bhagavad-gita* and devotional photographs of Prabhupäda, as well as devotional three-pin sockets and light switches.

Perched inside the door of the temple room are a series of wooden shelves for the footwear which must be removed at the threshold to this hallowed ground. Whenever devotees enter or leave, they drop to their knees and press their foreheads to the floor. The dedicated follower of Krishna will, I am told, prostrate his or her unworthy body up to 300 times a day.

"We understand that we are God's servants," affirms Mahotsäha. "That's why we're always bowing down to God. There is nothing more important than bowing down to God but, if we were doing that all day, we wouldn't accomplish anything else."

The dilemma is solved by the *tilaka*, the U-shaped ochre mark sported by devotees, most visibly from the bridge of the nose to the forehead, and which is often characterised as "a splash of birdshit" by astute Irish observers. The symbol represents the footprint of Krishna, and is actually worn on 12 individual locations on the body, such as the back and front of the chest, arms and legs.

Composed of clay from the bed of the river Ganges in India, the *tilaka* make-up comes in the form of soap-like bars from which a paste is created that is then sacramentally applied with the thumb and forefinger.

"By wearing Krishna's footprint on our heads, we are, in effect, always bowed down before him," explains Mahotsäha. "It reminds the devotee that his body isn't meant for his own enjoyment. His body is given to him only for Krishna's service."

Cookin' lasts, kissin' don't. That's as good a summary as you're likely to get of the difference between food and sex as far as Hare Krishnas are concerned. Devotees embrace the art of rustling up a bit of grub with an abandoned ardour. *Prasadam,* the chow that they prepare in their temples and offer to Krishna before cooking, is one of their proudest boasts, and justly regarded as a comprehensive argument in itself against the internment of people who bang *mridangas* in open municipal spaces.

My only complaint about dining in the Krishna temple is the agony it necessitates. Devotees eat all of their meals while squatting cross-legged on the floor. I am not, by temperament, inclination, practice or belief, a squatter. My attempts at a perfunctory hunker, therefore, involve a great deal of pain and considerable loss of self-respect.

"I feel a bit like Mister Bean here," I croak, in a vain effort to disguise my excruciation. The devotees stare blankly. They have never heard of Mister Bean. In their eyes, I am a clumsy original.

I gratefully accept the offer of a cushion, but my gratitude is rapidly deflated. In Hare-speak, a cushion is a slim, brown vinyl mat that is about as comfortable to sit on as an enormous After Eight mint.

Nevertheless, the tack *is* delicious. Transforming necessity into a virtue, Hare Krishnas have used the restrictions imposed by religion on their diet to develop a mouth-watering menu. Their kitchens are models of environmental and wholefood piety. They use only fresh, organic ingredients, they waste nothing and they recycle fanatically.

Fruit, vegetables (or *subji),* beans, carob, palate-scalding condiments and rice are their staples. Milk is regarded by the devotees as a "miracle-food." According to Prabhupäda, "Milk nurtures the finer tissues of the brain that help you to understand spiritual matters."

Eager to avail of only the purest creamery goodness, a couple of devotees travel down to Meath several times a week to buy cans of unadulterated, unpasteurised, sacred cow juice. They also separate their own curds and whey (now, there's a line you don't get to write very often).

A devotee will never eat food fixed by a non-devotee. Hare Krishnas believe that the consciousness of the cook enters food during its preparation. If they were to snork down any old product from the Findus Crispy Pancake range, for instance, they would be consuming false consciousness. For reasons that none of the Dublin disciples could quite explain, this especially applies to meals that are cooked over a flame and/or involve grain in their recipe.

Similarly, when *prasadam* is eaten even by a sinful and ignorant person from the materialistic realm, it helps free that person from their own bad karma. This is why devotees are so keen to dole out snacks on the street and why they welcome all-comers to their Sunday feasts.

Three years ago, Mick Duff was frontman with Dragonfly, one of the hottest young acts on the Dublin rock circuit. In September of 1994, at the age of 21, Mick caused consternation among his family, friends, and fellow band members when he announced that he was about to abandon the conventional world and join the Hare Krishnas.

An introvert from childhood, Mick says he was always plagued by intimations of mortality. At school, in his native Dundrum, he was more interested in death than in career guidance. While his contemporaries were enjoying carefree adolescence, he was in his bedroom writing poetry about the futility of life.

In fifth year, he discovered rock music, and believed he had found his vocation. He helped form Dragonfly, became a songwriter and learned the pleasures of dope-smoking. But it still wasn't enough.

It was at the 1992 Féile that Mick first encountered the Hare Krishnas. He spent the entire weekend in their marquee in the main campsite; chanting, listening to lectures and eating *prasadam*. Back home, he devoured the literature which the devotees had given him, and started to visit the Dublin ashram, which was then in Temple Lane.

18 months later, he sold his most prized possession, his huge record collection, and shaved his head. At first, his parents were shocked by his decision to become a devotee but his mother was relieved that, as he had long stopped going to mass, he was at least worshipping God in some manner. His father takes more convincing, and is still sceptical.

Mick will not be formally initiated and given his own Sanskrit name until he accepts an older and more experienced devotee as his Spiritual Master. At the moment, his chief duty is the distribution of Krishna books on the street. This is regarded as one of the most worthwhile jobs a devotee can have, a bountiful source of "spiritual nectar." It is said to be the quickest way of gaining advancement in Krishna consciousness through physical activity. Mick hopes to continue distributing books for at least another decade.

He spends five or six hours every day on his designated beat – Grafton Street, O'Connell Street and Temple Bar – handing out books and requesting donations from those who take them. He collects between £50 and £60 a day. Half this money goes to cover the cost of the publications, the rest goes to maintaining the temple. Among those to whom he has sold books are Adam Clayton and Paul McGuinness ("Paul McGuinness only had dollars but he gave me a few anyway," he recalls).

"I meet people from my band days, mates, on the streets," Mick avers. "They're gobsmacked when I tell them about my life now. I tell them that Krishna consciousness is better than sex or drugs or rock 'n' roll. Then I challenge them: Either I'm a nutcase because I've given those things up or else Krishna consciousness *is* better than those things. Are you calling me a nutcase?"

For visitors, the South William Street ashram is a temple. For the residents, it's a monastery. There are a number of devotees who live with their families, hold down jobs and practise Krishna consciousness in their own homes. But the ten people who live in South William Street are anchorites, austere purists who devote their every waking moment to worshipping their God.

The devotees are well used to people dropping by to sample the atmosphere, or the nosh, and then buggering off. The environment is carefully controlled to encourage such calm informality. Nobody interrogates newcomers or watches them too closely. In the background, meanwhile, a cassette of chanting replays itself over and over, just loud enough to create a constant buzz of low-level prayerfulness (but not quite loud enough to help me locate the tape machine so that I can accidentally unplug it – nothing brings on my migraine faster than a constant buzz of low-level prayerfulness).

In the midst of all this mellow forbearance, the Hare Krishna monks get on with the serious business of being Hare Krishna monks. The devotees are scathingly scornful of the materialist treadmill on which most of us spend our lives. Yet they blithely conform to a regimen of chanting, adoring and paying homage that is, by any definition, a ruthless daily grind.

These are people who arise at 4am, go to bed no later than 9pm, and spend their entire day scrupulously avoiding sense gratification. They have hopped out of the rat race alright, but only to substitute it with the hamster-wheel of Krishna consciousness.

The devotees are roused each morning by an electronic alarm which goes *de-de-de-de-da de-de-de-de-da*. I know this because, in keeping with their firm commitment to recycling, they put an onomatopoeic rendering of the noise to use as a metaphor during the 9am philosophy lecture.

"Just as the *de-de-de-de-da de-de-de-de-da* of our alarm awakens us from our slumbers," Sharma, today's lecturer, expounds, "so the spiritual vibration of the chanting of Hare Krishna awakens us from our illusory condition in the materialist realm."

The Hare Krishnas regard rock music as "a mundane sound vibration," and add it to their list of sense-gratifications to be avoided. Personal possessions are kept to a minimum. There is a TV set in the ashram but it is used only for the playing of videos of lectures by Prabhupäda, and for the occasional peek at the news.

Sport is also disdained by Hare Krishnas as "a waste of time of no value to the soul." The only athletic pursuits granted an official nod of the Godhead are swimming and wrestling, on the perfectly reasonable grounds that these were the recreations favoured by Krishna during his last incarnation on Earth.

Cleanliness is fundamental to the Hare Krishna way of life. A devotee's first task every day is a thorough wash. Though they are fond of dismissing human flesh, with a tastefulness worthy of artists working in the death metal genre, as "a bag of rotting meat" or "a sack of pus and blood," they also strenuously believe in keeping themselves spotless and fragrant at all times.

A fastidious concern for hygiene is also the primary reason male disciples shave their heads. "It's the best and simplest way of keeping clean," maintains Mahotsäha. "One of our devotees here is the son of Robert Chambers, the hairdresser. He told me how many hairdressing salons there are in Dublin alone. They are second only to the pubs in number.

People spend so much time and money grooming their hair. We just keep it simple and shave it all off. The girls keep their hair long but tie it up. It's a sign of renunciation. We want to become free from vanity but also to be clean."

At 4.30am, the daily veneration ceremonial begins. The devotees sing the 45 minute incantation of *mangal-arati,* and then spend a further 15 minutes chanting the Hare Krishna mantra. At 5.30am, the assembly disperses so that each individual may embark on his or her personal chanting regime.

Prabhupäda decreed that every devotee must complete 16 laps a day on a string of 108 *japa* beads (which, when not in use, is kept in an orange cloth-bag, sometimes worn at the waist). At each bead, he or she chants the full recitation of "Hare Krishna, Hare Krishna, Krishna Krishna, Hare Hare, Hare Rama, Hare Rama, Rama Rama, Hare Hare." This interminable ritual, which makes five decades of the Rosary seem as concise as an order for take-away spring rolls, requires two whole hours to complete.

"People think that it's very boring, chanting the same words for so long," says Mick Duff. "But those words are so special they don't lose their taste. As we chant, we're purifying our consciousness and becoming more attached to Krishna. With Krishna consciousness, you get the ultimate spiritual life and you don't hanker for anything else. Because the consciousness of a materialistic person is the same all the time, they have to change the externals. They have to change their hairstyles, their clothes, their sex life. Their consciousness is stagnant. All the time we chant, our consciousness is changing. We enter another realm."

Or, perhaps, it just feels that way. It's 7.30am, the day is half gone, when I first meet the devotees, and I am immediately struck by their haggard appearance. Most of them have big, black, refuse sacks beneath their eyes. A few also move with a twitchy, floppy, loose-limbed gait which could be an attempt to ape Eastern deportment and poise, or could just be the result of sheer physical exhaustion.

Unaccountably, they all seem thrilled giddy by my arrival. They wave and grin and bow in my direction like my very presence is enough to bring health to the afflicted, tranquillity to the tormented, and concord

On the third day, he rose again: Father Fay emerges from his confessional

i

Father Fran: The Heavy Petal Priest

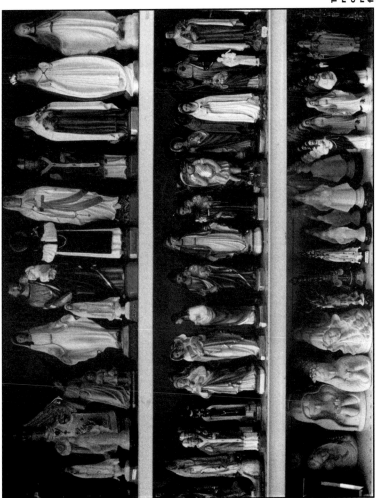

The first one to move gets its own shrine and merchandising franchise

Pic: Michael J.Quinn

iii

Is this a souvenir
Knock dagger I
see before me?

Pic: Michael J.Quinn

iv

Pic: Michael J.Quinn

Waiting for the call: Most Reverend Bishop Michael Cox will hear your confession now

v

Pic: Michael J.Quinn

Chant in the old-fashioned way: The Hare Krishnas enjoy a spot of Godhead-banging on Grafton Street

Staff outing: ring a ring a rosary on Croagh Patrick

Pic: Michael J.Quinn

vii

A Marriage Cake: the family that bakes together stays together

Pic: Michael J.Quinn

among the nations. *"Haribol!,"* they chirp, one after the other. "You are very welcome. Chant Hare Krishna."

Love-bombing is a classic Hare Krishna strategy. It's based on the proposition that, deep down, every one of us is convinced that we are singularly very special. If the Krishnas can persuade us that they think we're singularly very special too, they're well on the way to winning us over. For some, it proves an irresistible sales pitch.

Shortly after 7.30am, the daybreak rite of worship continues with *kirtan,* an ensemble adoration of the deity which entails more singing, more dancing and more chanting. The accompaniment is provided by Sharma on harmonium, and Mick Duff on *mridanga.* The men dance closest to the devotional wall, and the women dance behind the men.

For 60 minutes, the nine-strong congregation, some in socks but most in barefeet, shake their heads from side to side, jiggle about and spin in circles, their palms upraised in ecstatic adulation.

Beneath the photograph of Prabhupäda, Vince, one of the older devotees, wafts incense around the room with a peacock-feather. He also makes offerings to Krishna; a daisy, some water and a bowl of *halavah.*

The devotees sing, "Jaya Prabhupäda! Jaya Prabhupäda!" All glories to Prabhupäda!

Beryl and Ellen are childhood friends from Lucan, County Dublin. Three years ago, when they were both 15, they happened upon a *harinama* on the streets of Dublin. Intrigued by the brilliant, peach-coloured robes and the unusual music, they tagged along with the parade for as long as they could, but eventually lost it. A few days later, they plucked up the courage to follow a homeless man into the Dame Street temple, and they've been hanging around with devotees ever since.

Because they were, until recently, under 18, they had to be granted parental approval before they could be accepted into the ashram. Neither girl sleeps in the temple every night but they spend as many nights as possible there. Ellen attends a Youthreach course every weekday while Beryl is unemployed, but they both intend becoming full-time devotees within the next few weeks.

"The music is good, the devotees are real nice and I *love* the saris – they're the best thing of all," enthuses Beryl. "The Hares are not hypocritical about what they say. When they say they live by strict rules, they live by them, totally. Not like the Catholics. They just go to mass to make themselves feel better. Then, they go home, get drunk, smoke, take drugs and kill animals. The devotees are honest and real sweet."

Ellen is gleeful in her anticipation of life as *bona fide* monk. "I can't wait," she chirrups. "The devotees didn't want us to cause upset at home. They told us to wait until we're 18, and it's been a long wait. But we're lucky that our parents are fairly open-minded. Some of our friends thought that we were weird at the start, but a few of them think it's great now."

During stay-overs, Beryl and Ellen's duties include cleaning the kitchen, and helping to make the confectionery. They are not at all bothered by the degree of gender separation that is insisted upon in the temple. "It's nice, because you have privacy," asserts Beryl. "I like that. It's a good way to live."

The ultimate responsibility for the propagation in the West of the Hare Krishna dogma lies with The Beatles. Calcutta-born Srīla Prabhupāda (the most recent in a line of 32 disciples that stretches back to Lord Krishna himself) was a declining 69-year-old whose only possessions were a suitcase, seven dollars and a pair of *kartalas* cymbals when he landed in Boston on September 17th, 1965. "His mission," we are instructed, "was to take Krishna Consciousness to the most spiritually dark place on earth, the West."

The hippies of San Francisco (a portion of the populace renowned for their impeccable judgement) were the first to embrace his teaching. In July 1966, Prabhupāda and a retinue of excitable acid-heads founded ISKON, the International Society for Krishna Consciousness. One of ISKON's earliest allies was the poet Allen Ginsberg (however, Ginsberg's zeal soon cooled when he started to hear all that talk about abandoning sense gratification).

It was in 1969, when a group of Prabhupāda's acolytes, door-stepped the Fab Four outside the Apple offices in London's Saville Row, that Krishna consciousness achieved critical mass.

John Lennon placed his white Rolls Royce at Prabhupäda's disposal. The Beatles financed the setting up of a temple in Soho Street, and much else besides. George Harrison was their most enthusiastic champion. He recorded a single of the Hare Krishna mantra which reached number 12 in the U.K. Top 40 in August 1969.

Harrison later sold the movement his Hertfordshire mansion and estate for a nominal fee. Renamed Bhaktivedanta Manor, it is now one of the Krishnas' most palatial and busiest temples, much to the fury of upper-crust locals who have been campaigning to have it closed down for over two decades.

George Harrison is still a devotee. In early 1995, Mick Duff spent six weeks in India, at a world convention in Mayapur (Bengal). Harrison was a regular at the festivities, chanting his head off at every available opportunity.

When Prabhupäda died (or, as the devotees prefer, "left the planet") in 1977, the global Krishna movement went into a tailspin. Inevitably, power struggles erupted, and there was much internecine legal warfare over the phenomenal wealth which the founder had amassed during his short tenure as the hippest guru in the West. The very fact that Prabhupäda was exposed as a mortal human was enough to disillusion many with the faith. Throughout the '80s, Hare Krishna communities all over the world fell apart, not least in Dublin.

"There was a vacuum," admits Mahotsäha. "People drifted away. Some thought the movement had disappeared altogether. I know that a lot of the older Irish devotees are in India now, preaching. Their experience was lost to Dublin. We believe there is going to be a resurgence, especially in Ireland where the young people have been very demoralised by all the scandals in the Catholic Church. Eastern thought is very attractive to someone who has been oppressed by the fire and brimstone stuff, and the hypocrisy."

Up to a dozen British devotees have arrived in Dublin during the past year or so, all intent on rebuilding at least one strong ashram in the city. A Dublin posting has proven especially popular with U.K. disciples, who turned to Krishna consciousness as a route of escape from a degenerate youth.

"Necking E's, guzzling lager, goin' out ever night, I've done all that," states Matthew, a 25-year-old from Gloucestershire. "I was into the whole illegal rave scene in the early '90s. But I wanted out of all that. I grew to hate it, the drugs, the cheating, the sheer badness. I prefer to glorify God through music and dance, and Dublin is a great place to do that. In Britain, some devotees are making rave music that glorifies Krishna, and that's something that I'd like to bring over here too."

When the Dublin community's van isn't on the blink, a team of devotees travels to Cork, Limerick, Galway, Belfast, and points in-between, to stage miniature Hare Krishna festivals. Generally, they're received with bemused tolerance. In the confraternity city of Limerick though, they are invariably picketed by fractious platoons of Born Again Christians.

"We never condemn any other religion," insists Mick Duff. "We say they're all correct but that there's relative truth there. Born Again Christians are the only ones we find it difficult to deal with. Talking to them is like talking to a brick wall."

If amiability alone can clinch proselytes for Krishna then these people are onto a winner. An atmosphere of consummate courteousness and conviviality is maintained throughout the day in the temple.

By evening, I realise that the devotees possess at least one trait that is even more extraordinary than their unyielding fealty to Lord Krishna. None of them swear. Ever.

I mention the conspicuous lack of cussing to several disciples and they all respond by dazzling me with lavish smiles of pity and pained tolerance. The Hares don't need to utter expletives. They can simply look at you like you're a fucking gobshite.

"We are all striving to live saintly lives," claims Mick Duff. "Everything we think about, say and do is connected to Krishna. That doesn't leave a lot of opportunity for negative sound vibrations such as bad language. If we aren't going to say something about Krishna, we just say nothing."

AIN'T NO MOUNTAIN HIGH ENOUGH

If the annual Croagh Patrick climb were anything other than a religious ritual, it would be deemed a revolting bloodsport, and probably banned.

I was following closely behind the elderly man in the tattered pair of black and purple slippers for half an hour before I realised that he wasn't wearing slippers. It was his bare feet that were tattered, black and purple.

The man was 75 if he was a day. His face as dun and worn down as an old tu'penny piece, he assessed his every footstep deliberatively, like a farmer about to bid on livestock at a mart.

Despite his caution, almost every footstep he took turned out to be a mistake, as yet another shock of pain shot through his fragile limbs and exited through gritted teeth in the form of a despondent grunt.

When I last saw him, disappearing in to the mist, six of his toes had swollen to the size of baked apples. He was leaving bloodstains on the stones.

Croagh Patrick has the effect on bare feet that a cheese-grater has on a block of cheese. Ten minutes hiking on this craggy reek without shoes or boots and your feet are fit for nothing but sprinkling over pizza. 15 minutes, and they're Kraft Philadelphia.

I clambered up Croagh Patrick in a robust pair of brogues with brick-thick soles and there isn't a muscle or joint below my eyebrows that I didn't twist, injure, wrench, impair, tear or over-exert.

To remain even nominally vertical, it was necessary to slam a foot down on jagged rocks at least once every 45 seconds. Even the fern, heather and bracken up there are trip-wired to gash and pierce pilgrim flesh. The path on the mountainside is so narrow, crooked and treacherous that the very basics of walking have to be re-learnt. And that's when there is a path.

The hundreds who choose to scale the heights unshod have to deal with all of this, as *well* as the First Law of Rock Climbing, which states that there is a direct relation between how exposed and unprotected a foot is and how many mountain-boot studs will be ground into it.

Enthusiasts will tell you that those who conquer Croagh Patrick in bare feet are the most pleasing to Almighty God. It is they who will be most richly rewarded in the next life. This is probably because the shoeless tend to say more prayers on the way up. Well, they tend to utter more oaths anyway, which is close enough.

Croagh Patrick is the 2,710ft holy mountain on the north west coast of Mayo. Every year, during the last weekend in July, somewhere in the vicinity of 30,000 men, women and children toil and sweat their way to its summit, from where they can overlook Clew Bay and the absolute fatuity of the trek they have just endured.

As I write, three days have passed since I made it back down to *terra firma*. I still feel as weak and as tired as the RTE summer schedule. My face is fire-engine red with sunburn. In what is undoubtedly a medical first, I have both mild heat stroke and a touch of pleurisy.

The doctors tell me that my *joie de vivre* is scarred for life and that my chutzpah may never walk again.

Nevertheless, the thrill of being a landlubber once more is intoxicating. So harrowing was my day on the Croagh Patrick slopes that there have been times during the past 72 hours when I have found myself tearful with emotion at the mere sight of playing fields, the green baize of snooker tables and pancakes.

"Aren't level surfaces wonderful," I would chirp, miming uniform flatness with the palms of my hands and then holding my thumbs aloft in joyous approval.

When you stand at the foot of Croagh Patrick, you have two options. You can begin the arduous ascent or you can fling yourself to the ground and beg for a swift stoning. The only difference between the two alternatives is that the second one is quicker.

Before you commence the climb, it is recommended that you buy a reek stick, a roughly-cut, elbow-tall branch which acts as a staff. These sticks are sold by dozens of traders all around Croagh Patrick for £1 each. Some of the stick retailers are immediate locals, others come from nearby Westport, but the majority are travellers, many of them descendants of families who have been setting up stall here every year for generations.

When you take into consideration the cost of production, labour and overheads, the net profit on every stick sold for £1 works out at approximately £1. And there are people in the settled community who persist in believing that travellers are unsophisticated dolts.

The red letter date for visitors to Croagh Patrick is the last Sunday before August, or Reek Sunday. Local people make their pilgrimage on the previous Friday, or Garland Friday. This leaves them free to offer goods and services on the day the outsiders arrive, or Big Payday.

The locale which benefits most bountifully from Reek Sunday is the tiny village of Murrisk, directly beneath Croagh Patrick, a dreary, comatose hamlet whose inhabitants must look upon Bohola as downtown Manhattan. A road-sign just outside Murrisk makes a plea for motorists to DRIVE SLOWLY THROUGH THE VILLAGE. By the time you've finished reading it, it's too late to comply.

There is literally nothing to Murrisk apart from a couple of pubs, a grotto and a public phone box. The village has the feel of one of those rusted, discarded vehicles you often see rotting in the corners of fields in the west of Ireland. A scrapped Ford Anglia, perhaps – the height of automotive style in the 1950s but now a forlorn remnant of a dull and austere past.

The annual bloom of pilgri-tourism is the moss growing on the bonnet – it may not be much but at least it's a sign of life.

As well as taking care of business, hundreds of itinerants congregate in Murrisk, and around Westport, at this time every year because Reek Sunday is one of the most important holy days in the traveller calendar. All along the Louisburgh road, there are small encampments of caravans. Every hundred metres of grass verge has at least one grazing horse.

Westport is an affluent town, bristling with the kind of self-assured prosperity that is only possible in a district where the citizens can earn money by selling boughs to tourists. On Reek Sundays, it plays host to an extraordinary outdoor market which specialises in accessories for the Croagh Patrick expedition.

This might seem like a limited inventory. Apart from your stick, what could you possibly need to buy in order to trudge up a mountain? To ask such a naive question is to betray gross ignorance about one of the principal traditions of Reek Sunday – the capricious weather.

Though the public climb always takes place in the closing days of July, at the would-be zenith of the should-be summer, it is a long established convention that Mother Nature avails of the opportunity to pull the most devious tricks out of her meteorological bag.

"Expect the worst and you won't be disappointed," declared a ferret-featured man behind one of the makeshift counters at the Westport market. His stand stocked rainwear and straw hats, umbrellas and t-shirts, chunky sweaters and sun visors. He was doing a roaring trade in all lines.

It didn't take long before we realised why. The sky was a chilly zinc grey when photographer Mick Quinn and I set off up the mountain. We had barely travelled far enough to work up a flimsy pretext for our first drink when truncheon-shaped bursts of sunshine started to crash down on our backs.

A pounding surf of perspiration surged from my every pore. I stopped to remove my jumper and to tie its arms around my waist in what leading fashion consultants would recognise as a granny knot. Seconds later, the skies opened.

There is no shelter on Croagh Patrick, so everyone just marched onwards in the deluge, smiling, nodding and agreeing with each other that it was a dreadful downpour (not to be confused with those dreadful up-pours which are so commonplace in this country).

Gusts of wind flung rain in my face and rattled my teeth. I bowed my head as if that would somehow protect me from the shower. I was now so thoroughly wet that it didn't seem to matter whether or not I put my jumper back on. When I eventually did, it felt repellent, simultaneously hot, sopping and steamy, like laundry removed too soon from the dryer.

The early stages of the ascent are supposed to be easy, a gentle stroll in the hills. But not for me. I was already exhausted. My breathing had risen to a startling volume; the exhalations sounded like the brakes of the runaway bus in *Speed*. My heart was reprising the drum solo from Led Zeppelin's 'Moby Dick' (live version).

Everywhere I looked, people were in good spirits, striding through what they knew were the lowlands with poise and aplomb. I, meanwhile, exuded all the poise and aplomb of a wobbling vase on a toppling shelf in a demolished china shop just after the bull has left.

About an hour into the climb, I latched onto a female with a pink rucksack who seemed to know what she was doing. She was certainly making more steady headway than I had been. Staying a few discrete steps behind, I mimicked her every movement; leaning low at certain points like she did, taking breathers when her radar decreed that it was safe and smart to do so.

It seemed to be paying off. With only a slight exertion, I was able to keep pace with her. I was delighted with myself. She must have been nearly seven years of age.

When her father periodically turned and told her that she was a great girl and that it wouldn't be long now, I took his words as personal encouragement. A re-assuring smile for my pathfinder was a re-assuring smile for me.

The only awkward moment came when we hit a bad slope and the father said, 'Give me your hand, darling'. I honestly didn't mean to push his daughter out of the way like that. It was a reflex action.

According to legend, Croagh Patrick was originally known as Cruachan Aigli and belonged to Crom Dubh, the pagan harvest goddess.

Having overwhelmed Crom with his (tarantara!) miraculous powers, Patrick took control of the mountain around A.D. 441. To celebrate his victory, he adjourned to the summit where he fasted and did penance for the statutory 40 days and 40 nights.

It was from the sheer slopes on the south side of the mountain that Patrick banished the serpents from Ireland. The story goes that he rang his mighty iron bell until every snake in the country had been driven into the sea. Today, the only reptiles which survive on Irish soil are natterjack toads and barristers.

The fable about Patrick's novel programme of snake-expatriation is accepted as fact by a sizeable number of those who climb Croagh Patrick. Speak to some of the older people about it and they become almost dewy-eyed with admiration for the efficiency and thoroughness of Patrick's achievement.

Start talking about how the land bridge between this island and the continent was inundated by the sea before the reptiles made it back after their retreat south during the Ice Age, and they'll look you up and down with an expression of converging commiseration and contempt which loosely translates as, "I didn't know they could stack shite that high."

I guess if you believe in the concepts of a 'holy mountain' and a 'Saint' Patrick then the idea of a bell that impels serpents to mass suicide is not a huge stretch. Especially if you're an unfortunate graduate from the crack-er-barrel school of Christian infomercials which passed as basic education in a country where the three R's have frequently meant religion, religious studies and religious instruction.

The tradition of the communal Croagh Patrick climb is said to be 5,000 years old. It was a pagan ritual which was incorporated into the Christian schedule sometime after the fifth century. The designation of the last weekend in July as the occasion for the ascent has strictly heathen roots. Reek Sunday is the last Sunday before the harvest festival of Lughnasa, which falls on August 1st.

The pagan custom was that the climbing of the reek was accompanied by tremendous revelry. By all accounts, the carousing, feasting and, no doubt, fornication took place at both the summit and the foot of the mountain where our pre-Patrick ancestors would generally party their unbaptised asses like it was 1999 B.C.

Gradually, however, as Reek Sunday became more and more Christianised, the clergy strove to ensure that the climb was no longer used as an excuse to get ripped to the tits. It was to be a day dedicated solely to repentance and atonement.

William Makepeace Thackery, who visited Croagh Patrick on the last Sunday in July, 1842, shortly before the Great Famine, recounts that "The priests going up the mountain took care that there should be no sports nor dancing."

Where once people had merrily ascended the reek to celebrate the gods of wine, food, song and jiggy-jig, they were now being kept under surveillance by the spiritual forbears of Una Bean Mhic Mháthúna. Language historians have recorded a dramatic rise in the use of the phrase *Ochón agus Ochón O* during this period.

After a decline in popularity, the Catholic hierarchy instituted a revival in the observance of Reek Sunday in 1903. Thus began an era of intense zealotry which regularly saw over 50,000 penitents scale Croagh Patrick. This was the heyday, or heynight, of the 'darkness climb', the tradition of beginning the ascent at midnight on Saturday and, all going well, reaching the summit before dawn.

The night pilgrimage was officially ended by the Church in 1973, ostensibly because of the multiple accidents which occurred on the mountainside in the murk and gloom. But the casualty figures have always been worse during daylight climbs, when the reckless and the greenhorns take more gambles with life and limb.

The real reason for halting night pilgrimages was that an increasing number of 1970s penitents had begun to reclaim their pagan heritage by turning the climb into a booze crawl, and getting blazingly lit-up in the dark.

Though no longer ecclesiastically endorsed, dozens of people, especially travellers, continue to make the darkness climb. Some because they feel it is a more purging penitential exercise.

Others because, well, let's put it this way, there are an awful lot of empty Blackthorn cider cans crushed into the clay up there, and not all of them can date from the Bronze Age.

Until today, I hadn't realised that it was possible to fall upwards but it is. I did so several times on Croagh Patrick. And just as well too. If it hadn't been for the falls and the stumbles, I wouldn't have made any progress at all.

The weather was still acting the bollocks. Within one 45-minute interval, we had been treated to hailstones, hurricane winds, melanoma-hatching sun rays and a curious spume which looked like regular mist, but felt like mist on performance-enhancing drugs.

The staff was indispensable. Not everybody had bought a reek stick. Loads of people had brought their own homemade versions, made from broom handles, canes, walking sticks, old crutches, shillelaghs, even a strip of aluminium doorframe. But some sort of solid stave was essential for the climb.

The higher we got, the more painful movement became. It wasn't just that the muscles of my thighs and back had begun to ache with the stinging agony of raw sunlight on hungover eyeballs. It was also the fact that the smallest action, such as a blink, a scowl or the expression of a scatological profanity, now required an Ardnacrusha of energy to accomplish.

At an inlet in the rockface, a Born Again Christian choir of four toothy young people were lashing away at 'Nearer My God To Thee' and 'Saint Patrick's Breastplate'. Thanks to the felicitous acoustics on Croagh Patrick, they were virtually impossible to hear until you passed straight in front of them.

As soon as you came within earshot, you were instantly filled with respect for the bravery of these kids. It took a helluva lot of guts to bring their unique style of melody-free gospel to this particular location. The ground is littered with potential missiles.

Cleverly, however, the choristers diverted the attention (and the hands) of climbers from thoughts of brickbat-slinging by inviting everyone to clap along with a chant of, *"O Glorious Saint Patrick, dear saint of our isle, upon the people of Ireland, bestow your sweet smile!"*

For a brief moment, I caught a glimpse of my reflection in a puddle of water, an offshoot from the creek which bubbles down the mountainside with infuriating nonchalance. I had the hollow stare of a man whose life had abruptly gone completely to shit.

As the slope steepled ever more sharply upwards, and the atmosphere grew thinner, most climbers fell silent. An air of solemnity settled on even the giddiest groups of young people. I, however, reacted to the exacerbation of conditions by starting to make a strange, loud and involuntary sound: *"Heek!"*

This unusual, helium squawk first surfaced as a sort of hiccup of exertion, a little like the noise weight-lifters make when they hoist an especially formidable barbell. Pretty soon, it became the *only* utterance of which I was capable.

Every time I stirred so much as an inch, I wheezed another *"Heek!"* A pause for breath was bookended by a coming-to-rest *"Heek!"* and a starting-off-again *"Heek!"*

I have no idea what *"Heek!"* means or why I kept repeating it. But, in my personal lexicon, it will forever-more be code for a private incantation, which goes, *"O Glorious Saint Patrick, dear saint of our isle, if I make it home in one piece, I am going to hunt down all of your living relatives and skin them like pigs!"*

For some time, the fog that enveloped us on the reek had been so dense that immediate visibility extended to no more than ten metres. Suddenly, the haze seemed to melt away in the sunlight, and I could see where the mountain tapered off. I could even see the silhouette of a structure of some kind. We were obviously on the threshold of the Croagh Patrick peak.

I spun around to alert Mick Quinn. *"Heek!"* I bellowed excitably, pointing towards the horizon. *"Heek! Heek!"*

To my spine-curving horror, I soon discovered that we had not reached the top of the mountain at all but merely what's known as the First Summit, a plateau which provides a respite from climbing for a few hundred metres, only to give way to an even more precipitous and arduous incline.

If nothing else, the First Summit was at least a watering hole. A rudimentary shop had been constructed from stones, planks and riven fertiliser bags. But there was nothing rudimentary about the shop's *modus operandi,* that was forged from the stainless steel of unsentimental and unadulterated market economics. Cans of minerals retailed for £1, bars of chocolate for 50 pence. If you didn't like those prices, the alternative was mashed dirt and spit.

The plateau reminded me of the original *Star Trek* series, and specifically of the single, unconvincing set which used to constitute the variety of alien planets onto which Kirk, Spock and co. would habitually beam down. The mud path was so hardened and frost-glazed, it could easily have been a camouflaged studio floor. There was too much spectral fog around the place and it was far too quiet to be the real outdoors.

The shoulder-height rocks have been hewn by the elements into monumental but oddly synthetic-looking pieces of modernist sculpture. You'd to have try and budge one of them before you'd be convinced that they are not actually fibreglass props.

The other-worldly ambience is amplified by the graffiti of names and messages which previous migrants have written, with the help of pebbles and stones, on the grassy slopes just beneath the plateau: NIRVANA, PEACE, RADJ WOZ HERE, TYRONE McBRIDE, UP THE IRA.

As Gaeilge, the First Summit is called Leacht Benain. A stone cairn honouring Benen, Patrick's boy attendant, stands at the centre of the plateau. Hey, I bet this is the first time you've heard tell that Patrick even had a boy attendant. It's just another one of those little details they leave out of the Official Version. But it goes to prove what the song says: Saint Patrick *was* a gentleman.

A true gent, even when busy fasting and abstaining, likes to keep his domestic staff around him to provide those little touches which separate a civilised man from his social inferiors. The 40 days and 40 nights valet service. The impeccably-pressed sackcloth and carefully temperature-controlled ashes. The gong striking promptly at 6pm each evening to announce that, "Dinner is not served."

As a penitential rite, there's more to the Croagh Patrick climb than simply mutilating your feet or paying through the nose for a slurp of warm Lilt. There is a prayerful procedure, a ceremonial rubric, which must be assiduously followed if one is to obtain the full spiritual benefit from the holy mountain. A sequence of 'stations' are located at strategic sites, instructing the faithful in the fine print of the drill.

On reaching the First Summit, for instance, the pilgrim must walk seven times around the Leacht Benain mound of stones, saying seven Our Fathers, seven Hail Marys and One Creed. At the second summit (the top of mountain), the pilgrim first kneels and says seven Our Fathers, seven Hail Marys and One Creed. Then, the pilgrim walks 15 times around the church saying 15 Our Fathers, 15 Hail Marys and one Creed.

This isn't religion, it's algebra. But it is perfectly in keeping with the pedantic, weights-and-measures ethos which girdles Croagh Patrick like a bewildering smog. Believers come here for the most selfish reason imaginable, to pile up the chips against the day they meet that great croupier in the sky.

"Every pilgrim who ascends the mountain," affirms a wooden sign at the foot of the reek, "and prays in, or near, the church for the intentions of our Holy Father, the Pope, may gain a plenary indulgence, on condition of going to confession and holy communion within the week."

There is much about Reek Sunday that is distasteful. To my mind, however, the most repulsive aspect is the grim fetishising of hardship, the glorification of the peasant mentality. The clergy have long mined this particular seam in order to keep their flock in fearful servitude, distracted from their true lot by scratching at the scabby old sores of nationalism and the need to defend the one, holy Catholic and apostolic Church.

But we can't blame the clerics for everything. Individuals must take responsibility for their own actions. The people who come to worship at Croagh Patrick are not stupid, not all of them anyway.

Deep down, they must have some sort of qualms about precisely what sort of force or creature their God really is. A deity who is appeased by a nonsensical rigmarole on the side of a Mayo mountain! A Supreme Being who demands that His faithful demonstrate their devotion by literally walking around in circles . . .

Nothing I had survived thus far had prepared me for the final part of the climb. Below the plateau, the slope was abrupt and the terrain both difficult and deceptive. But there were plenty of knolls and valleys where the clay was as black and as moist as fresh Black Forest Gateaux. You might get covered in, eh, Black Forest Gateaux but at least it was possible to occasionally retreat from the precipice and to get some sort of stable purchase on the mountainside.

From the First Summit upwards, the rise was pure, sheer rockface, unrelieved by footholds of any kind. I felt faint just looking at it. I didn't feel any less faint when I stopped looking at it and tried to climb.

Rocks have a reputation for being reliable and sturdy. It's all hype. Whoever does their PR deserves a raise. The truth is that rocks are the slippiest customers this side of the patrons who shop at Squidsavers, the cephalopods superstore (Manager: Maurice Sprat).

What galled me was that the rocks on Croagh Patrick, like rocks everywhere, have had gigayears to snuggle into positions they find comfortable. All of geological time has been one long settling-in period during which they could put down roots at a spot on the mountain that most thoroughly suited their needs.

They've had eons and epochs to get acquainted with their environment, to develop a relationship with their neighbours and to turn their houses into homes.

And yet, the instant I place so much as toecap on a single stone, scores of them decide to totter and tumble, slide and slither, and generally terminate their leases without leaving a forwarding address.

All of a sudden, this imposing, unyielding cliff-face becomes the crum-

106

bliest, flakiest holy mountain in the world. Granite turns to fleece beneath your boots, slabs to sponge. Every foothold gives way like a trapdoor. You'd find more solid ground if you tried to cross a lake by stepping on the lily pads.

"Look out, below!" boomed a many-voiced roar in the foggy distance. A boulder the size of Bernard Manning came hurtling down the slope. With the lithesome grace for which my name is a byword, I avoided being crushed by deftly keeling over, out of its path, and landing on my coccyx.

The guy behind me only managed to dodge the boulder by launching skyward with split second precision, and allowing it to pass beneath his airborne knees. That's no mean trick when your launching pad is a San Andreas fault in full fracture.

The attrition rate on Croagh Patrick is immense. Today, mountain rescue teams from Dublin, Galway and several locations in Britain were strategically based all over the reek. They were kept busy; a stream of stretchers ferrying down the injured and the maimed was a constant presence in the peripheral vision of climbers. A helicopter darted back and forth in the clouds above us, on the look out for flares signalling emergency cases which had be winched to safety.

If the Croagh Patrick climb were anything other than a religious ritual, there would be calls for it to be banned. It is unquestionably dangerous and regularly results in hospitalisations, most commonly for head injuries. It is probable that, sooner or later, somebody will be killed on the reek. This, apparently, is an acceptable risk.

The mountain rescue personnel seem to treat their work with a large degree of black humour. Early on in the day, Mick Quinn and I stood aside to allow a stretcher to pass, on which was strapped an unconscious man with a generously bloodied bandage around his skull. When Mick started to take photographs, the stretcher-bearers smiled and posed briefly. "Is that for the In Memorium card," one of them quipped.

The last hundred metres of my ascent were completed on my hands and knees. My memory of this half-hour is jerky and fragmented, shot in unsteadicam. I seem to have been moving more from muscle memory than from any sense of purpose or direction.

I wanted to sing with relief when I eventually made it to the top of Croagh Patrick. However, at that precise moment, I couldn't seem to generate enough saliva to free my tongue from the roof of my mouth. I marked my arrival, therefore, with a ceremonial running of a wrist across my forehead, and a shout of, "Thant Thight thor thant!" (or "Thank Christ for that!" in English).

It had taken two hours and 50 minutes to get here, and would take another 90 minutes to get back down again. But, for the moment, I was happier than I could remember being for a very long time.

Masses and confessions had been held every half hour, from 8am to 3pm, in the white-washed oratory which stood at the centre of the summit. It was now after 5pm and the church was locked and bolted. Pilgrims crouched and knelt in prayer outside the strapped oak doors.

Others encircled the perimeter, still following the commands of the stations to the letter. An aged man in a tweed cap huddled with his arms around the shoulders of three twentysomethings I took to be his sons. They were all singing 'Hail Queen Of Heaven' at the tops of their lungs.

The atmosphere up here was eerily hushed and tranquil. The summit was surrounded by a halo of fog, mist and cloud. It felt like we were cast adrift aboard a large raft on an ocean of steam somewhere close to the edge of the world. Or something.

It was the kind of spooky environment from which an ominous and foreboding figure will suddenly emerge in a horror movie. And that's precisely what happened next.

The first thing I noticed was the dog, a vicious-looking Alsatian or bloodhound, with the proportions of a small horse. My eyes traced their way along the leash to the beast's owner. There was no mistaking his identity. I'd recognise that beard anywhere. It looks like a weird species of lichen which has taken hold of a human chin.

The mysterious stranger was Peter Scully, the former ovum-groupie and zygote cheerleader with Youth Defence and, latterly, Human Life International's Irish supremo and wiseacre. The young man whose impas-

sioned campaign against the introduction of divorce was the deciding factor in the resolve of many to vote in favour of the introduction of divorce.

Peter's palms were caked with mud and slime. With expressions of
furious determination on both their faces, man and mutt began to march
around and around the oratory, Peter's lips moving frantically as he recited his litany of 15 Our Fathers, 15 Hail Marys and one Creed.

When they had concluded their benediction, Peter lead his dog to the
edge of the summit and gazed contemplatively into the abyss. There was
a smile amid his beard. Despite his obvious exhaustion and discomfort,
he looked pleased with himself, as thoughts of future battles, perhaps,
fluttered into his mind.

It was time to go home.

NOWT SO QUEER AS FOLK

The Rathmines folk mass is one of the country's longest-running musical productions. Isn't it about time the gig was afforded a proper review?

The inscription above the lofty colonnaded entrance reads SUB INVOC MARIAE IMMACULATAE REFUGII PECCATORUM. Unfortunately, having slept it out the morning we did Latin at school, I can't render a precise translation but I presume it means something along the lines of LICENSED PREMISES. PROP: JESUS H. CHRIST. EST. 000. BREAD' N' WINE A SPECIALITY. LIVE MUSIC TONITE!

It's the Church of Our Lady Of Refuge, Rathmines, it's Sunday evening, and that can only mean one thing: it's folk mass time, the biggest holy show in town, or at least in the greater Dublin 6 area. This ritual takes place religiously every Sabbath evening at 6pm sharp, and has been a conspicuous part of life in flatland for longer than anyone cares to remember. Even today, in this the year of our landlord 1993, it would still appear to be as popular as ever.

For the uninitiated, allow me to explain. The folk mass is a musical sub-species characterised by giddy melodies, Christianised lyrics and the tendency of many of its exponents to wear dungarees in public. In its Rathmines incarnation, it is performed by an ensemble comprising two acoustic guitarists, a keyboard player, a flautist and a chorus of 11 vocalists.

The group is fronted by a guy in a funny-looking get-up who neither sings nor plays an instrument but who spends the entire gig making strange gestures and muttering incomprehensible slogans into his mike. Technically known as 'a priest', this character is to the folk mass what Bez was to the Happy Mondays.

Folk mass music is very similar to death metal. Both genres concentrate explicitly on themes such as blood sacrifice, mutilation and life beyond the grave.

One major difference between the two forms is that people who sing death metal have the good grace to look and sound convincingly appalled by the content of their songs. The Rathmines liturgical folk group, on the other hand, croooooon their way through their gore-spattered ditties with the vacuously chirpy, bouncy demeanours of glue-sniffing cheerleaders. They even smile, wink and chirrup while mouthing such gruesome lines as *"This is my body broken for you/This is my blood poured out for you."* ('In Love For Me').

Mention of which suggests another and, to my mind, crucial distinction between death metal and the folk mass. At least with death metal you can't hear the lyrics.

Thematically, most of the songs featured in the Rathmines set actively encourage their listeners (among whom, on the night, were probably many impressionable College of Commerce students) to engage in the heinous act of cannibalism. Could anything, for instance, be more blatant than the following exhortation from 'Seek The Lord': *"Oh, taste and see, taste and see that the Lord is good."*

111

To the best of my knowledge, no other religion or movement apart from Christianity has ever attempted to further its aims by advertising the succulence of its founder.

Most leaders ask only that their followers administer the occasional wet smackeroo to their buttocks. Christians, it seems, are required to use a knife and fork.

If nothing else, this reviewer learned one valuable lesson tonight. The Devil *does* have all the best tunes. All God has are tricky harmonies and complicated chord changes. It has to be said that the musicians do their best but they are ultimately defeated by songs which are what we professional music critics would describe as *a pile of shit*.

The audience is regularly invited to "sing along" and one or two people actually try, but the only number that arouses any kind of genuine participation from the congregation is a version of 'Grrrmmm Frrrmmm Wrrrmmm'.

That particular song is probably better known to you as 'Gale Force Wind', but here it was performed during the distribution of holy communion and, when sung by several hundred folk fans with their mouths full of transubstantiated hosts, it comes across as 'Grrrmmm Frrrmmm Wrrrmmm', I can assure you.

The merchandising stand at the back of the arena appeared busy throughout the evening, with fanzines like *The Irish Catholic* and *The Universe* emerging as the best sellers. Sales of memorabilia such as crucifixes (clever variations on the Satanic inverted cross) were also brisk.

For the record, the group managed to get through their entire set in a little over 47 minutes. There was no encore. There was no round of applause either.

Come next Sunday, I'll certainly be sauntering up to Our Lady Of Refuge Church. However, I'll be taking the advice of a very well-known folk mass hymn which has a line about *"travelling the few extra yards"* – all the way up to the beer garden of The Rathmines Inn, to be exact.

THE CURSE OF P.M.T.

That's pre-marriage tension, of course. And there's
plenty of it about at a weekend-long pre-marriage
course organised by the Catholic Marriage Advisory
Service.

In the beady eyes of the Catholic Church, marriage is a serious business. *Serious* in the sense that the clergy deem weddings to be more than just opportunities to pour champagne over our heads and to holler obscenities in limerick form. *Business* in the sense that the servicing of the sacrament of matrimony is one of the most profitable rackets in the Roman shakedown canon.

Take pre-marriage courses. These finishing schools for the betrothed are run by a body which glories in the title of the Catholic Marriage Advisory Service but now prefers to be called Accord. A couple wishing to be married in a Catholic ceremony will almost certainly be compelled to attend one of these courses before a priest will agree to perform their nuptials. They are not compulsory, but you have to do them.

An Accord marriage preparation course lasts eight hours. It can be completed in a series of four weekly two-hour sessions or over a single weekend. In the Dublin bailiwick, the course costs £36 per couple. In most rural areas, the charge is £30. The genius of the scam is that this fee entitles the bride-and-groom-to-be to a detailed summary of their additional obligations to swell Church coffers.

The Accord motto is: "Caring for Marriage, Building Relationships." A catchier and more honest slogan might be: "Pay us £36, and find out how much more you owe us!"

But pre-marriage courses are not merely a Church scheme to bilk, gyp and diddle young lovers wherever they are. They also have a more sinister intent. Accord's mission is to gleefully prescribe the nitty gritty of the Catholic marriage ethos, those myriad malign means by which a soulmate can be turned into a cellmate.

In the noble tradition of undercover journalism and the even nobler tradition of capering japery, I recently attended an Accord marriage preparation course in a border county town. Out of compassion for the other individuals who participated in that particular course, I will be no more specific about the location. They have already suffered enough.

Statistics show that most engaged couples are composed of at least two people. Therefore, for optimum effect, I needed an accomplice, a position which was ably filled by my girlfriend, Anne. In reality, Anne and I are not engaged, but we do both share the ownership of several Johnny Cash albums which, legally-speaking, amounts to the same thing.

Our course was held over a weekend, with the schedule stretching from 8pm to 10.30pm on the Friday night and from 10am to 5pm on the Saturday. The Accord counsellors need this length of time to allow every one of their doctrinal prejudices a good chance to roll up its sleeves and work up an abundant sweat.

To an extent, I can't blame Accord. The only folk obliged to partake in their pre-marriage courses are those sufficiently gullible or malleable to want a Catholic wedding. If you're going to hold the gig in the church hall, you play by their rules, simple as that. It is a nonsense, however, for anyone to pretend that these bizarre seminars are anything other than PR exercises – shabby, patronising and over-priced PR exercises at that.

The notions about relationships which underpinned the specific course for which we signed up were fascinating, but they did not square with reality as it is known anywhere outside of the Mhic Mháthúna household. This was very much a zealous Catholic's vision of what marriage is all about. But then, the Moving Crib is very much a zealous Catholic's vision of what spectacular, high-tech Christmas entertainment is all about.

The facts of life, for instance, were outlined for us in a talk by a middle-aged woman who we will refer to as 'Ursula'. By profession, Ursula was a district nurse who spent much of her time among psychiatric patients. Her lecture was first class – not in the sense that it was top notch, but in the sense that it was fit only for kids in first class.

That it was a rudimentary re-statement of the basics of human reproduction was not itself the problem. No-one should ever underestimate the depth of elementary biological ignorance in which the ecclesiastical affiliates of Accord have conspired to keep some citizens. There are men and women of marrying age in this country whose life skills amount to a knowledge of which solvents provide the quickest buzz.

What was truly laughable about Ursula's presentation was how shamelessly amateurish it was. Her visual demonstration, displayed via an overhead projector, consisted of a series of crudely hand-drawn sketches which looked like the work of a six-year-old in the throes of heroin withdrawal.

The diagram of the uterus, fallopian tubes and ovaries was extremely disturbing. The uterus resembled the back of a hairy, hulking beast of some sort. It was Bigfoot with its arms around the necks of two small Hendersons.

Despite Ursula's proclamation that this was meant to be an exercise in candour, in frankly calling a sperm a sperm, there was a coy and folksy tone to the discourse. She spoke about the testes, for instance, as though they were sons of hers who were studying too intently for the Junior Cert. "Those poor little fellows never get a day off," Ursula sighed. "They're working all day every day, even at weekends."

The graph comparing the climaxing speeds of males and females was odd, to say the least. It appeared to contend that if a man reached orgasm after, say, two minutes of intercourse, his female partner wouldn't come until the next time Ireland assumes the presidency of the European Union.

"Men are microwaves," insisted Ursula. "Women are cookers." Obviously, if you want to know the real facts of life, your best bet is Power City.

A total of 13 couples had enrolled for our course, the setting for which was a wood-panelled, second floor room in a large church annex. The coosome twosomes arrived in dribs and drabs, the harsh fluorescent strip-lighting bringing up the textures and tones of the discomfort on their faces.

Straight-backed chairs were arranged along three of the four walls, giving the room the feel of a school disco in a village hall. This was appropriate given that at least a half dozen of the couples looked as if they had gotten together in just such an environment, and earlier this very evening at that.

As classrooms go, this temporary one was extremely well equipped; alongside the standard desk and chalkboard, there was an overhead projector, a flipchart, a TV and video unit and an audio cassette player.

A family Bible was lying open on the desk, presumably at a particularly fortifying text. To its side sat the journal recording a list of the couples who had and had not yet paid their course fees. A marriage made in Heaven.

On entry, we were each handed a folder for our "notes and worksheets." We were then presented with Band Aid sized name-tag stickers. I was 'Tom', a name which I felt, after due deliberation, struck the perfect note of stability and responsibility, making me sound like a mellowing young swain who had played the field but was now ready to settle down and have little Toms. To protect her identity, Anne had also chosen a pseudonym. She called herself 'Ann'.

116

Our tutors for the weekend were three Accord counsellors, two women and a priest. All three would remain in the room during every talk, but each individual claimed a particular expertise in certain fields and would lead the instruction on topics related to this expertise.

The woman who delivered the welcoming address shall be known as 'Rita'. "I was reading about the Oasis boys today," she said ho-hoingly, keen to prove how hip she was to the yoof of today. "I was just thinking that they would probably have learned a lot more about how to get on with one another if they had done a course like this."

Rita was a small, smiley-featured lady in her 40s who worked as a professional fertility counsellor. Rita's specialist subject was family planning but she also gave us the benefit of her wisdom on family budgeting and house purchasing.

The aforementioned Ursula was an older, leaner, more authoritarian kind of dame, a school marmish sort who would have stared out over the top of her spectacles when she spoke but for the fact that she didn't wear spectacles. As well as outlining the inner workings of the reproductive system, she was here to warn us about the perils of alcoholism.

Every other facet of marriage – from "sexual loving" through "effective male/female communication" to "the overcoming of relationship difficulties" – was to be the domain of 'Father Jim', a respected authority on the nuptial bond in the same way that I am a respected authority on Gödel's Incompleteness Theorem.

Fr. Jim was a brusque, bearded, self-satisfied man in his mid 30s; one of those natural born priests who resemble over-grown fifth years and who walk, elbows akimbo, at a permanent slope because they have to lug around arses the size of three-seater electoral constituencies.

To help loosen the knot of formality and break down the barriers between us and him, Fr. Jim eschewed his clerical collar and mixed freely among the couples during teabreaks. The aim was that we would gradually forget that he was a clergyman. This objective was somewhat undermined by the fact that his name tag read "Fr. Jim."

By day, Fr. Jim dealt in the evil trade in human misery that is secondary school teaching. He carried with him to the pre-marriage course many of the most loathsome trademarks of that squalid occupation: the steely gaze demanding absolute capitulation, the why-don't-you-share-the-joke-with-the-rest-of-the-class hauteur when he caught people talking amongst themselves, the gross clearing of the throat just when I was about to nod off.

Worst of all, though, was that irritating rhetorical habit, indigenous to religious and lay teachers alike, of leaving sentences unfinished and expecting the students to complete them.

"You are about to experience one of the most precious sacraments there is," affirmed Fr. Jim, "and that is the sacrament of?" His eyebrows shot halfway up his forehead, and he paused expectantly. This was the cue for us couples to chime in with the word *Marriage!* (This teacherly practice can be turned into a fun game for all the family – all you need is a statement concluding with a blank, which can then be filled in by the other players. Eg: "Bite the back end of my?" *Bollocks!* Or: "Shut your hole, you filthy?" *Scum!*).

Fr. Jim maintained that a weekend course like this was the least we could do to prepare for embarking on a lifetime pledge. He spoke at length, width, breadth and depth on this theme, and, in the process, simultaneously provided corroborative evidence for the twin propositions that, a) a sense of humour is a fundamental necessity for married people and, b) we will never see married priests.

"I spent six years in Maynooth before I became a priest," he averred. "And what I learned in those six years about myself still helps me every day. I get on fairly well with myself now. I don't fall out with myself too often."

As our first assignment, Rita announced that we were going to bake a cake. "Ooooh," I thought to myself, this course may not be as bad I expected; at least, we're starting with the important stuff, the reception edibles. However, I had oooohed too soon. What Rita had in mind was not a wedding cake but a *marriage* cake, an infinitely less toothsome prospect.

"I want each couple to think about their life together as if it were a cake," explained Rita. "We know that there are some ingredients that are essential for a good cake, like yeast and baking powder. What are the ingredients that you think are essential to the recipe for a good marriage?"

The 13 couples were divided up into two groups of four couples, and one group of five couples. The first group was taken to a room downstairs. The two remaining groups were positioned at opposite ends of the main room so that recipe copying was rendered virtually impossible, unless of course you were prepared to go the extraordinary lengths of listening to the other group's recipe and then copying it.

The group in which Anne and I found ourselves sat around in a circle. A glass cooking bowl was placed at our feet. We were issued with strips of notepaper and biros, with which we were to write down what we felt to be the most important requirements for a happy marriage. These "ingredients" (or "pieces of paper") would then be mixed up in the bowl to create a "marriage cake" (or "pile of pieces of paper").

There was a lengthy silence in our group before anyone spoke.

I was thinking along the lines of the basic necessities, those household prerequisites which are as crucial to domestic bliss as the Morphy Richards product range. You know the kinda stuff; anti-depressants, Prozac, mood regulators, tranquillisers, bottles of Chivas Regal Scotch liquor. But this wasn't where my colleagues were coming from at all, so I decided to keep my powder dry.

"Trust!" trilled a scarifyingly perky young woman who I henceforth suspected of having boned up for this test in advance. How else could she arrive at something as hoity-toity as *Trust?*

"Loyalty!" chirruped the red-haired girl in the seat beside her. Another swot, obviously. They must have had inside information about what questions were going to come up.

"Communication!" proffered the red head's boyfriend. Sweet swinging Jesus, even the blokes were at it now! Anxious not to be seen as some sort of emotional dunce, I began nodding at every suggestion; of course, of course, of course. Now and again, I'd make a frowny face before I nodded, an experienced man of the world weighing up the merits of the proposition.

"Patience!"

"Understanding!"

"Love!"

"Helping around the house!"

The ingredients were coming thick and fast. Some of the bakers were more enthusiastic than others, however. Throughout the weekend, most of the couples had the decency to look bored and bemused by this absurd burlesque. But there were one or two eager beavers (predominantly female, it has to be said) who acted as if the sole reason they were getting hitched was so that they could bamboozle with bullshit at a pre-marriage course. These people positively oozed ingredients.

"House and home would have to be a big part of the recipe," proclaimed the eagerest beaver of them all, a tall, slender, blonde girl with a countenance that resembled a pot of make-up with the lid unscrewed. "But they should be separate ingredients. A house is not a home. A house has to be turned *into* a home. That's the job of the blushing bride." All things considered, in this particular case, I think the groom has more to blush about.

At the opposite extreme, there were those among the group who felt that the quickest way to get this baloney over with was to just spew out what they thought the Accord counsellors wanted to hear. "I suppose we might as well throw in 'Religion'," drawled a laconic local man with a weary grimace which suggested that his personal feeling was that religion was about as essential to a marriage as a writing desk is to a giraffe.

In for a buck, in for a bundle, I decided to make a modest proposal myself. "Two televisions," I submitted. "Vital ingredients if you want to avoid friction in the marital home." There was a murmur of assent from most members of the group, all bar one in fact.

"No, I don't think so," demurred Ms. Eager Beaver icily. "That's too frivolous." Fortunately, her opposition was enough to galvanise support behind the motion and "2 x TV" was eventually added to the mix but with a "?" appended to make clear that it was not an unanimous selection.

Recipes completed, we all re-assembled. A spokesperson read out each group's table of ingredients and a master list was complied on the flipchart. The flipchart lists were not treated as starting points for further discussion. The various suggestions were recorded and the lists were then stuck up on the wall as the final word on the subject, end of lesson. The fact that, for the most part, they were either top-of-the-head statements of the blindingly obvious or mere eruptions of sexist prejudice was irrelevant. They were up on the wall, gleaming in the white light of revealed truth.

With the marriage cake in the oven, Rita set us a further series of tasks. The men and the women were separated into two groups and sent to different rooms. Both genders then had to catalogue what they felt would be "the major changes" to their lifestyles after their weddings.

The females' inventory of anticipated changes was quite short and not all that major. They expected that they would have to do more housework, and more ironing in particular. They would have to get used to being called "Mrs." and to having a different surname. Some were saddened that they wouldn't be able to go home to their Mammies and Daddies every evening. All were apprehensive about having to endure close proximity to "a man snoring in bed every night."

To the males' eternal credit, we topped our list of major post-wedding lifestyle changes with, "Reduction in sex life." Later, when this was read out to Rita, she feigned confusion.

"You mean reduction in social life," she informed us.

"No, reduction in sex life."

"Oh, you mean you won't be able to go out with other girls."

"No, reduction in sex life with our partners."

"What do you mean?" she asked.

"Don't people have less sex with each other after they get married?"

"Well," mused Rita, a disheartened slump in her voice. "That would suggest that you have a sex life with your partner *before* you get married which isn't always the situation." Case closed.

The full male list of predicted changes to lifestyle included "having less money," "having less time to spend with friends," "fewer visits to the pub," "getting used to baby-sitters," "learning to change nappies," and having to endure close proximity to "women with PMT."

PMT was repeatedly cited by a number of males as a potential source of strife amid the connubial harmony. Ursula responded to these concerns by delivering a discourse on what PMT is and how it affects different women in different ways. Which was fine, except for the fact that she seemed to believe that the initials stood for *Post* Menstrual Tension.

It was time for the next "workshop." Still divided into unisex halves, the men had to draw up a roster of the primary characteristics of women, and vice versa. "We're not talking about the obvious physical differences," warranted Rita, to a collective groan of disappointment. "We're talking about the emotional and intellectual differences that make men distinct from women."

According to the men, women were "soft," "sensitive," "gentle," "more responsible," "generous," and "hospitable" but also (deep breath!) "moody," "unpredictable," "too cautious," "hypocritical – they smile at people but bitch about them behind their backs," "vindictive," "vicious," "PMT," "too influenced by what their families say," "they expect men to be mind-readers," and "they're too worried about keeping up with the Joneses."

The list would've been even longer but we ran out of paper and Fr. Jim stuck his head around the door to tell us that the time was up ("Are we right there, men!" were his exact words. "This kind of exercise is helpful because it gives you an insight into your partner's?" *Personality!*)

Returning to the main classroom, I expected to encounter a mujahideen of female vengefulness. Because the men had been so critical in their comments about women, I assumed that the girls would have levelled an even more trenchant charge sheet at the boys, synopsising the popular view that guys are invariably worthless, irresponsible trash. But, on the contrary, males emerged from their portrait smelling sweeter than a dozen long-stemmed roses.

According to the women, we were "even-tempered," "less excitable," "fair," "generous," "less inclined to worry," "more independent" and "hard-working." Nevertheless, we were also "moody," "aggressive," and "lazy around the house."

Curiously enough, apart from those last three examples of typically excessive female fault-finding, this is precisely the way most of us guys see ourselves. Women from the border counties are obviously ahead of their time and the rest of their gender in appreciating what admirable and precious folk we men are. Surely, it cannot be too long before these most perceptive ladies learn to love some of our other great qualities too, such as beer-bellies, ear-hair, a fondness for recreational spitting and those super-fast ejaculations that Ursula told us about.

Saturday morning, I arrived at the classroom late and with a hangover but just in time to catch an educational video about the problem of alcoholism within marriage. "You'll enjoy this," Ursula assured us. "It's a good story."

The film was about a fictional couple called Joe and Dervla. Joe was a big boozer before he married Dervla. To illustrate this fact, we saw Joe boozing bigly at a variety of different locations. While Dervla enjoyed a sociable tipple with her demure pals in a sophisticated wine bar, Joe was shown demolishing pints and baring his yellow teeth in coarse laughter with a gang of obvious ne'er-do-wells in a dark, scuzzy dive.

It was manifest from the start that Joe was headed for trouble. Early on, he is depicted drinking bottles of Harp. By the neck. In the kitchen. This is not the kind of activity you see being practised by movie characters who are going to lead contented, successful lives. In the lexicon of late 20th century cinema imagery, a scene in which a protagonist drinks bottles of Harp by the neck in the kitchen means only one thing: uh oh.

Joe and Dervla went to Miami for their honeymoon. We know this because we saw a shot of an Aer Lingus jet in flight above the ocean followed by a shot of Miami airport followed by a shot of some flamingos followed by a shot of some palm trees. And because, in what may have been the key expositional clue, the narrator told us that Joe and Dervla went to Miami for their honeymoon.

A sudden, jerky cut-away and we're in the happy couple's honeymoon suite where Joe has passed out on the bed. Another shaky jump-cut later (evidently, the cinematographer wasn't beyond strangling the occasional carafe of Harp by the cutlery drawer himself) we see Joe performing a raucous 'Upchucky Ar Lá' into the wash-hand basin.

The honeymoon was a disaster. Joe was either as drunk as a skunk or as sick as a pig throughout. He was certainly too consistently mouldy to even consider parking the conjugal Pontiac. Dervla said she didn't mind, but attentive viewers could tell what she was really thinking. You could hear it in her voice. She was gagging for it.

Back home, matters went from bad to worse. Joe became an even more enthusiastic Harpist. His grip on reality (not to mention the cinematographer's grip on the camera) became increasingly unsteady. There were quarrels, embarrassing falls and flashes of violence, many of them part of the plot and not entirely the director's fault.

Eventually, Joe was signed into a drying-out clinic, There, he received treatment and counselling and, it appeared, a guarantee that there would be no more close-ups of his mouth every time he laughed. He stopped drinking and was reconciled with Dervla. In a matter of seconds, they had a child.

Hot on the heels of a baby Joe came a baby Dervla. Joe and Dervla senior were elated. They went on to live happily ever after, while remaining callously oblivious to the fate of the dozens of employees of Harp breweries who were thrown on the scrap heap because of the steep decline in demand for their product. THE END.

For the kind of people who like their cautionary tales told slowly and in large bold type, *When Joe Met Dervla* may well have been an eye-opener. For the rest of us, watching such a film about the horrors of drink addiction is almost enough to make a person swear off the practise for life, the practise of watching films that is.

After the morning teabreak, we returned to the classroom to find a scummy-looking, gruel-grey sheet laid out on the floor with a yellowing, limp pillow at one end. Fr. Jim was kneeling at the foot of the sheet with a low-slung grin swinging like a hammock between his ears.

All trace of conversation amid the couples thinned to a hush. We sat down warily, as if we'd heard a vague rumour outside that our seats had been surreptitiously replaced with electric chairs during the recess. A splitsecond later, we realised that the rumour was truer than we'd liked to believe. Still on his knees and still grinning, Fr. Jim flicked the switch and fricasseed our butts.

"Now, I'm gonna show ye all how it really *should* be done," he sniggered, indicating the makeshift bed with a nod and a wink, a nod and a wink being the most important teaching aid in the repertory of an Accord counsellor. "We're going to talk for a while about what happens in the bedroom."

The palpable haze of embarrassment which descended on the assembly had little to do with the subject of sex *per se*. My impression of almost all of my fellow fiancés was that they were perfectly well-versed in the potential pleasure, distress and havoc that can ensue when the beefy bayonet meets the love muffin.

What was making us squirm like slugs in salt was the phoney cockiness of Fr. Jim who was trying far, far too hard to illustrate how comfortable he was talking about life beneath the marital duvet.

His demeanour, tone of voice and rictus grin were as convincingly relaxed as the adolescent who brays too vigorously and too loudly at dirty jokes he clearly doesn't understand. The intended impression was that of a cool cat; the achieved effect was that of a yipping coyote.

Fr. Jim would have appeared considerably more sympathetic if he had even tersely acknowledged the absurdity of the situation. There he was, a celibate male cleric who probably ain't had pussy since pussy had him, and he was stretching himself up to the full height of his hubris to talk to a soon-to-be bridal party about the ins and outs of sexual intercourse.

The centrepiece of this treatise on "sexual loving" was what Fr. Jim termed a "sculpt," or what the French would describe as a *tableau vivant*. Those of us with a lower preponderance of the poncyness gene in our DNA than Fr. Jim or the French would call it a group of silent and motionless people arranged to represent a scene.

"I want to show you the different pressures that can bear down on the average couple's marital bed," stated Fr. Jim with a Benny Hill smirk. To act as the totemic couple, he chose a boy from one side of the room and a girl from the other. The boy sat on the 'bed' while the girl sat off to his right, facing him. "The husband's name is Mork and his wife is Mindy," decreed Fr. Jim, the imperious Creator anointing His handiwork in the Garden of Eden.

Fr. Jim told another girl to sit at the foot of the 'bed' to symbolise "the couple's desire for a child." He then nominated two boys to kneel down behind the 'headboard'. This pair would represent "natural family planning" and "artificial contraception" respectively.

Two more girls were selected and ordered to sit at either side of Mork and Mindy. One to act as "Mork's mother, who's getting impatient for a grandchild." The other to personify "Mindy's sister, who has two lovely children that Mindy is very fond of."

As you can imagine, the space on and around Mork and Mindy's crib was now getting pretty crowded. The participants in this stationary scrum remained heroically stoic and did their best to retain some semblance of dignity. But they still looked like they were assuming positions for the start of a riotous gang-bang.

Fr. Jim continued with his random conscription. He chose the guy sitting to my immediate right to play the role of "Mindy's well-paid job which she is very reluctant to give up." The rat's feet of panic skittered down my spine. What if I was roped into this ludicrous farce next?

I hatched a cunning plan. I scrunched up my features, hunched my shoulders and slowly slid down in the wooden chair in the hope that Fr. Jim would mistake me for a coat of varnish or a large cushion. The disguise worked a treat. The sculpt was complete and I was still safely seated.

"Now, when all these pressures have been taken into consideration," purred Fr. Jim. "Mork and Mindy are finally ready to close the door on everybody else, and to make their own decisions. We'll leave that part to your imaginations."

"If there's people of different religions here, *great!*" burbled Fr. Jim, croaking that last word as if it had literally gotten stuck in his throat. "There's no problem with that whatsoever. But, right now, I'm going to give you the Catholic Church's perspective on marriage."

Fr. Jim began by telling us that marriage is a sacrament, and that the term 'sacrament' comes from the Latin words meaning *make holy*. This was Movietone News to me. Having grown up as part of an extended family where the passing of the seasons was marked by the migration of herds of relations to our frontdoor with their paws out for first holy communion money, confirmation money or wedding gifts, I had always believed that the term 'sacrament' comes from the Latin words meaning *nobody move, this is a stick up.*

Fr. Jim then showed us a diagram juxtaposing two high-jump bars, one higher than the other. Displaying a fundamental misunderstanding of the concept of the high jump, two matchstick couples were trying to limbo dance *beneath* the bars. These idiosyncratic, by which I mean stupid, drawings were meant to illustrate the point that "civil marriage is not as demanding as a Church marriage because the Church has higher standards."

Tightly lacing up his dogma bovverboots, Fr. Jim stopped farting about with limbo-dancing high jumpers and cut straight to the chase. "The purpose of Catholic marriage," he stated, "is the procreation of children." The happiness of the couple themselves is secondary, he expanded. Even after they have had one child, and assuming that both parents are healthy, it would be selfish of them not to have more.

After another ten minutes or so of this kind of guff, Fr. Jim finally moved on to the heart of his disquisition, if not the entire course: the couple's responsibilities in terms of wedding day dos, don'ts and dosh. "You shouldn't forget that you have to pay the priest who marries you," he declared. "Priests usually get between £25 and £100 for the ceremony."

Fr. Jim made it clear that, in most areas, convention would tilt this scale a lot closer to the £100 end. The stipend we pay the priest must *not* be confused with the fee we would be expected to pay for the use of the church. That is entirely separate and could be anything up to £200.

On the day, if there is a sacristan on hand to open and shut the church door, we should give him about £10 in an envelope. Presumably, it is crucial that we hand this envelope personally to the sacristan and that we do not fall into the trap of slipping the envelope underneath the church door. To do so would oblige the sacristan to re-open and re-shut the door, a task for which, at going rates in the competitive sacristanian market place, he would expect to be paid *another* £10.

We should discourage our guests from throwing confetti outside the church. "It looks terrible on a wet day," moaned Fr. Jim, "and *we're* the ones that have to clean it up after you."

As far as wedding music is concerned, "pop songs are out." Only religious music and hymns are permitted. If the church is being decorated by a florist, we should "make sure that some flowers are left behind in the church, and remember, at all times, that the church is the priest's domain." Evidently, all that old stuff about the church being the House of God no longer applies.

Out of courtesy, we should send the priest an invitation to the reception and not just expect him to turn up. On the subject of reading out cards and telegrams after the wedding breakfast, Fr. Jim was adamant. Every care should be taken to avoid "dirty messages" which might "put the priest under pressure." (It is, after all, the priest's day.)

Fr. Jim recalled the occasion when he attended a reception at which Niall Toibín was one of the speech makers. "Ordinarily, I love Niall Toibín's humour," he testified. "But every time Toibín made a joke relating to, shall we say, the bridal suite, everyone looked at me first to see if I was laughing. I felt very awkward."

To avert this kind of calamity, Fr. Jim recommended that the best man should be instructed to scour through the good wishes and excise all ribald or bawdy remarks which might bring a splash of crimson to the sacerdotal cheeks of the poor old padre.

Like so much else, however, this is a question of degree. The intensity of a clerical blush is not always easy to measure. I've attended wedding hooleys where the priest has chug-a-lugged so much wine and brandy by the soup course that his face is already the colour of the salmon bisque. Even Niall Toibín at his most navy couldn't darken that kind of glow.

When it came time for Rita to talk to us about contraception, she more or less endorsed everything that Fr. Jim had said about marriage's primary purpose being for the procreation of children. But she did so while holding a packet of contraceptive pills in her hand so that no-one could accuse of her of not providing us with both sides of the argument.

After a luridly-hued film about the development of the foetus (a sort of Dick Warner's *Waterways* of the birth canals), Rita held up what she described as her "box of tricks." She promised to pass this around the room so we could see for ourselves what items such as a coil, a condom, a diaphragm and a contraceptive pill actually looked like.

However, she never did pass it around, perhaps for security reasons. Rita told us that there used to be a Femidom in her box of tricks until her last pre-marriage course. Since then, she's only had a Femidom wrapper.

Her parting shot on the topic left us in little doubt about her own views about contraception. "There is a moral dimension to all of that," she opined. "We must never forget that. Taking the pill is not like taking a Panadol."

Having spent so long on the foetus, there was little time left to discuss children. Rita simply gave us some more hand-outs and a Health Promotion Unit booklet entitled *The Book Of The Child*. The couples were encouraged to chat among themselves for a while about the issues raised in this literature. It would be a good idea, Rita said, if the men in particular asserted their ideas and views about child-rearing.

Anne and I flicked through the booklet in search of something to discuss. Ah, breast-feeding. "I'm all in favour of breast-feeding," I asserted. "But I just don't see why it should be restricted to children."

Discipline. To spank or not to spank? "I'm all in favour of spanking," I asserted. "But I just don't see why it should be restricted to children."

Helping around the house. Is a rota for household chores a good idea? "I'm all in favour of a rota for household chores," I asserted. "But it should definitely be restricted to children."

From children to money. All three Accord counsellors were beginning to suffer from GMT. It was late in the afternoon, and they still had the whole area of family finance and budgeting to cover. "We'll just have to scoot through it," said Rita.

I had actually been looking forward to this section all weekend. I'm getting on in years now and know little of matters such as mortgages, stamp duty, bridging loans and endowment assurance. In fact, until very recently, I thought that endowment assurance was that crafty old routine whereby some of us guys cram a sock down the front of our trousers before we hit the disco.

However, it wasn't the pre-marriage course which relieved me of that particular misapprehension (it was actually the Dunnes Stores strike, during which I ran out of socks). By comparison with the quantity of time expended on other matters (such as confetti), the financial education element of the Accord weekend was extremely skimpy and weak.

We were provided with a questionnaire entitled ATTITUDES TO MONEY which the partners in each couple were to answer privately and then analyse with one another.

One major deficiency in the questionnaire was that there wasn't always enough space to write down the answers. The multiple choice options were fine, as were those queries that merely required a Yes or No response.

But there were also more exacting questions such as, "Are you the kind of person who likes to buy presents for your friends?" I had terrible difficulty trying to fit in the full text of my reply, *to wit* "There *are* people who buy presents for their friends?"

Having carefully analysed both sets of answers, Anne and I came to the conclusion that we both retain very healthy attitudes to money, so healthy in fact that it would be selfish of us not to have more.

As Andrew Strong's parents know better than anybody else, marriage involves the making of a massive commitment.

A fiesta of the cheapest kind of bottom-linery imaginable, an Accord pre-marriage course is of no practical use to people who live in the real world, where *sculpt* is a verb. The most dangerous aspect of it all is that some of those who come away from these courses with an Accord certificate (i.e. everyone who attends these courses) may believe that they now know everything they need to know about cultivating a successful marriage. This is the sort of thinking that made John Wayne Bobbitt a household name.

The closing ceremony of our course was a truly touching affair. While Rita and Ursula signed our certs, Fr. Jim went around the room blessing each individual couple to the strains of (I shit you not) Christy Moore's 'The Voyage'. Asking someone like me not to scoff at spectacles such as this is a bit like asking hedgehogs to lay off the traffic.

If I have a favourite memory of this unforgettable weekend, it is the thought of Fr. Jim explaining to 13 rapt couples how they should go about having their rows. He accomplished this astonishing feat with the help of pie-charts and pin-wheel diagrams, two of which I reproduce below for your personal edification:

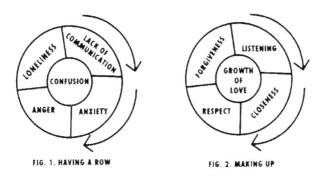

FIG. 1. HAVING A ROW   FIG. 2. MAKING UP

This is exactly the sort of thing that would give marriage a bad name, if it didn't already have one. Call it an unjust generalisation if you like but it *is* only married couples who get divorced.

LET'S FACE THE MUSIC AND DANCE!

Father Neil Horan predicts that the end of the world is very nigh indeed, less than five years away. But he's not too down-hearted. In the Heaven on Earth that will follow Armageddon, he hopes to perform reels and jigs for Jesus Christ in Jerusalem.

Gingerly, deftly, reverently, Father Neil Horan unfurls the cellophane dry cleaning bag which holds his Irish dancing costume. Beneath the diaphanous sheath, the outfit looks like some sort of mutant Saint Patrick's Day butterfly still in the chrysalis, its distended wings covered with gaudy Republican lineaments.

The uniform is based on a traditional arrangement but has been adapted slightly by Fr. Horan himself. It comprises an emerald tunic, Kelly green cap (with shamrock crest), saffron kilt with tapestry border, and knee-high tricolour socks, all topped off with a Tara brooch impaled on the tunic's breast pocket. The standard Irish Harp, usually embroidered on the front of the kilt, has been replaced by an unusual emblematic refinement: an appliqué Star of David.

Over mugs of sugary tea, doorstep-sized slices of fruitcake and a Giant's Causeway of (his favourites) Fig Rolls, Fr. Horan had burbled effusively about his passion for jigs and reels. Asserting that he dances in public to "do my part to increase joy in the world now, and to point to the much greater joy to come," he reminisced about the time, in 1988, when he travelled from Dublin to Belfast by bicycle, and shook a leg in all of the towns and villages *en route,* for peace.

He also gleefully poured forth his hopes for his designer dancing duds. Now, he wants me to see and touch the ensemble for myself.

"There's no such thing as an Irish national costume," he laments. "I think this is the nearest thing we can get to it. I'm trying to make it more acceptable to the wider world. We have spent so much time in conflict as a nation. Our history has been so dogged by the attempt to free our country that, in many ways, we haven't built up the country at all. The lack of a national costume is one example. Nearly all countries have a national costume of some sort. I would like to think that by wearing this in public I can encourage other Irish men and Irish women to follow suit. I want to help in some way towards a consciousness of national dress.

"I wear the Star of David on my kilt to express my admiration for the Jewish people. The Star of David is the symbol of Israel, the land that God gave to Abraham and his descendants. By wearing it on my costume along with the small shamrocks and Celtic symbols, and the Tara brooch, I want to express unity between the Irish and the Jews. The kilt itself corresponds to the ephod cloth which King David wore around his waist when he danced in Biblical times."

Aged 48, with the build of a fastidious jockey, Fr. Horan's hair is an unconvincing jet black, but, as he sprints up the precipitous stairs to his bedroom, he moves with an effortless, lissom grace which belies any concerns he may have about the onset of silver-locked middle age.

A native of Knockeenahone, Scartaglin, in the celebrated Slieve

Luachra area of County Kerry, Fr. Horan has lived and worked here in London for close to a quarter of a century, but he still retains a symphonic Kingdom brogue that is as robust and brawny as The Bomber Liston. He almost busts his buttons with pride at the very mention of placenames from his mellifluous home county. When he walks, even the thickly polished leather of his transcendentally sparkling shoes seems to squeak with a Kerry accent.

We're sitting in the tiny attic chamber of a rambling suburban house on the King's Hall Road, in Beckenham, Kent, but it's clear from the wistful look on Fr. Horan's face as he talks about his childhood in Scartaglin that, in his imagination, he has never really left the place. "If we only had old Ireland over here," he muses with a rueful smile.

On a narrow wooden ledge by his bed, Fr. Horan keeps a display of homemade Irish mementoes: a half dozen black'n'white photographs cut from newspapers and glued onto pieces of cardboard. The stars of this Auld Sod gallery include Pat Kenny, Gay Byrne, PJ Mara and Charlie Haughey, the latter pictured shaking hands with Francois Mitterrand.

"My heart is still back in Kerry," he says plaintively. "I've never fully adapted to life in London. I don't think I could ever adapt to city life. I miss the green fields. On a hot summer's day, I feel I should be out in the fields working, or just lying down on the warm grass. I think that we are literally shaped by the landscape around us while we're growing up and that it becomes part of our beings, both body and soul.

"If you go to my village in Scartaglin, you'll see a memorial in the village green to a man called Padraig O'Keefe. O'Keefe was the last of the fiddle masters. Slieve Luachra is famous for its musicians: great people like O'Keefe, Dennis Murphy, many others. The music they made, I can hear it now. It was literally divine."

Smoothing down the plastic wrap over his dancing uniform and rolling the shoulders of the tunic so that the cloth sits better on the wire hanger, Fr. Horan casually changes tack and amiably but forcefully discloses the fate which he confidently expects to befall not only his beloved Ireland but the entire world sometime within the next five years.

"There is no doubt that we are in the last days and that the nuclear holocaust, Armageddon, is very close at hand," he declares, in a tone of voice that is shocking not because it is too melodramatic but because it is insufficiently so. "There will be an enormous number of people wiped out in the war. Two thirds of the world's population, at least, will be wiped out. It appears that two thirds of the world's nations will disappear completely too. There will only be about 70 nations left.

"The prophet Zachariah gives us the most vivid description of what it will be like during Armageddon. He talks about the flesh dissolving on the bodies of men, women and children as they stand on their feet. Eyes will melt away in their sockets, tongues will melt and fall out of mouths. It is almost exactly what happened in Hiroshima when the atom bomb was dropped and that was also accurately predicted by prophets such as Zachariah.

"Unfortunately, we know that the annihilation will be even more horrific and widespread this time round," he concludes ominously. "There is no doubt about it."

The English Authorised Version of the Bible is made up of 1,189 chapters, 31,173 verses and 774,746 words. Fr. Neil Horan knows almost all of them by heart.

His own copy of the Good Book looks like it has had to endure daily 12-round bouts with a team of Bible thumpers who take their job description a little too literally. Its fat leather spine has snapped in two. An enormous drift of loose paper bulges from between the severed covers like thawing ice cream between sodden wafers, each page creased, pleated, doubled or crimped with overuse.

Fr. Horan regards every statement in the Bible as if it were, well, Bible. "The basis of the Bible as a whole is literal," he asserts. "It is not merely made up of figurative stories as some would have you believe. You can take it literally, Old Testament *and* New Testament, just like you'd take today's newspaper. We are real beings. We face a real beginning and a real death at the end. Yes, there's a lot of symbolic language at times. It takes us to the depths of our intellect to understand it. But, when we do understand it, it's very, very plain."

Historically, the dying years of a century and, more especially, of a millennium are boom times for doom and gloom merchants. Like others who have studied Biblical prophesy, however, Fr. Horan is adamant that the signs and portents presaging the end of the world in or around the year 2000 are irrefutable, and that they have nothing to do with doltish superstition.

He has written a 292 page book, entitled *A Glorious New World Very Soon To Come,* in which he outlines in minute detail the scriptural foundation for his contention that Armageddon is at hand.

"The return of the Jews to Israel is a clear fulfilment of the prophesies," he insists. "May 1948 saw the foundation of the state of Israel. The Bible tells us that the Third World War will begin in the century which witnesses Israel's rebirth. That leaves less than five years. Other events also point to Armageddon. The commission given by God to Adam and Eve was 'to fill the Earth and subdue it'. Man was told to conquer the Earth. That only happened finally in 1953 when Hillary and Tensing went to the top of Mount Everest. Man's arrival at the North and South Poles only happened in this century also.

"The fact that the nuclear and atom bomb exist for the first time in this century is important. We are the first generation who could wipe out humanity in one day. The landing on the moon was hugely significant. The day that man landed on another planet was definitely ushering in a new era. We have completed our mission on Earth. It's time for God to take back the landlordship, the trusteeship, of the Earth which He gave man."

To his eternal credit, Fr. Horan has the courage of his convictions. Logic dictates, he argues, that if the prophesies turn out to have no basis in reality, the Bible itself "will be shown to have the spiritual worth of the London A to Z street directory." It's piss or get off the pot time for Holy Scripture. Either this stuff is the word of God, or it isn't.

"It is safe to say," Fr. Horan avers, "that if Armageddon doesn't happen very soon, if the Kingdom of God doesn't emerge within the next few years and if Christ doesn't come within this generation, the Bible is a totally fallacious document, a fraud."

Quick to spot that there's only a modest feelgood factor in a doctrine preaching the imminent extinction of 66% of the world's populace, Neil Horan's superiors in the Catholic Church have moved to sack and discredit him. Rather than attempting to counter his arguments, which are above all else canonically based, they have striven to depict him as a disturbed and demented individual, crazier than a snake humping a goat.

Stripped of his income, his home and his job, Fr. Horan has been driven into the attics and spare rooms of sympathisers throughout his former parishes in London. He has become a clerical Anne Frank, forced into internal exile by ecclesiastical Nazis. This week, he's a guest of a Maltese family in Beckenham. Next week, he takes refuge in the home of a widow in Nunhead.

What appears to have infuriated the high muckety-mucks of the London hierarchy is the credence being accorded to Horan's views by substantial pockets of the faithful. For some months now, Neil has had to stop lecturing at Speakers' Corner in Hyde Park, where he had become a regular sight, because he has become so immersed in the writing and dissemination of pamphlets, leaflets and letters warning of the impending apocalypse. Assisting him in this onerous task is a network of about 40 devotees, "mostly retired people," who are keen that others will share the "understanding of the prophesies" which they have been lucky enough to receive with Neil's help.

Such are the dark complexities, fine nuances and, of course, bladder-shrivelling implications of Neil Horan's central text, *A Glorious New World Very Soon To Come,* that it cannot be described as an easy read. This is a book which encompasses the entire history of life on this planet, up to and including its grand finale. After a couple of pages, you find yourself anticipating a pounding big headache very soon to come.

At its core, however, lies the simple but seismic revelation that everything that has ever happened has been leading inexorably, and increasingly rapidly, towards a nuclear immolation of humanity which will indisputably occur before the millennium countdown reaches its climactic conclusion.

"The final war will be an attempt to wipe the state of Israel off the map, to wipe the descendants of Isaac *(the Jews)* off the face of the Earth," explains Fr. Neil. "It will be an Arab attack. The main purpose of the Arab attack will be a religious reason, to win back Jerusalem. That's why the rise of Islamic fundamentalism is fulfilling prophesy. It is a religious voice crying, 'We want Jerusalem back!'.

"It does seem definite from the prophesy of Daniel that Russia will, first of all, invade Turkey, and that it will be from that point that they will join the Arabs in their attack. America will back Israel. Iran will join Israel. Many of the Muslim nations created since Russia's fall will join Russia. Libya will join, so too will Ethiopia and Sudan. They're named by the prophets. Muslim counties like Bangladesh and quite possibly India and Pakistan will become involved. It will be a truly world war.

"It's almost certain that Islamic fundamentalists will come to power soon in countries like Algeria. If they come to power in one, it could easily spread. That has been going on gradually now since Ayatollah Khomeini, an unstoppable process of fundamentalism spreading among the descendants of Ishmael *(the Arabs)*. Anyone who examines world affairs will see that events are already heading in this direction. These are the times of the final events. There is no way of mistaking it."

Fr. Neil is reluctant to nominate a specific date for the beginning of the end but he hints that late 1998/early 1999 might be a more-than-safe each way bet. "It is extremely likely to commence this side of the year 2000," he claims. "Saint Paul tells us in a letter to the Thessalonians (First letter, Chapter 5, Verse 3) that the day of the Lord will come, suddenly, at a time when they are saying 'peace and safety'. We know that there is much talk now about peace and safety in the Middle East. We have seen Arafat and Rabin shake hands, sign peace agreements and so on. The peace and safety cry is in full force.

"1998 is a jubilee year in Israel, 50 years after the founding of the state. In Israel, before Christ, they always had a great celebration every 50 years. I believe, therefore, that 1998 will be very important. Events will speed up from now until then, when the war may well begin. It is a matter of a few years."

For those who survive the approaching horrors of World War 111, an estimated two billion happy campers in all, says Fr. Horan, there will be many reasons to be cheerful. "The prophesies are explicit," he stresses. "Jesus Christ will return to Earth in glory. He will become King of Israel and reign for 1,000 years. There will follow a time of unrestricted joy."

Christ's first duty on His Jerusalem comeback will be to emcee the long-awaited and much-hyped Judgement Day jamboree. "The bodies of everyone who has ever lived will be raised up," states Fr. Horan solemnly. "Those who are condemned will merely receive the final sentence of condemnation. Obviously, they cannot enter the kingdom. The saints, however, will be sent from Jerusalem to preach what is called the Everlasting Gospel. Many of these saints will be totally unknown and unsung. Their names are not written in any history book, only in the Book of Life."

Saints and mortals will thenceforth live side by side, cheek by halo. It will literally be Heaven on Earth, the Garden of Eden before the Fall. A world free from war, pestilence, poverty, pain and television programmes hosted by Aonghus McAnally.

"Many people expect Christ to come as a purely spiritual person to save us all," submits Fr. Horan. "They're not prepared for the fact that He will be a literal King, reigning in a literal city, and that He will ask the whole world to submit to Him as King of Israel. All remaining countries will become part of a great Hebrew commonwealth.

"'Every man shall dwell under his vine, under his fig tree, and none shall make him afraid', say the prophesies. Everyone will be given a piece of land to live on. There are enormous and beautiful prophesies about nations beating their swords into ploughshares, their spears into reaping hooks. The thought of war will no longer exist. Neither will the thought of killing or attacking another human being. Or the thought of husband and wife fighting. Harmony will be within each human being. Even people who are cripples will get their footing back, and there'll be a tremendous sense of peace and joy.

"The ordinary citizens like, hopefully, you and me, if we are admitted, will live to vast ages but they will be not immortal. It appears that they will live to 900 years or more. Those who die will be raised up immediately at the end of the 1,000 years and then they too will be made immortal. Death itself will be destroyed. Even the person who knows he's going to die tomorrow will be so certain that he'll be resurrected in, say, 20 years that he will not mind dying.

"Daniel says that, 'The saints of the most high will possess the kingdom, and will reign forever, and ever'. Why is the phrase 'forever and ever' always used in religion? Shouldn't 'forever' be enough? This is a Hebrew phrase meaning 'the hidden period and beyond'. The first period is the 1,000 years of Christ's reign. The other period is after that 1,000 years, which is the final resurrection and eternity."

In this glorious new world very soon to come, the day-to-day running of each country will be overseen by saints from that country. It seems that the saints will even take over the relatively minor legislative and administrative functions, effectively filling every position, in an Irish context, from Mayor to Ceann Comhairle to Treasurer of the local Urban District Council.

National saints will become heads of state. Given that Saint Patrick was by birth a Welshman, however, Fr. Horan conjectures that Saint Brigid is the probable successor to Mary Robinson at Áras an Uachtaráin.

"The world will have come to an end as we know it and the new world will have begun," exults Fr. Horan. "The rulers of mankind will not be politicians, who are prone to mistakes, but Princes associated with the King, the saints. Obviously, there will be countless millions of saints, but there will be a job found for each one. There's no doubt about that.

"You will even have saints ruling areas as small as a parish. Christ said, 'Some will rule over ten cities, some over five, some over one'. The word 'city', in many cases, was used for a fairly small town – even Nazareth was a city. All of the saints will have different roles. They will all be immortal. They will never again suffer or die. They will never have to be elected. There will be no question of elections because they will be immortal rulers forever."

At this point in my discourse with Fr. Horan, one or two practical questions arise. Saints, as we know them, are inviolate, sacred beings, venerated for their sanctity, whose very body parts are often revered as consecrated relics with special supernatural powers. They can perform miracles with just a flick of their wrists or a nod of their heads. Why should they bother walking when they can fly? Why hold a conversation with one person when they can speak in tongues to multitudes? Why eat, for that matter, when it will only necessitate the taking of a holy shit?

"The saints *will* eat food," Fr. Horan states categorically. "They won't have to eat food to sustain life. They will eat totally for enjoyment. For that reason, it is speculated that the circulation of blood will not need to operate in the same way in the saints as it does in the ordinary human beings. Christ said, 'They will come from north, south, east and west and sit down with Abraham, Isaac and Jacob in the Kingdom Of God'. He also said that the Son of Man will put on an apron and serve them Himself. The saints will live real literal lives. They will walk and talk and move just like they did when they first lived on Earth."

Will the saints have any interest in making the beast with two backs?

"They won't marry or reproduce," replies Fr. Horan. "The love that will fill the world will have no need of that kind of physical expression. Christ again said that, 'They will neither marry nor be given in marriage but will be as the angels in Heaven'."

Will they use filthy lucre?

"I don't know if there will be any need for money as we have it now. Bartering was very much a part of ancient times. In the time of Christ, every Israelite had to make an offering to the temple of the half shekel, the Hebrew coin. If there is money, I have no doubt that it will almost certainly be all Hebrew money.

"Amazingly enough, the shekel has been re-introduced as the Israeli currency during the last ten years. I'm sure there will be a need for trade and buying and selling, for houses, food and so on. All people will have a real connection with the land. Farming and agriculture will be the main pursuits, but there will be a place for cities as well, of course."

If Fr. Neil Horan seems remarkably unperturbed by his certitude that Armageddon will be upon us no later (barring miracles) than the year

2000, it is because he has made an intimate study of the "bliss and sheer fun" which will be the hallmark of the post-apocalypse era.

"I have no doubt but that music and dancing will be very important in the New Jerusalem," he asserts, grinning like a house ablaze. "Everybody will travel to Jerusalem once every single year. First of all, to worship and to see the King. That worship will be in a great new temple that will be built in Jerusalem. We don't have to wait for the future to know all about the architecture and the measurements of that building. They were given two and a half thousand years ago to the prophet Ezekiel, as the last six chapters of his book. Every single detail is given. It will be roughly a square mile in size. Even the gate which Christ will enter is described. He will come in through the East Gate. The temple will be built after Christ returns to Earth. Christ will be its chief architect, and it will be the finest building ever seen on Earth.

"As well as prayer, there is no doubt that there will be festivities and music. There's many references to this, such as, 'Let the saints be joyful, let them play the harp, let them play the pipes, let them sing and dance'.

"We can take it for certain that the cultures of all the remaining nations will play a big part. I like to think that our beautiful Irish music and dancing will be to the fore at this wonderful time. It is the best thing I can think of that we have to offer."

John McColgan, Moya Doherty *et al* will no doubt be pleased to hear that Fr. Neil believes that the *Riverdance* extravaganza is precisely the kind of "very good cultural entertainment" which is likely to be staged for the King of the Jews at His annual knees-ups – assuming of course that its performers and mentors are deemed spiritually pure enough to survive the great chastisement. The bad news, though, is that he is not quite so sure that Irish, or indeed any, rock music would be appropriate fare for such a notoriously finicky audience.

"It isn't for me to say what kind of music that Christ and His saints will accept," affirms Fr. Horan. "It would be presumptuous of me to say, as it would be to say what form of dress will be prescribed then or what form of transport. What I do know is that it will be music of quality from all eras. That would certainly include the great classical composers. Things like rock 'n' roll or things like the music of Gilbert and Sullivan, or the opera of Puccini, I'm sure there'll be a place for them. I'm not so sure they'll be at the top table. Variety will be the main feature. That's how the 'wealth of the nations will be taken to Christ'. Not as money, but as culture."

It was on June 17th, 1973, that Cornelius Horan formally put his hand in the hand of the Man from Galilee. On that date, he was ordained by the priapic Bishop Eamon Casey, in Saint Mary's Cathedral, Killarney.

The second oldest of a family of 13, Fr. Horan describes his childhood as "conventionally Catholic and very happy." He decided to become a priest at the age of 16, as much to follow in the footsteps of his beloved uncle, Fr. John, as anything else.

A brief consultation with *Forbidden Fruit* reveals that it is entirely probable that Bishop Casey struggled out of the love sack he shared with Annie Murphy on the very morning he consecrated Fr. Horan's Holy Orders. On purely sacramental grounds, I wonder if this realisation detracts in any way from the validity of the ordination?

"No," he insists. "The office of a bishop or a priest performing a sacrament does not actually depend on the priest being good or bad. The sacrament is valid anyway. There are very few, if any, priests who are really worthy of performing the consecration. A priest is human too and his thoughts wander, even at the consecration.

"I was shocked by the Bishop Casey scandal. I was disappointed in him, disappointed because there's no doubt he was good friends with Annie Murphy at the time of my ordination. Secondly, it wasn't just the fact that he was friends with a woman – that's a natural thing for a human being even though it is wrong for a priest – but it was the fact that it went on for so long. The worst thing was that he was a very popular bishop in Kerry and so it shook a lot of people. It shook me."

While still preparing for the priesthood at Saint Peter's College, in Wexford, Neil Horan was one of a number of young seminarians earmarked for positions with London dioceses. Immediately after his ordination, he went to work for the Archbishop of Southwark, in the parish of Saint John Fisher, Bexley.

Life in this alien, heathen metropolis was both daunting and difficult for Fr. Horan but he says that he was "a hard-working and conscientious priest." He was not a "troublemaker" by any means, and had, indeed *has*, no major differences of opinion with Catholic teaching on subjects such as divorce, contraception, celibacy and so on.

Then, while cycling through Dartford, on the second Sunday of February, 1974, he stumbled upon something that was to change his live forever, and ever. Amen.

"As I was passing the local hall, I noticed a lecture advertised, entitled *Signs Of The End Of This Present Age,*" he recounts. "On entering, I found the talk was being given by a religious sect called the Apostolic Fellowship of Christ. They were Christadelphians, a word which means 'Brothers of Christ' in Greek. The Christadelphians were established in England about 150 years ago and have a worldwide membership of no more than 10,000.

"What these people were saying impressed me deeply. It was against all my raising. These people were Protestants, a people to be wary of. But I couldn't deny their truth. The prophesies foretelling the future make up perhaps one third of the whole book of the scriptures. They have to be important. But I didn't just accept their word for it. I went to libraries and read up on Israel, the history of the Jewish people, and on other prophesies that have already been fulfilled. I was very excited to find that everything they said was true."

Posing as a building labourer so as not to disturb anyone with his Roman collar, Fr. Horan attended Christadelphian meetings every Sunday and Friday evenings. He found himself becoming more and more convinced by their philosophy. In August 1975, he invited two of the elders from the Dartford group to Scartaglin, to speak to his family who were, after all, the baptismal font of his faith.

"They spent a week at home," he recalls, his face illuminated at the thought. "They spoke to my parents, brothers and sisters and an uncle that was there, for a full week. And, gosh, my family said they had never heard things put so simply before. They could so easily identify with the idea of every man dwelling under his vine or under his fig tree, or even the odd sycamore, as my father said. They loved the thought of Christ

144

building the temple in Jerusalem. There was a builder at the time, a local mason, who had just died called Maurice Horan, or Mossy Paddy. They could imagine Mossy Paddy coming back with Christ and working at it.

"The trouble about religion generally is that the ordinary small farmer or workman, they find it very hard to believe that it really has something directly to offer to them. Do good to your neighbour and so on is fine. And doing good now is an essential part of religion. But, within each human being is the question, 'What will I get in the end?'. That's not a selfish question. It's a realistic one. It's a question the apostles asked Christ.

"The idea of going to Heaven is okay but it's a bit vague. The question people in a place like Kerry would ask, especially the farmers, is, 'What will happen to my land in coming generations? Who will be farming it?'. We know we live in the real world but where does the real world go when we die? The prophesies struck an enormous chord with my family, simple country folk. They could understand it, no problem.

"Like I am, they were quite sure that figures like Padraig O'Keefe and Mossy Paddy will play a part in the Kingdom of God. It's the simplicity and wholesomeness of their background."

Holy See, holy do. Fr. Neil has an interesting take on the flood of sexual and financial scandals which has threatened to burst the banks, both metaphorical and literal, of the Catholic Church in recent years. Paedophile priests, philandering bishops, crooked cardinals – according to prophesy, they are all merely carrying out God's plan.

"Christ prophesied that, in the last generation, the sun and the moon would be dark and would not give their light," explains Fr. Horan. "That sort of language is used not just by Christ but by all the prophets. The 'sun' would generally refer to the governments of the world. The 'moon' is speaking about the religious leaders – Catholic, Protestant, Hindu, Muslim. It is said that the 'moon' will be darkened which really means that the religious leaders will not be able to give any great leadership. Without doubt, part of the reason is that their own moral standing will be low in the last days.

"Jesus Himself makes the comparison that it will be like the days of Noah. Noah was, of course, a great religious preacher, but there's no doubt there were other religious preachers in his day as well. And what happened? Eight people was all he managed to convert in a whole long lifetime. Christ said it will be the exact same in the final generation, which I believe is now. I have no doubt that the scandals about Bishop Casey or Fr. Michael Cleary fit in with the prophesies of the end of days.

"Just before the most glorious period in history, when Christ comes back, will come the darkest period. The moral state of the world in the last days is very bad, according to the prophesies. The Church is losing its moral authority because of the scandals. That is fulfilling God's plan."

Similarly, if you want to know why there's so much carnage, slaughter and butchery in the world, all you have to do is go back to the Creator's drawing board.

"War is another thing that has God's blessing because war is to teach us human beings that we cannot manage our own affairs," maintains Fr. Horan. "There is only one Prince of Peace and that is Christ. He is the only one who will bring world peace. When He does so, the whole of humanity will realise that we can forget about our human leaders, politicians, diplomats and our peace troops. They would never succeed.

"We have to give all the honour to this Prince of Peace. War is of God. Regarding Armageddon, it will be the gateway to the Golden Age. God will be gathering all the nations of the world together for Armageddon to show that the world leaders have not got it within their power to bring about eternal peace."

God never closes one door but he treble-locks, bolts and chains another. This is especially true in His treatment of the Jews, His, would you believe it?, *Chosen* People.

"Anti-Semitism is of God," asserts Fr. Horan. "Moses himself foretold the history of the Jewish people from his day to the end. There's a celebrated chapter in the Book of Deuteronomy, Chapter 28, in which he says that if they did not live up to God's plan, curses would come. The reality is that they never did live up to the plan, so the curses always came. God said He would scatter them among the nations, from one end of the Earth to the other.

146

"The prophet Jeremiah foretold that, 'They will chase you under the dens of rocks of the Earth and in the dark holes of the Earth'. The Nazis literally chased the Jews into sewers. Every aspect of the prophesy is fulfilled. But it's God that's doing it. He always says, 'I' will do it. Therefore, although the persecution of the Jews has been a dreadful thing, it was God's way of keeping His people separate and of punishing them. The same way as God crucified His own Son."

So Adolf Hitler was doing God's work when he ordered the extermination of six million Jews? "Hitler was doing God's work, yes. Not doing God's will, but doing God's work. It was never the will of God that His Son should die – but God knew that because the Fall took place, everything that would happen in human history would be tragedy. The only way to get back the New Paradise was through a series of tragedies, including the death of His own Son and including the long, long persecution of the Jewish people and the persecution that is yet to come.

"Adolf Hitler's given role was to put six million of God's chosen people to death. He was certainly fulfilling God's plan because that was prophesied 3,000 years ago by Moses. Although it was a most frightful event, and the concentration camps are an incredible blot on this century, bad and good things fulfil God's plan. God's plan is to move forward step by step towards the final events.

"Famine, murders, disease, all disasters are from God, and have been from the start. It's important to go back to the story of creation. It all has a purpose."

Even child abuse? Was Fr. Brendan Smith another of God's little helpers? "It has a purpose in the sense that it shows that innocence is gone," replies Fr. Horan. "Innocence is gone from the Earth but innocence will be one day restored. God is not in favour of what people like child abusers do. But because God knows of the Fallen state of humankind, God now approves of what they do, in this limited sense."

For Neil Horan, the Biblical account of God's creation of the Universe in seven days, and the Fall of Adam and Eve in the Garden Of Eden, are not mere stories or fables. Like every other passage in the Bible, he sees these narratives as works of hardnosed, bluntly factual reportage.

Inevitably then, he regards the theory of evolution as "a lie, a false belief." He corroborates his case by using the New Testament to verify the Old Testament. With considerable rational justification, he attests that you cannot have one without the other.

"The idea that things progressed from a low form of life to human life is directly contrary to the Bible and contrary to the belief of Christ Himself," he states. "The early part of the Bible is not made up of stories. It's fact. Close study even reveals the literal location of the Garden of Eden. It was in the fertile area at the mouths of Tigris and Euphrates, near what is today the Basra region of Iraq.

"Why did Jesus refer to a character like Noah as a real person? If Noah was just a mythical figure who never existed, was Christ mistaken? If Christ was mistaken, then we've all had it. There are dozens upon dozens of references to Abraham in the New Testament, all suggesting that he was a real person. Why do we have a seven-day week, other than the fact that there were seven days at the start and that seven is the most symbolic of all numbers in the scriptures, the most perfect of all numbers."

With the jaunty assurance of a man who is absolutely secure in the precision of his faith, Fr. Horan even takes in his stride that perennial creationist teaser: If the brothers Cain and Abel were Adam and Eve's only children, how did they manage to reproduce?

"There's a simple answer to that one," he chirrups. "The human race at the start did not have a fraction, naturally, of the inherited disease that exists today. They had nothing inherited because they were the first people. God never said that you cannot have intercourse with your mother or sister. The only reason that the Church says it nowadays is that it is proven to double disease. Any inherited disease in the family is doubled through incest.

"With Adam and Eve, there was no such thing. They lived to 900 years of age. The air was perfect, as clean as could be. There was no pollution. Their blood had nothing in it, in the way of disease. Even death itself only came very gradually to them. Cain had intercourse with his mother, Eve, and their offspring are our ancestors.

"Incest is morally wrong now because of the Fallen state of human health. Since Christ, we are allowed only one husband and one wife. All the figures before Christ were allowed more than one wife. God, strictly

148

speaking, did not say that it is wrong for you to have more than one wife. After Christ, yes, but there's a reason for that. Not because it is morally wrong, but because it's put forward as a symbol of Christ marrying His bride, the Church.

"It is still morally right to have more than one wife but it's not right for a Christian because of the symbolism of the one bride and the one King."

In September 1975, Neil Horan was baptised into The Apostolic Fellowship of Christ. He left the priesthood shortly afterwards. Within a year, two of the Dartford Elders had died and the group began to fracture over what he saw as "silly power struggles." Drifting aimlessly in a career sense, but still a zealous student of prophesy, he eventually travelled to Italy to do a course on Church history, sustaining himself with a job as a kitchen porter in a Florence *trattoria*.

"I remember being in Florence one Sunday, visiting one of the beautiful palaces, the Belvedera Palace," he relates. "I remember looking around at all the Italians there and wondering how much did they know about the prophesies. Gosh, at least I had been given some understanding of these prophesies but I was making no use of that knowledge. That very day, I decided to avail of my position as a priest and to use my knowledge to teach Catholics."

In the summer of 1980, Neil Horan rejoined the priesthood and was welcomed back with open arms by the Archbishop of Southwark, Rev. Michael Bowen. Over the coming years, he was stationed as a curate in Plumstead, Clapham, Anerley (near Crystal Palace) and Nunhead. Throughout this time, he became increasingly engrossed in a campaign of "publicising prophesy," which reached a peak with the printing and distribution of 500 copies of *A Glorious New World Very Soon To Come,* with the help of lay support, in November 1985.

At first, Neil's colleagues merely clucked and ummed impatiently whenever he began to speak about his prophesy studies. When the book was published and started attracting more widespread attention, however, the response of the top brass in the London Church was to invite Fr. Horan to pursue his studies in a more secure environment, *to wit* a booby hatch.

He was ordered to seek psychiatric assessment, which he obediently did, first in Killarney, later in Harley Street, and later still in Greenwich Hospital. The doctors differed but none was prepared to pronounce him insane, or in need of any mental therapy. The Harley Street shrink went so far as to give him "a clean bill of health" on two occasions.

Believing himself to be of sound mind, Fr. Horan co-operated fully with all the psychiatric investigations requested and became angry only when he learned that one doctor was recommending that he be pre-scribed Risperidone, a drug usually used in the treatment of psychosis.

Rather than engage with his arguments, it seems that the institutional Church would prefer to see Fr. Horan coldcocked with pharmaceuticals.

"They have no intention at all of tackling my beliefs," he charges, with the first flicker of rage he's evinced all day. "They have decided that the only way to deal with me is psychiatric treatment. A priest in Nunhead said to my brother Dan, 'Many of those who think that they have a mes-sage for mankind are mentally ill'. But they too are supposed to believe that the Bible has a message for mankind.

"They are as nice as you can get, as open as you can get, but not one of them has sat down and gone through what I'm saying. They won't dis-cuss it. They prefer to paint me as a disturbed person."

We will leave aside here the rich, corn-fed irony of people who claim to drink the blood of Christ every day trying to suggest that *anybody* is a bit loopy. For the record though, I do not believe that Neil Horan is in the least bit mad.

Sure, he can be a little pedantic and compulsive with the details at times. He is also self-evidently obsessed with the subject of God, but that's an occupational hazard in the profession of faith. He has none of the numb, unfocused, thousand-miles-away glare that I have encountered among genuine screwballs. At the very minimum, he's as sane as any other priest I've ever met.

All he has done is to take Christianity at its word. With characteristical-ly sinuous duplicity, Vatican gurus themselves have been perfectly happy to deploy the Bible as a crossword puzzle when convenient, and to peri-odically exhume cryptic passages which can be twisted to obliquely outlaw and condemn whatever it is that they would like to see outlawed and condemned for their own contemporary and inevitably corporate reasons.

Equally, embarrassing interpretations can mysteriously vanish when appropriate. You don't hear a lot these days about the explicit scriptural justification for slavery, witch-burning, the shunning of shellfish, or the prohibition on women wearing trousers. Yet, at various times in Christian history, these Biblical sanctions were all decreed to be written in stone.

In July of 1995, after a lengthy saga of censure and reprimand, Fr. Neil Horan was officially sacked by the parish priest of Nunhead, Fr. Jeff Cridland, because he was "using the pulpit to advance his sensationalist views." In statements to the press, Fr. Cridland categorised Fr. Horan's theories as "complete and utter tosh." (A phonecall from this reporter to the Archbishop of Southwark's Private Secretary, Rev. Richard Moth, elicited nothing but a lengthy silence and a stern, "We have nothing to say about Fr. Horan.")

Effectively banished from "even setting foot within the bounds of the parish," Fr. Horan stayed in a convent in Hertfordshire for three months after his dismissal but now lives like a fugitive, availing of the safe-house hospitality of friends and admirers. "Officially, I'm a priest on leave of absence, on a sabbatical," he says. "I get the social security, that's all I have. I say mass for myself every day. Sometimes, I'm invited to say mass in the homes of others. I do a lot of walking. I don't drink or smoke. My role publicising prophesies is not finished. There's a lot more I want to do. I would like to republish my book. I may also go home to Kerry. Events themselves will dictate what I have to do."

Fr. Horan insists that he is not bitter, merely sad for his misguided brothers of the cloth. "The prophesies are part of the sacred book that the Church has accepted for 2,000 years. There's no dispute about that at all. But it is the interpretation that the Church puts on it that Catholics must accept. They say there are two sources of revelation from God: scripture and tradition. What they mean by tradition is that you cannot interpret anything if it disagrees with the Church's interpretation. It's a vicious circle.

"The Church does not believe in the Bible. That's the bottom line of this controversy."

151

Fr. Neil Horan does not have a messiah complex. He takes pains to emphasise that he is not a prophet. He says he has never had a vision or a supernatural experience. He simply sees himself as a man condemned to live in interesting times.

"I'm as sure and certain about the Kingdom of God and the nearness of Christ's coming as I am that next year is 1997," he proclaims. "I don't feel I need any apparitions or messages from God. All the necessary revelations were already given by God, finishing 1900 years ago this year when Saint John, the beloved disciple, received the final book of the Apocalypse, The Book Of Revelation. It's just as exciting to read as if I had received those revelations myself."

A tirelessly modest man by temperament, Fr. Horan is nevertheless demonstrably certain that he will be selected to be among the citizens of the New Kingdom. "I have no doubt that people who are studying the prophesies and who know a little bit about the state of Israel and its history will have a role to play at the end," he says, marshalling as much humility as he can in the circumstances.

He shows me his freshly laundered dancing vestments again. He admits that the reason he takes such assiduous care of the garments is that he is confident that these will be the very threads he will wear when he achieves his greatest ambition: to dance a jig for Jesus Christ while He sits on the throne of David in the New Jerusalem.

"That's speculation of course, but it's a speculation that I don't mind going in for," he smiles, pausing to allow me to form a mental picture of the scene. "It would be a great privilege to go to Jerusalem in my national costume and to dance for Jesus. I'd love to know what He would think of my dancing.

"I would also love to meet King David himself. He was the greatest King of Israel. He reigned 3,000 years ago. It is on David's throne that Jesus will sit. He had a tremendous understanding of the soothing power of music. He wrote many of the great psalms. He played the harp and he danced. I'm sure he would appreciate Irish dancing.

"I do definitely think that we will be able to meet figures like David and even The Blessed Virgin Mary. There'll be no question then of having to depend on visions. It will be real encounters, face to face. We will be able to shake hands with them. I look forward to meeting Abraham. It was to Abraham that God promised the land of Israel, yet he had no field of his own to bury his wife in. I would say to him, 'Now you have the land of Israel, are you really delighted?'.

"Our Lady was only a 15-year-old girl when she prophesied of these times. 'Gosh', I would say to Our Lady, 'it has all come true, you must be very happy'."

Rising from his chair, Fr. Horan produces from his bedside locker a small gilt replica of the Menorah, the seven-branched candelabrum used in Jewish worship. "There will only be one religion in the Kingdom of God," he asserts. "We will have absolute clarity of belief. The Judaeo-Christian religion will be truth, not opinion. Everyone is entitled to religious freedom but that will not operate then, because we will all know the truth. We will worship together. Human wisdom will be finished."

Fr. Horan warns that even at the moment of "Christ's triumph," there will be one last fly in the Elysium ointment. "The Antichrist will come after Christ has returned," he counsels. "There is a real fear that the main Common Market countries will mistake Christ for the Antichrist. They may not necessarily join the original attack on Israel but they certainly will join later to win it back from the Antichrist.

"Disturbingly, a lot of religions are building up the idea that the Antichrist will come first and that he will set himself up in Jerusalem. I'm not saying that they're not entitled to their view. But if that is true, it will be true. If it's false, it's frightening. If it's false, the real Christ will come to Jerusalem and they will mistake Him as the Antichrist, which I think is what will happen.

"There's no doubt that the Antichrist will arise in Rome, chiefly as a military leader. He will also have religious trappings. He certainly will be identifiable at the time and he will oppose Christ.

"I would make no attempt to name any figure. He could well be living as some sort of Christian figure now. Suppose there was a split in the Church, as there was during the Great Schism. We'd have a Pope and an

Antipope. That's quite possible."

Against such a backdrop, Fr. Horan has an urgent message for An Taoiseach, John Bruton. "Acquaint yourself with the prophesies, Mr. Bruton, and learn as much as you can about the state of Israel," he beseeches. "Above all though, if you get an ultimatum from Jerusalem, you must accept it. It will not be from an Antichrist. It will be from the real Christ. My final plea to you, Mr. Bruton, is to investigate everything I say. Not because I say it but because the evidence fits. People of the opposite view are not able to offer any kind of adequate explanation for what is happening.

"The Bible does not tell us what will happen to Ireland during Armageddon. In Saint Patrick's own prophesies, he suggests that Ireland will be submerged beneath water until the Antichrist has been defeated and that it will then re-emerge. We know that tidal waves and so on are more predictable nowadays but it is unclear. The people could, of course, survive by living abroad temporarily, or even on some of those huge modern liners."

Beneath the slightly open window of his bedroom, a passing British Rail train gnashes and natters on the tracks. Inside, however, the room goes as quiet as cotton wool while Fr. Horan, his face glowing like a hot coal, reveals what is, perhaps, the supreme source of his trust in the prophesies.

"Both of my parents are gone now," he sighs, rapids of emotion gathering in his eyes. "My father died recently and my mother died eight years ago. I had a handicapped brother, Denis, who passed away in 1992 and a sister, Hanna, died of a brain tumour in 1968. They're all buried in Scartaglin cemetery but we won't have too much longer to wait now. More than anything else, I look forward to meeting them at the resurrection. That will be a wonderful day."

ONWARD CHRISTIAN SOLDIER!

The streets of Dublin are a battleground. Dozens of religious sects vie with each other daily for the deeds to yet more Irish souls. One man, however, has pledged himself to opposing those groups and to thwarting all of their evangelical efforts.

The cluster of serpentine Dublin streets which runs from the swarming thoroughfares of Stephen's Green to the darkest corners of Parnell Square may seem like an unlikely setting for a *jihad,* or holy war, yet that is precisely what engulfs this territory every day of the week.

This mottled terrain constitutes the frontline in a battle for souls that is straight out of the Old Testament. It's a conflict in which you and I may not be interested but it's a conflict which is most certainly interested in you and I. We, after all, are the human fodder that these spiritual rivals so badly need to feed their massed canons.

By their brand names shall ye know them! At any given moment on this city-centre strip, you could be stopped and evangelised by Jehovah's Witnesses, Mormons, Moonies, Scientologists, Hare Krishnas, Eckankars, Christadelphians, any number of American fundamentalists and the peddlers of a variety of other proselytising sects whose titles and beliefs are too arcane or newly-minted to be found in any reliable textbook.

Relations between all of these competing cults are cordial but distant. Their footsoldiers never seem to fraternise with one another or pool information, but nor have there been very many cases of them actually fighting over which team gets to bag a particular soul.

Why bother? These spiritual anglers have got other fish to poach. Any minute now, there'll be another potential recruit barrelling along; one more sappy greenhorn with a gullible grin and the words BRAINWASH ME all but tattooed across the forehead. Sometimes, winning converts is like taking candy *to* a baby.

Unless, that is, Noel Deane happens to be around. Deane is the scourge of the evangelists who ply their tirades in Dublin's city centre. For longer than he cares to remember, this self-styled "cult-buster" has been waging a one-man guerrilla war against the Moonies, the Jehovah's Witnesses and the Mormons in particular, but also against all the religious sects who work the streets and estates of the nation's capital.

The Deane *modus operandi* is simple. First, he collates as much information as possible about each individual cult and its Dublin division, and then he hits them where it hurts: in the sales pitch.

"I decide which group I'm going to target on a particular day and I go out on the streets and follow them," he asserts. "I try and stick right behind them no matter where they go, and I try to speak to everyone that they speak to. I give out leaflets and explain that a lot of what these cults say about themselves is untrue."

There have been scuffles and slanging matches between Noel Deane and some of the evangelists he shadows. He has also been reported to the Gardaí several times for "harassment" and has been arrested at least once. None of this deters Deane from what he sees as his mission.

"I believe in planting seeds of doubt," he says. "Cults in this country have it too easy. Nobody wants to be seen to be intolerant, so people are afraid to come out and say plainly that these groups are dishonest and dangerous. I believe in giving people that information. A little bit of information before a person gets involved with a cult goes a long way.

"That same bit of information after they get involved is useless," he adds. "That's why I feel I have to go out on the streets and get to people at the same time the cults do. I have to fight them on their own battleground."

It's just after 7.30am on a cold Wednesday morning in late July, and this latterday Saint George is preparing for another day of slaying dragons. Rather than a sword, the only weapons which Noel Deane carries are a shoulder bag of leaflets and anti-cult books, a small wooden card-table and a sheet of plywood.

The question "Could Jehovah's Witnesses Be Wrong?" is stencilled on one side of the plywood. A warning to "Beware of Moonies, Please" is printed on the other (note that *Please* – this cult-buster is nothing if not polite).

Since his mother died a couple of years ago, Deane has lived alone in what was the family home in Rory O'Connor House, a drab and poorly-preserved block of flats in Dublin's north inner city. Now in his mid 40s, he has been unemployed for well over a decade, and survives on the small invalidity pension to which he is entitled as a result of the severe dose of brucellosis he contracted while working in a meat-packing plant during the early '70s.

"A lot of people think that fighting the cults is my job," he observes with a rueful smile. "But it's not a job because I don't get paid for it. At the same time, it's a lot more than a job because it's my whole life. It's what I do all day, every day – and what I hope to do for the rest of my life. It's like a crusade, I suppose."

While nobody grants Noel Deane a wage for pursuing his crusade, his work does require both money and resources. These he receives from

Irish Church Missions. Based at 28, Bachelor's Walk, I.C.M. is a Church of Ireland-funded operation which was set up, as its superintendent Reverend William Bridcut explains, "to assist and propagate the Church of Ireland's mission to the Irish people."

In practical terms, the I.C.M. do little proselytising but they do host Bible study classes, run a religious bookshop and provide facilities for a variety of C of I youth groups. They also underwrite a Cult Department, in the portly shape of Noel Deane.

"It has always been Irish Church Missions policy and ethos not to avoid controversy," insists Rev. Bridcut, a lean, dapper, Alastair Sim looka-like. "Our attitude has always been that if people came along with a different point of view, you examined that point of view and then you sought to prove them wrong. Therefore, what Noel Deane is doing on the streets of Dublin is very much in keeping with our history."

I.C.M. have equipped Deane with an extensive library of background material, including videos, books, pamphlets and an indispensable American dictionary of cults outlining the beliefs, origins and financing systems of most known sects. Full stencilling and photocopying facilities have been provided, with which Deane produces a vast array of fact-sheets and newsletters. He also pens a regular "cult column" in I.C.M.'s modestly titled quarterly magazine, *The Banner Of Truth In Ireland*.

More crucially, from the point of view of Deane's on-the-ground activities, is the fact that I.C.M. afford him free use of a suite of fully furnished rooms on the top floor of their Bachelor's Walk premises. Deane uses this base as an unofficial information and "counselling" centre for the relatives and friends of people who have become involved with cults or are on the verge of doing so.

"I get callers all the time," he says. "The fact that I'm based here has spread by word of mouth. Parents of kids who are getting sucked into one of these groups come over and I'll give them all the relevant background information, and show them a video. It's great that the place is so central because if I meet someone on the street who wants information, we can go back and get it immediately.

"I also try to get some of the young people involved with the Jehovah's Witnesses to come back and watch some of the videos. I had a couple of Mormons back here recently. I gave them some milk – Mormons love milk for some reason – and they watched a video documentary called *The Mormon Dilemma*. They pretended to me that it didn't bother them, but it might have planted that seed of doubt, and that's what I want."

At this point, it's essential to place Noel Deane's own religious cards firmly on the table. Shortly before he began his cult-busting activities in late '87, Deane became a Born Again Christian. He has rejected his Catholic upbringing as the product of "Christianity in error." He attends weekly Church of Ireland services and regular Bible classes.

Right now, on this particular Wednesday morning, it's getting perilously close to 7.45am and Deane is keen to get down to O'Connell Street. His targets are the Jehovah's Witnesses. At this time every Wednesday morning, a group of Witnesses usually convene outside the G.P.O., to sell copies of their magazine *(Watchtower)* and to plan their proselytising strategy for the days ahead. Today, however, they obviously expect Deane to appear (he has, after all, been here on the three previous Wednesday mornings) and they don't turn up.

Relations between the Witnesses and Deane have been especially strained in recent times. Infuriated by the attention they'd been receiving from the cult-buster, the Witnesses embarked upon a policy of reporting him to the Gardaí for harassment, and even stalking. Most of the time, the cops decide that no real crime is being committed and stay out of it.

Deane is undaunted by the non-appearance of the Witnesses. He sets up his little table of booklets and leaflets and holds his "Could Jehovah's Witnesses Be Wrong?" sign aloft. He is joined this morning by a young accomplice called John Scanlon, a resident of Oliver Bond Flats, who often accompanies Deane on his anti-Witnesses ventures.

"A while back, a friend of mine joined the Witnesses," attests John, a tall, angular, moustachioed man in his mid 20s. "His personality changed very quickly and he wouldn't listen to anything any of us would say. I tried to find out as much as I could about the cult and that's how I met Noel. I like what he's doing. People should be warned off these groups."

Noel and John stand outside the G.P.O. for over two hours. Most passers-by ignore them. Some point, some even laugh. Only a handful of people bother to accept a pamphlet. Then, at almost 10am, an alarmingly thin and wrinkled elderly woman approaches. There are tears in her eyes.

"I wish you'd been here three years ago," she tells Deane. "My son got involved with that crowd. He changed completely. He doesn't even come home anymore. I haven't seen him for months."

Listening to Noel Deane talk about his battle with Dublin's cults is like listening to an army General discussing military intelligence.

MOONIES:

"They're usually based outside Telecom Eireann at the top of O'Connell Street. They never call themselves Moonies, it's always Unification Church or even just evangelical Christians. They like it at the top of O'Connell Street because it's near their headquarters where they like to bring people back and show them videos.

"They've recently bought a big Georgian house on North Great Georges Street which cost £80,000 – so you can see how much money they have. They used to attract people by having a sketchboard, but now they just use a questionnaire. They stop you and ask you all these nice questions about the purpose of life and God and the Messiah. Most people will give pretty general answers and then they say, 'Oh yes, you're very spiritual, you should come to one of our meetings'.

"One of their great tricks is that they get your address and the next thing is that someone arrives at your door selling pot plants. They get you talking about religion and start saying what a great coincidence it is that you've met someone from the Unification Church again so quickly, how God has led them to your door. The whole thing is a set-up.

"They make money by selling those pot plants door-to-door. They've a big garden somewhere down the country growing these things. They're also behind a lot of those people who go around pubs in Dublin selling roses.

"Whenever I arrive on the scene beside them, they usually move off. But there have been a few slagging matches. Their leader in Ireland, a fella called David Hanna, got the Gardaí once, because I was standing beside them when himself and his wife – a Korean woman called Kyung Ja – were handing out leaflets. Usually though, they try to avoid anything which would get publicity.

"Internationally, I believe that they are a very dishonest organisation. They have a lot of different fronts. They had an anti-communist group here called C.A.U.S.A. (Confederation of Associations for Unification of Societies of the Americas) and they're behind a student group called C.A.R.P. (Collegiate Association for the Research of Principles). I believe also that they were involved in one of those religious political parties that were set up a while ago."

The Moonies have been in Ireland since 1972 and claim to have between 80 and 100 full-time Irish members and a further 1,000 supporters.

MORMONS:

"Everyone knows what they look like. They have bases in several places but the main ones are in Glasnevin and Terenure. They do a lot of door-to-door stuff but they also have a couple of city-centre spots, especially around Grafton Street.

"Everything they believe comes out of the *Book Of Mormon*, that's all they read. They say that when they read the truth in the *Book Of Mormon*, it gives them a burning in their bosom. But, sure that could be indigestion.

"Most of the time, the Mormons on Grafton Street try to ignore me and pretend that I'm not bothering them by being there. But things have gotten heated at times. One time, one of them went for me and tried to hit me and the others had to hold him back. I said to them that I was glad that I wasn't living in Utah (the Mormon's global H.Q.) because I'd probably be dead by now.

"In Utah, if a Mormon converts he's in danger of losing his life. And anyone who speaks out against them is also taking a big risk. They basically rule the roost in Utah.

"I'd say that, in Dublin, the Mormons are one of the most successful cults at getting new recruits, especially among young people. They get

161

you to go to meetings and then they invite you to one of their dances. The Mormons have a wonderful social life. You go to a lot of these dances and entertainment evenings and you meet only Mormons.

"One particular lad who left the Mormons explained it to me in this fashion: there's a kind of smell in their buildings that is very attractive or hypnotic or something and, when you're away from this, you start to have a longing for it. The whole set-up, even down to how Mormons dress and look so clean-cut, is designed to be attractive and to draw you into the cult.

"Another thing they do is they go to big housing estates and offer to baby-sit or to do the ironing or the gardening or clean your windows, all free of charge. A lot of people let them do these things too, because it's free. Once inside the house, they befriend you and start talking about religion. They have you then. The Mormons are very persistent and very crafty."

As full-time Mormons are regularly sent abroad for lengthy periods of "missionary" work, community numbers in each country fluctuate. Nevertheless, there are believed to be several hundred Irish Mormons.

JEHOVAH'S WITNESSES:

"They have bases which they call Kingdom Halls all over the place, but most of the Witnesses I know are based either in Finglas or Rathgar. Selling *Watchtower* is their big thing. They're each forced to buy a large bundle of these magazines out of their own money, and only break even when they sell them all. They move around a lot. Sometimes, you see them outside Eason's on O'Connell Street or outside the G.P.O. They also hang around the ILAC Centre and outside some office blocks around the city.

"I've gotten to know a good few of the younger Witnesses over the years. They're mostly nice kids but it's like they've been programmed about what to say. If you ask one of them how long he or she has been a Witness, they'll always say three months, even if I know well that they've been around longer than that. They're also trained very well about how to entice people to their meetings, especially with their door-to-door canvassing.

"They target specific people, usually women living on their own, and they turn up selling their magazine or offering free Bible classes. They also use the Moonie trick of visiting someone who's been visited before and then saying that it's God's will. They're great spoofers!"

Despite having already predicted the end of the world three times this century (in 1914, 1925 and 1975), Jehovah's Witnesses still manage to attract a sizeable number of converts. They profess an Irish membership of over 5,000.

ECKANKAR:

"This is a very weird religion. It was founded in 1964 by an American called Paul Twitchell. They believe in soul travel and all this sort of stuff. They have an office somewhere on Lower Mount Street, and they seem to have a good bit of money behind them. They're hard to track down too. They had a meeting a while back in Buswell's Hotel and I picketed that, but they're usually very secretive."

Eckankar has had an Irish chapter for almost 20 years and claims a rank and file here of over 50.

✚ ✚ ✚ ✚ ✚ ✚ ✚

There is, of course, something inherently comical about the idea of this short, stocky Born Again Christian harrying and chasing Moonies, Mormons and the like up and down the streets of Dublin. As far as Noel Deane himself is concerned, however, it's a deadly serious business. Deane is earnest about his cult-busting to the point of obsession.

"I don't read papers or watch television anymore," he admits. "People often talk to me about some current event or controversy and I won't have a clue what they're on about. I know I should but I'm just not that interested. I've buried myself completely in the cults."

Deane's commitment to tackling the cults is grounded not only in his own religious beliefs but also in personal experience of sect indoctrination. For almost two years during the mid '80s, Noel was a practising member of the Unification Church, the group more widely known as the Moonies.

Though born and raised in a strict Catholic household, Deane says that he had grown lukewarm about his religion during his late teens and early 20s. He still prayed regularly but rarely went to mass.

Then, one day towards the end of 1984, he was shopping in the Saint Stephen's Green area when he came upon a small knot of people preaching about God with the aid of a sketchpad and easel. He got chatting to them, liked what he heard and soon started attending meetings in their then headquarters, at 13, Lord Edward Street.

"They made feel very welcome," he recalls. "I also liked the fact that there were a lot of people there of different nationalities. It was a very nice environment."

Gradually, over a period of months, Deane became more and more involved with the Unification Church. An avid thirst for religious knowledge and devotion, which had been dormant since his childhood, was re-aroused. He threw himself into feverish study of *The Divine Principle,* the Moonie Bible. He ate most evenings at the Lord Edward Street premises, and usually stayed on for the night workshops. It was at these that he started to experience strange visions.

"I'd be looking at someone and suddenly I'd see an aura around their head," he says. "Or else I'd be looking up at one of the leaders speaking to us and I'd see these spirit bodies flying out of him. They were all sorts of different shapes and sizes but always very brightly coloured. They'd move very quickly away from whoever they came from and then settle, as though they were watching. Sometimes, they'd float over a particular person's head for a while. It was very weird."

With hindsight, Deane believes that these apparitions were induced by "something in the food." The hallucinations continued for lengthy intervals, often just after one of the daily meals. During this period, he routinely met other "learner" Moonies who claimed to have seen similar phantasms.

All of which only served to deepen Deane's credence in the cult. He travelled regularly to Unification Church seminars (which could last anything from two to 40 days) at a variety of locations throughout Ireland, but most frequently at a large Moonie-owned deer farm near Mullingar, in County Westmeath. There were also conferences at Moonie centres in

England, primarily in Lancaster Gate and Chiselhurst, the fees for which were subsidised by the Dublin chapter.

"To describe what they do as 'brainwashing' makes it sound very glamorous," he avers. "It's more like a constant bombardment of their teaching and rules, and nothing else. They keep you away from newspapers and television and radio and the world in general. You're mixing with Moonies all the time and it takes over your life. It changes your character and your personality.

"When you're away from the group, they get you to do these 'conditions', which are like penances, doing without food or sleep. The one I was given was cold showers, in and out about seven times a go, and I had to do that several times a day. This is the kind of stuff that occupies your free time. After a while, they get into your head so much that it's no wonder you start to see spirit bodies."

It was Noel Deane's excessive eagerness which eventually caused him to leave the Moonies. Totally convinced of the truth of *The Divine Principle,* he took to the streets in order "to see how the teaching would stand up when attacked by evangelists of other faiths." He also started reading the Bible voraciously so that he could back up what he now believed with scripture from the Lord's book.

To his horror, he came to realise that much of the Bible was incompatible with *The Divine Principle.* This distressed Noel because he had thought that what the Unification Church preached was itself "true Christianity." He eventually quit the cult with the help and counselling of Reverend Bridcut, whom he had met at a Bible study evening.

"Over the years, I'd had a lot of hassles with doctors and the Social Welfare, and I'd become very good at standing up for myself," Noel explains. "I was belligerent and outspoken and was becoming a nuisance to the leaders of the Dublin Moonies. I'd started asking a lot of questions in front of other people and this embarrassed them.

"I was a troublemaker to them. They were glad to see me leave. In most other cases, they don't let go so easily. I've heard cases of them following people around and calling at their houses all the time. If you're a Moonie, all your friends are Moonies. If you leave, they all have to shun you. This is the kind of blackmail that they use. If you're at all weak as a person, they'll take advantage. It can be very hard to get away from them."

Noel Deane's primary objection to religious cults is itself a religious one. He believes that these sects are wrong, not because they are self-evidently a carnival of barking buffoons but because they are not Christians.

When he grapples with one of these groups, he does so on the basis of scripture. Deane believes that he has been chosen by God to carry out this work. While he insists that he doesn't actively seek to convert cult members or former cult members to "true Christianity," he does like to point them in that direction.

"If you haven't got something better to offer then you'll never get people to leave a cult," he maintains. "That's why I believe God allows these cults to be successful. At least, they give people who are searching *some* sense of religion. What they believe is wrong, but I don't fight the people, I fight the religion. And, at least, these people are now on common ground with me. We're both talking about God and I have a chance to win them from a false one to a true one."

So, it turns out that the cult-buster is actually a secret agent for the biggest cult of them all, Christianity. Noel Deane concedes that, yes, in order to be thoroughly consistent, he should be out "tackling" the members of all non-Christian denominations, and not just the so-called cults. As is the nature of these things though, there's a handy "theological explanation" for why he chooses not to.

"Even though they are non-Christian, religions such as Islam, Hinduism and Buddhism are not classified as a cults," he argues. "They're classed as 'other religions', albeit false religions. The cults are seen as new groups who use some scripture, but then deny the reality of Jesus Christ. This is the distinction that is made by Christian theologians who know a lot more than I do. But, in the end, it all hinges on Jesus Christ.

"If you have the right Jesus Christ, then you're right for all eternity. If you have the wrong Jesus Christ, then you're wrong for all eternity. That's why I confront people who are spreading a false teaching of Jesus Christ. In a respectful and loving way, I'd also tackle people in other religions about the scriptural basis for what they believe.

"For example, there's a lot of things in Roman Catholicism that are scripturally wrong and I would point that out whenever possible. Roman Catholics are Christians in error."

Why then doesn't Noel Deane take to the streets with a sign urging us to "Beware of Roman Catholics, Please"?

"Well, they're not the most dangerous group," he replies. "There's a lot worse than the Roman Catholics out there."

Before I can take issue with this dubious statement, the Irish Church Missions superintendent, Reverend Bridcut, pops by and offers his own take on why and how the appeal of the cults should be challenged.

"You can't blame these groups themselves," he attests. "They exist because the major denominations have created a huge vacuum. You don't meet that many sincere people among the major religions who are ardently devoted to a cause anymore. Therefore, when young people encounter these groups, they are gripped by their zeal and commitment. The major religions have become too bland. They're all trying to merge into each other. They're almost afraid to stand up and say, 'This is our gospel, this is what we believe'.

"If any of the major religions in this country were starting from scratch today, they wouldn't have a ghost of a chance against the zeal and fire of these new cults. I say that as a member of a major religion. If the major religions want to survive, they'll have to start fighting for their people and winning their stripes rather than just coasting along.

"They should be out on the streets like Noel, pitting their truths against other truths, and standing up for what they believe."

There is a fine old joke about Southern Baptists which perfectly encapsulates my attitude to devotees of cults and religions, *all* cults and religions: The only thing wrong with Southern Baptists is that they don't hold them underwater long enough.

However, for all its innate contradictions and hypocrisies, it is an undeniable fact that there is considerable demand for the service that Noel Deane provides. He receives numerous calls and requests for information every week, usually from the parents of people who have become ensnared by one or other of the cults.

And, who knows? Perhaps his presence on the streets does alert some of the more impressionable citizens to the darker sides of these ostensibly bright and beaming organisations. Noel Deane himself certainly believes so, and is doggedly determined to continue his fight, no matter what the perceived personal cost.

"It has crossed my mind," he says, with a defiant smirk, "that what I'm doing could be dangerous. If I become too much of a nuisance, some of these groups might decide to become very heavy about it. It's certainly not beyond some of them. But if I have to suffer, it will be for doing the will of God. It'll all be worth it in the end."

THE EX-FILES

Just what does a person have to do to get excommunicated around here?

Being born a Catholic is a lot like being
sent to prison. It can be interesting, enlightening, even self-improving, if
you treat it as an educational experience, but there comes a day when
you are ready to graduate.

The perils of incarceration are as widely advertised. Caged humans
neither grow nor prosper. The body atrophies, the brain softens and the
spirit hardens with calluses and carbuncles. The simple act of stooping in
the shower to retrieve a dropped bar of soap within reach of some big,
sweaty thug can become the prelude to intimacies that have no place outside the context of a stable, loving relationship. All of these phenomena
are also considerations for those who are sent to prison.

The primary difference between detention in the calaboose and in the

Catholicism penitentiary is the duration of the stretch. When it is deemed that a custodial term has served its purpose, there are many mechanisms by which interned criminals can regain their freedom. They are given parole, they are given time off for good behaviour, they are given official pardons, or, as is increasingly the case in this country, they are given the cell keys and a head start of 24 hours.

Things are not quite so simple for us convicted Catholics. We are condemned to a life sentence, without remission. And the alleged felony for which we must suffer this incessant penal servitude? A single lousy count apiece of aggravated baptism, to which we were no more than mere accessories in the first place.

The fact is that it's virtually impossible to genuinely leave the Catholic Church. Oh sure, one can become lapsed or non-practising. But this strikes me as a rather half-hearted way to abandon one's faith. I, for one, have no intention of going gently into that good night. I want to storm out and slam the door behind me. I want to thumb my nose and cock my snook. If I can fire off a parting *Harrumph!,* all the better.

Lapsed and non-practising Catholics are still Catholics, of a sort. Nobody would like to be known as a lapsed handbag-snatcher or a non-practising ringleader of angry lynch mobs. And, generally speaking, both of these categories of citizens make a more constructive contribution to society than the sky pilots, or their stooges in the national control tower.

Lapsing implies culpability on the part of the lapsee. It suggests, at best, a degree of default and, at worst, a failure to fulfil one's duty. It certainly does not suggest the truth of the matter, that one wants out of this warped organisation because one is sickened by the charnel-house stench of corruption, fraud and depravity.

Week after week, ever more twisted branches of clerical disgrace are welded onto the Church's sprawling scandalabra. So commonplace are the indictments of priests and religious on paedophilia charges, for instance, that their trials will soon no longer even make the evening news. They have become predictable enough to be reported as part of the weather forecast. ("Tomorrow will see sunny spells in the north, moderate south-westerly winds veering towards westerly on the east coast, and the prosecutions of 6 Franciscans, 3 Cistercians, and a scattered shower of Christian Brothers.")

It is now the widespread view that, collectively, the Irish Catholic clergy are a bunch of whoring, degenerate boozehounds. However, it is wrong to tar every individual cleric with the same sleazy brush. To be fair, the child molesters aren't always drunks and most of the womanisers draw the line at pederasty. These curs are already fitted with dog collars but it's way past time they had leashes put on as well.

To my mind, the sole dignified and ethical course that remains available to the thinking Catholic is to seek excommunication. Force them to kick us out and we can hold our heads up high. A dishonourable discharge from a club such as the Roman See can only be a badge of honour.

Unfortunately, getting excommunicated is easier said than done. *The Code Of Canon Law,* the user's manual of Catholicism, reserves its ultimate sanction for those who commit "the most grave offences." But they mean *grave* by ecclesiastical standards, *grave* in the eyes of men who have all the moral sense of a three-peckered billy goat. It ain't easy to sicken or appall these guys.

Unless, of course, they feel threatened. Canon number 1370 decrees that a *latae sententiae* (automatic) excommunication is incurred by anyone who "uses physical force against the Roman Pontiff." There are many, many references to the evils of such behaviour in *The Code Of Canon Law.* Indeed, "striking the Pope" is listed as the principal and most grievous transgression under the catalogue of *Offences Against Church Authorities And The Freedom Of The Church.*

At first, I thought that the injunction against "striking the Pope" was a metaphor, a Jesuitical euphemism perhaps for some advanced autoerotic technique practised only by the most skilled specialists, seasoned masters for whom bashing the bishop no longer holds either challenge or thrill.

But no. It is meant literally. While clobbering a prelate, a cleric or a member of a religious order will get you a *latae sententiae* suspension (Canon 1370, again), smacking the Holy Father means curtains, immediately. One strike and you're out.

Elsewhere, Canon 1367 states that those who "scatter the sacred species" are also instantaneously excommunicated. This is one for the prank-loving Catholic, as it involves the strewing about, the stealing and/or "the keeping for a sacrilegious purpose" of the consecrated host.

Like all practical jokes, it will appeal only to a niche segment, specifically the very sad and heavily-anoraked crank without very many other calls on his or her time. In Ireland at least, the sacred species is pretty safe then, given that the vast majority of such people here are kept constantly busy on Youth Defence business.

The procuring of an abortion is another fast track to excommunication, as outlined in Canon 1398. Again though, this is not a course of action that is readily open to all of us. We might therefore have to consider apostasy, heresy or causing a schism. (Note: a schism is a split which periodically arises in Catholicism over whether 'schism' is pronounced *sizzum* or *skizum*.)

The statute covering apostasy, heresy and schism, Canon 1364, is the most detailed of all the get-out clauses, and is essentially concerned with the bringing into disrepute of Catholicism's good name. How exactly it is anticipated that a mere mortal could do this is far from clear.

Especially when you recall that not one of the hierarchy's innumerable paedophiles, perverts, philanderers and crooks whose lurid exploits have been fouling the airwaves in recent years have yet qualified for excommunication. Some forms of wrongdoing are obviously so serious they are regarded by the Church as cardinal sins, except when it is cardinals who commit them.

Sooner or later, the Catholic establishment is going to have to eliminate all the red tape. There's an increasing backlog of excommunication applicants out there, and we're starting to get impatient. The Vatican simply has to update its criteria and adapt to the needs of the modern infidel.

Otherwise, there are thousands of us who will be left with no option. We will just have to travel to Rome and form an orderly queue outside Saint Peter's Basilica, so that we can all ceremonially headbutt the Pope.

THE LAST OF THE HIGH KINGS

Where better to survey the rich landscape of paganism and witchcraft in '90s Ireland than from the summit of a windswept Hill of Tara in the dead of Oíche Samhna?

The Hill of Tara is a modest peak, 500 feet above sea level, situated about six miles from the Meath town of Navan. The hill rises gently amid acres of upland pasture, its flanks a wilderness of scar, tor, knap, brae, wold, fell and other peculiar topographical phenomena that you would normally only encounter if you were to stray onto the vast, untamed tracts of a rolling thesaurus.

On a bright summer's day, Tara would make the perfect location for a picnic with your loved ones or, if necessary, your family. It is a very, very different proposition on a savage Saturday night in late October, with a howling hurricane threatening to blow whole stretches of Leinster to Hell, if not to Connaught. And it is on precisely such a night that I join a congregation of hardy pagans, witches and druids as they celebrate the Celtic festival of Samhain, the pre-Christian New Year's Eve.

The moment I step off the early evening bus, I am concussed by a gale. "That's as close to Tara as I go," shouts the bus driver with a gloating smirk. "I hope you had your Weetabix this morning." As he pulls out onto the motorway, his wheels raise a tidal wave from the gutter.

Squalls of wind and rain rip open my overcoat and frisk me from my armpits to my ankles. My cheeks billow and bloat sideways in the whirl-blast; I feel like a Loony Tune that's been whacked in the face with a shovel. I try to stand firm for a moment at the crossroads to grasp my bearings but I'm propelled up a muddy laneway by a bulldozing gust before I know what's happened.

Fortunately, I'm catapulted in the right direction. A man in a purple felt hat stops and gives me a lift (he's also in a purple Ford Escort). It's not yet 7.30pm but already the roads are virtually deserted. Fallen electricity poles have caused a local power-cut, and the muted glow of a candle burning in the odd window is the only proof that this part of the country is even inhabited.

"It's going to be a ferocious night, one of the worst of the year, I believe," the man in the hat reassures me, as I shiver and drip on his backseat. "It's a night for sitting in by the fire. I hope you had your Ready Brek this morning."

He drops me off by the turnstile leading onto the tourist trail, outside the converted church that serves as the Tara interpretative centre. The *Dúnta* sign on the door suggests that the centre is closed (or at least that's my interpretation).

It's pitch dark and I can see no sign of pagan life or light anywhere on the horizon. Having clambered over the gates, I strive to stay close to the high stone wall for shelter and support but it's impossible. I am tossed about in the tempest like a dirty sock in a washing machine.

If one were prone to such thoughts, it's a night when it's easy to believe that the planet is wreaking some sort of angry vengeance on humanity. The Hill of Tara itself seems alive with fury and ferocity. In the beam of a flashlamp, the grass looks ink-black, hostile and alien. The rabbit holes and badger burrows are treacherous, loath to release any foot they snare.

Gradually, I discern the silhouettes of two approaching figures, their shapes only marginally less murky than the background from which they emerge. One of them is carrying a lantern on a stick, the swinging beacon guttering in the gale.

I scramble over to meet them. They speak to me but I haven't a clue what they're saying, what with the caterwauling storm and the fact that my ears are liquefied and sizzling like eggs on a frying pan. Turning, they beckon me to follow. I resolve that if either of these people ask if I had a bowl of cereal for breakfast, I will strangle them both with my bare hands.

The two men lead the way and I straggle behind. Through the gloom, I can see that they are dressed like twin bargain bins in a second-hand clothes store. They're draped with thick furs, woollen shawls and what are known in the rag trade as rags. One is wearing sandals, the other is in bare feet.

After about ten minutes of silent hiking, we come to a track which snakes up and over a bluff escarpment. In the basin at the other side, there is an astonishing scene: a neat and orderly campsite, almost impervious to the weather conditions.

A ring of tents wobble in the cyclone like giant jellies but hold their ground. A row of flags bearing Celtic insignia flap and snap as though there is nothing whipping about but a bracing breeze. In the centre of the glen, an enormous fire dances in the air like a living thing. Zigzag pillars of smoke waft into the atmosphere and the flames are a primitive strobe-lamp, casting erratic washes of light hither and thither.

About a dozen men and women sit around the fire on tree trunks and bulky branches, laughing and talking. Immediately I appear, a brawny, bull-necked bloke leaps to his feet. He moves like a wrecking ball. He's attired in sheepskin pelts, a fox fur cloak, Donegal tweed breeches and a green cap, and wears a dagger at his waist. He has an unruly moustache and his cheekbones are as bristly as a hairy chest.

Judging by his mean-hombre expression, I half expect this guy to lunge forward and pummel me to a bloody mist. Instead, he produces a bottle and tankard from under his cloak, and pours me a draught of warm, mulled wine. He then hands me a wooden spike on which he has skewered a small roast potato and a testicular chunk of hot sausage.

"Welcome stranger," he says, refilling the tankard when it has barely left my lips. "Happy Samhian! Have a drink and join the party."

It turns out that the toastmaster's name is Martin. The emblem of the braying wolf on his cap attests to his membership of Cú Glas, the Dublin-based Celtic battle re-enactment unit, in which he holds the rank of captain.

Not everyone in Cú Glas is pagan, and vice versa. However, the remarkable growth in the popularity of battle re-enactment (there are a half-dozen fighting clans in the Republic alone) has been mirrored by a tremendous upsurge of interest in pre-Christian lifestyles and spirituality. As far as we know, there are now pagan groups in Cork, Clare, Leitrim, Sligo, Wexford, Meath and Dublin.

"An awful lot of people are getting more and more curious about Celtic paganism," asserts Martin, leaning towards the fire, his shoulders raised against the cold. "It's a natural progression. People start researching how the Celts lived, how they dressed, how they fought, how they built their stockades and forts, how they made their equipment. It's only natural to ask what did they believe in. How did they see the greater picture?"

The wardrobe of those in the encampment includes twice as many furs, jerkins and tunics as oilskins or anoraks. The Cú Glas boys and girls (females routinely participated in inter-tribal combat in Celtic times) are the more impressively clad among the assembly. The most elegant is an Oriental guy called Mike, a Malaysian-born martial arts expert who has lived in Dublin for over 15 years, and was one of the founding fathers of Cú Glas. His robes are black and heavily-padded, topped off with a cape that shines like satin in the firelight.

For most of these gladiators, battle re-enactment is more than a hobby, it's a vocation. When not rolling about in the muck of tournament, they spend one half of their free time drilling themselves in the use of swords, spears, claymores and war hammers, and the other half scouring junk shops and charity sales for the right props and duds.

"The amazing thing about Celtic wool and fur costumes is how incredibly warm they are," Martin avers. "Rain just doesn't get through a real fur mantle. The synthetic stuff doesn't stand up to the weather, it falls asunder, and is no real protection. Most people in the clans make their own clothes. You beg, borrow and steal bits and pieces where you can.

"A lot of the people involved in paganism are vegetarians and into animal rights. We try only to use old fur that's been used before. If we can get old fur coats and adapt them into clan gear, that's ideal. The way the Celts lived off the land 1,000 years ago, they *had* to kill to survive, but they honoured the spirit of the animals they took and used every part of them, for food and clothing. We don't kill for sport."

The atmosphere around the campsite is genial and jolly. It is extraordinary how pleasant it can feel to be out in a furious hurricane provided one is adequately insulated and in close proximity to a roaring fire. This cosy sensation is greatly enhanced by the beer, wine and mead which flow like Niagaras, and the uninterrupted supply of joints the size of baguettes.

Fortunately, when it comes to a soundtrack, the pagans prefer folk music to anything from the dreaded New Age canon (is there a more heinous locution in the English language than the phrase *the haunting sound of the pan pipes?*). They sing songs by Christy Moore, Moving Hearts, Clannad and The Bothy Band, and play a number of Davy Spillane tapes. A couple of people also desultorily rap bodhrans and bongos.

As I sit oiling my inner motor with Heineken's finest liquid engineering, my eyes are drawn to a short, muscular man sitting alone with his thoughts in the smoky shadows beyond the flames. My gaze is attracted towards him not so much by his raw animal magnetism as by the glint of light off his gigantic golden brooch.

This is Albert Coen, one of the most zealous pagans in the country and the impetus behind an information group entitled C.R.O.W., Celtic Revival Of Witchcraft. By day, Albert runs his own city centre recording studio, Sonic, on Gardiner Row, and has been involved in the music business for almost 20 years. A former drummer, he has bashed the skins for such diverse outfits as Sacre Blue, Rocky De Valera and The Gravediggers, Paranoid Visions and Caliban.

A keen student of ethnic and Native American spiritualities and tribal philosophies, Albert has been into paganism since his early teens. He is proud to be a witch, and is one of the few Irish pagans willing to go public about his beliefs.

"I know pagans who are Gardaí, solicitors, social workers, mechanics, shop assistants, artists, musicians, writers, the lot," he professes. "They do not want to come out because of the ill-founded prejudice against paganism. There are some pretty influential people in very high-powered jobs in this country who, for their own sakes and the sakes of their families, have to keep their paganism very private.

"C.R.O.W. provide a safe way in for people because there *are* some nutballs out there. There *are* Satanic groups, there are people who would exploit the innocent, but they're not pagans. In the last few years, I've been instrumental in trying to dispel some of the misconceptions that people have about paganism; that we're Devil-worshippers, that we're into blood-letting, that we're into ritual sacrifice, that we steal babies, that we eat human flesh, desecrate churches, abuse children, abuse animals.

"We leave ritual abuse up to the Catholic clergy, they're much better and have more experience than we have. If people are looking for sensationalism, join the Scientologists! Join a Satanic group and go slaughter a donkey on Howth Head! We don't do that, we despise people who do that kind of thing. Heavy Metal music has an awful lot to answer for."

Another Cú Glasian, Albert is swathed in a filamore, the ancient Irish kilt. This is a 12-foot long bolt of tweedy material, folded, pleated and belted around the hips. Its upper part can be worn as a cloak or a *bráth*, pulled across the shoulder. Albert's face is smeared with eye-patches of black greasepaint, a declaration that Cú Glas are mercenaries and not a clan. He looks like Zorro sitting down, Batman's Robin standing up.

"People build up their own kits," Albert attests, brandishing his arsenal. "As well as weapons, everyone likes to have his or her own ritual knife, goblet, staff and wand. It's the paraphernalia, the little fetishes people like. The wand is an empowerment tool, people cut a limb from a sacred tree, like a rowan or hazel. If you're performing magic, the magic doesn't come out of the end of the wand, it comes out of the heart of the person who's doing the work.

"These are tools that we use to attune us mentally. It's like a priest putting on vestments before he goes out on the altar. He alters his persona for the role he's about to take on."

Aside from boasting a mighty individual armoury and a lavish collection of personal ornamentation, Albert is also a master brewer in the pagan tradition. He vints his own wines at his house in Finglas and his home-made ales and mead are much-admired.

"Mead is made with honey," he explains, replenishing my eager goblet with a double measure of some-he-made-earlier. "Take a straightforward wine recipe: a couple of pounds of grapes, a gallon of water, and a pound of honey. Brew the whole thing up, get it nice and hot, add a couple of pounds of sugar, a spoonful of brewer's yeast, put in a nice warm place for three or four weeks. It's the drink of Kings, literally."

Every boulder, incline and knoll on Tara has its own name. The hill was the capital of ancient Ireland, the seat of High Kings from earliest times until the 6th century. Like every great Irish landmark, its history is seamed and snarled with legend.

In mythical terms, Tara is an Aladdin's Cave. For instance, Cúchulainn's shield (with his right hand attached to it) is said to buried here, as is Finn Mac Cumhail's fork and cooking cauldron. However, the hill has also provided archaeologists with a rich fund of authentic weaponry, torques, brooches and jewellery, dating from the Bronze Age and beyond.

The remains of forts and ramparts encircle the foothills. Pre-historic tribes gathered at Tara in times of war and invasion. It was a holy ground, a place of worship. It was also a sacred graveyard. Huge burial mounds still dot the landscape, some containing the tombs of real people, many raised in commemoration of Celtic gods and other divine figures.

The burial mounds have faintly absurd, portentous titles such as The Mound Of The Cow, The Mound Of The Hostages and The House Of The Women. The voices of the more dour pagans always drop a few octaves whenever they enunciate these hallowed words. Their painfully reverent parroting of the nomenclature is reminiscent of nothing so much as the witterings of The Knights Who Say Ni from *Monty Python & The Holy Grail*.

Monty Python is evidently to paganism what death metallers Deuicide are to Devil-worshipping. There are numerous Python fanatics among the Tara throng: frenetic, obsessive types who delight in ostentatiously enacting entire sketches while sitting around the campfire.

One young chap is so intent on performing a song from *The Holy Grail* directly into my earhole that, eventually, I have to ask him to cease and desist. What I should have said, of course, was, "I wave my private parts at your Auntie, you tiny-brained wiper of other people's bottoms."

To the north of the Mound Of Hostages, a fat, phallic, six-foot limestone pillar juts from the earth. This is known as the Stone of Fál (or Destiny), the rock which reputedly "used to roar beneath the feet of every King that took possession of Ireland." Legend has it that the roar of the Stone of Fál was "fearsome and shrill, frightening to behold." It was probably roaring, "Get the fuck off me, King!"

But there is more to the story of this hill than noisy rocks and bloodthirsty monarchs. Daniel O'Connell held some of his most successful mass meetings on its brow. Tara was also the site of the first mill in Ireland, the mill of Cormac Mac Airt.

Today, under the tutelage of that 20th century druid Sean Boylan, the Meath football team train on the hill. During the run-up to All-Ireland season, they are regularly to be seen jogging up and down its slopes. The Meath players in turn feel a tremendous fealty to Tara and are keen to fete its noble past. Perhaps this explains why they stage their own mill during almost every game they play.

For the pagan, Tara is a site of tremendous ritual significance, a corridor linking the present with the fabled days of yore. The High Kings of Tara were also High Priests, pagan shamen who led the way in paying homage to the Celtic gods. There was a long-standing prohibition against the lighting of sacred fires in the district until the druids of Tara had first kindled theirs. Contemporary witches and druids see themselves as the remnants of that priesthood.

Its practitioners do not regard paganism as a religion, but rather "a spirituality, a way to see the world." They maintain that if a human being was brought up unschooled, in a natural environment, without indoctrination into any religion or contact with any religious people, he or she would inevitably become pagan. Unfortunately, he or she would also be a deaf mute yak herder in darkest Siberia.

Pagans do not believe in a single 'God', a white, elderly, heterosexual male with unkempt facial hair. Nor do they believe in the Devil, Original Sin, saints, or any such man-made constructs. While rejecting the idea of a god personified, pagans do defer to "a higher power, a divine guiding-power."

They are the ultimate tree-huggers. They worship the Earth Mother Goddess (female energy) and the Horned God (male energy) as manifest in every aspect of nature, and in all living things.

They do not claim to have 'faith' because they are surrounded by what they consider irrefutable proof of the reality of their deities, *to wit* the trees, the grass, the stars etc. "Nature is the bloodcells of the creator," they exult.

The term *witchcraft* comes from an old Saxon word *wiccy,* meaning "to bend or to shape." "The wiccys were the people who could bend or shape nature through their spell work," adduces Albert Coen. "They were the people you went to if you needed a problem sorting out, infertility, sickness, whatever. They performed a combination of herbalism and magic."

For pagans, difference does not logically entail inferiority. All sincere religions, they contend, are distinct paths to the same truth. The only facet of organised religion to which they explicitly object is dogmatic hierarchies. They respect the notion of karma, expect to experience an afterlife and see reincarnation as a definite possibility.

"We have only one commandment," enthuses Albert Coen. "If it harm none, do what you wilt! Christianity is a religion of thou-shalt-not. Paganism is a spiritual path of do-what-you-want but do not wantonly hurt another creature. We are only here for a set period of time as caretakers of the Earth. We must tread lightly."

There are four main Sabbats (feast days), glorifying the cycle of the seasons, in the Celtic pagan year: Imbolg (February), Bealtine (May), Lunaghsa (Mid-Summer) and Samhain (Early-Winter). The movement of the Sun in relation to the Earth is marked with observance of the two equinoxes and two solstices. Witches, in particular, also honour the lunar calendar, getting together at full moon for "magical workings" which they call Esbats.

The gathering on Tara tonight is to mark the most solemn festival of all, the full moon rite before Samhain (pronounced *sough-en)* aka Oiche Samhna, All Hallow's Night or Halloween.

Samhain literally means the end of Summer. In pre-Christian Ireland, it was the time when the people gave thanksgiving to the Earth for its bounty and steeled themselves for the hardship of the barren winter ahead. The crops were harvested, the last of the livestock had been slaughtered and the meat had been salted and stored. Samhain therefore was an excuse for a hooley, but also an opportunity for veneration and sacrifice, through which the gods could be appeased.

As the Earth entered what the Celts considered to be "her death mode," it was also a night for remembering the deceased, "the ones that have gone over to the other side." The tradition was that "the veil between this world and the next was at its thinnest" underneath the full moon before Samhain. By summoning up the dead, it was believed that they could be called back to join in the festivities.

"On this night, we think back to the summer," proclaims Albert Coen. "When you're lying down in a summer meadow, the decay of winter is just an inch beneath you. For new life, for growth, there must be death. We're part of that cycle. Paganism is a fertility religion, a religion which venerates the regenerative forces in nature. We venerate the cycle of the year as the planet revolves, the cycle of life: growth followed by death followed by life anew.

"Standing barefoot in a place like Tara is not everyone's idea of a good time, but being aware of the Earth beneath you, being aware of the energies that are Mother Earth travelling up through you, empowering you. Feeling your connection with the Earth and all things in nature. That's what we get out of it. There is no feeling like it."

✚ ✚ ✚ ✚ ✚ ✚ ✚

The only thing new is the history we don't know. The truth is that we were all pagans once. The notion that Catholicism, or even Christianity, is innate to either the character or the people of Ireland is an unsustainable nonsense. "Scratch the topsoil of Irish Christianity," declaimed a witch to me at Tara, "and you come at once to the bedrock of paganism."

There are all sorts of examples which illustrate this point. Take marriage. Under the Brehon Laws (the ancient Irish legal system which prevailed well into the 17th century), husbands and wives were free to divorce. Couples married provisionally for a year and a day. At the end of that time, they returned to their pagan priest and declared whether or not they wanted to renew their vows for another period. If they chose not to, they simply turned their backs on each other and walked away.

A preference for this enlightened brand of matrimony was evident among ordinary Irish citizens long after the imposition of, first, Catholic and, later, Saxon law on the populace. Marriage in the church didn't even become legal in Ireland until the 1300s. Therefore, though denied legal status in contemporary society, it is the pagans with their handfasting nuptial ceremonies who are the real upholders of those much-vaunted *traditional Irish values*.

Pagan races inhabited these islands (and continental Europe) for thousands of years before the Christians arrived. Shame and guilt about carnality is consequently a relatively new phenomenon among the Irish.

As modern pagans gleefully attest, this country was essentially an open air knocking shop until the Christians got their sweaty paws on the levers of authority. Bealtine festivals were especially notorious. The likelihood is that most of our ancestors were conceived during these saturnalian sprees in what were known as "merry-begots," carnivals of revelry and lust.

It was believed that a child procreated at this time was divine, the offspring of the gods. Young lovers would run up the mountains or down the valleys and copulate for hours. Intercourse in fields was encouraged as a method of re-fertilising the land, and assuring the growth of healthy crops. I am reliably informed that, to this very day, there are dozens of pagan farmers all over Ireland who swear by this form of organic husbandry. ·

Throughout Europe, the onslaught of Christianity meant the persecution of pagans. The Roman empire was determined to enforce brand loyalty to its concept of God, with the help of dungeon, fire and sword. But it didn't work. The Celtic people, especially, clung to their old ways, staunchly resisting the Jesus *jihad*.

Around the turn of the millennium, the Church launched what was to become an extremely effective black propaganda campaign against paganism. The Christian spindoctors deftest agit-prop coup was to endow their anti-Christ figure, the Devil, with horns, when no-one was watching. They then highlighted the prominence of horned figures among the pantheon of pagan gods, glossing over the inconvenient detail of horns being a venerable old Celtic symbol representing spiritual power and the magnificence of nature.

There is no mention in the Bible of Satan having horns. Indeed, there is a statue of Moses with horns in The Vatican. In early Christian art, horns were actually a prototype for what was to become the halo. However, the association of pagans with horns and of horns with Beelzebub was a neat and durable equation. Right into the 1990s, you will find people who assume that pagans are Satanists, irrespective of the fact that, as defiant non-Christians, they believe in neither God nor Satan.

Up to the Middle Ages, in most pagan communities, medicine was the prerogative of women; women were the herbalists, the midwives, the potion mixers. The Christians put their inherent abhorrence of all things female to good use by demonising these women as agents of evil. What ensued was The Burning Times.

Historians estimate that up to nine million individuals were put to death during the witch-hunt hysteria that spread through Europe between the start of the 15th century and the end of the 18th, the overwhelming majority of them women. As the shadow of the pyres and the gallows grew longer and longer, paganism went underground.

It was not to re-emerge in any substantial manner until the 1950s, when the British Witchcraft Act was finally repealed, and people like Alex Sanders and Gerald Gardiner came forward and openly proclaimed themselves witches.

In Ireland, the pre-Christian beliefs were never obliterated. Here, the Church managed to successfully bottle and cork the genie by absorbing huge reservoirs of pagan practice into their own doctrine. Even a catechism junkie like myself was amazed to discover precisely how much of the one, true, apostolic faith was brazenly cribbed from the pagans.

Where to begin? For a start, the global Christian church stole the Celtic pagan calendar. Stretching back for several millennia, the feast of Yule had been celebrated on the shortest day of the year; from that day onwards, the sun commenced its climb, the daylight hours got longer and the skies were regenerated. The pre-Christians saw this as the re-birth of the sun god. The Christians came along and decreed that the festival should mark the birth of the Son of God.

Easter was originally the time set aside for honouring the goddess Esther. It was a full moon Esbat at which eggs (pagan fertility symbols) were exchanged as gifts. Even after it had been appropriated by the Church, the date of Easter was, and is, determined by the lunar timetable.

In Ireland, the pagan druids of antiquity, such as Columba, became 'monks'. The feast days, legends and mythical powers associated with the pagan goddess Bríd were simply hijacked by the Church and ascribed to a 'Saint' Brigid. Dozens of other pagan feast days were also subsumed in this manner, as were pagan healing wells, pagan rituals (such as the famous bread 'n' wine palaver), and destinations of pagan pilgrimage, most notably the mountain now known as Croagh Patrick.

The most audacious Christian stunt was the elevation of the Virgin Mary, a woman who had never been held in high celestial esteem by the founding fathers of The Vatican empire because, well, she was a woman, and what kind of namby-pamby church do you think we're running here?

"The first Christians arrived and were met with this stone wall," maintains Albert Coen. "The ordinary people were saying to them, 'Your god is a barren god, he doesn't have a partner, a balance'. So, the early Celtic Christian Church raised Christ's mother to the status of being a demi-goddess. That is how she is venerated by many people in this country, even today."

Hey presto! The ransacking of the pagan bag of tricks gave the Church an off-the-peg credibility, and a ready-made pedigree. Without such credentials, the Christian fiction might otherwise have had all the shelf-life of an ice cube.

"You still see the figure of the Sheela-na-Gig, the fertility goddess, holding the lips of her vagina open, over very old church doors," avows Coen. "Churches were built on sacred sites that were already being used by pagans. The Christians used images like the Sheela-na-Gigs to entice people into the Christian ceremonies, the implication being that one church was the same as another. It made the transition of conversion a lot easier."

"Let's sacrifice a 16-year-old virgin," bellows a hoarse voice from beyond the Tara campfire.

"Where would you find a 16-year-old virgin in this day and age!," comes the reply.

At around 10pm, the pagans decide to commence their ceremonial. The gusts are still fierce, each one quilted with a cold so cruel it could crack your bones like they were sprigs. The full moon, the focal point of tonight's devotion, is only sporadically visible behind the sulphurous-looking and fast-scudding clouds.

Nevertheless, there is a lot of booze being consumed around the fire-side and it is deemed prudent to get started before the assembly gets too snockered to tell the difference between a badger burrow and a hole in the ground.

By now, maybe 20 people in all have made it to the campsite. Reluctantly, we manage to drag ourselves away from the warmth and the liquor. We fall in line behind our priest, Mark, and priestess, Lisa, as they lead us up to a wide grassy plateau, the spot most popularly favoured as a ritual altar.

Both in their late 20s, Mark and Lisa were married on Tara about a year ago in a pagan nuptial rite known as a handfasting. It is the convention that the priest and priestess be either wed to each other or an established couple.

Atop the plateau, Lisa draws a broad ring in the grass with her sword, and walks three times around. It is explained to me later that the purpose

Here comes the hotstepper: Father Neil Horan shakes a leg

Pic: Deirdre O'Callaghan

Pic: Cathal Dawson

Who you gonna call? Cultbusters: Noel Deane and John Scanlon hold court outside the GPO

A meeting of remarkable men: Des Hanafin has a public audience with Fr. Fay

A pagan face: Albert Coen in full druidic splendour on the Hill of Tara

Pic: Brendan Duffy

The loaves and fishes will be along in a minute: Daniel addresses the faithful at Kincasslagh

Pic: Cathal Dawson

xiii

Pic: Michael J. Quinn

Reverend Cleophus Fay stops the traffic

Eating to forget: breakfast the morning after the Lough Derg vigil

**Come dancing:
Mary Margaret
Doyle Dunne on
O'Connell Street**

Pic: Michael J. Quinn

of this action is to "create a temple and cleanse the area of bad energies." Unfortunately, she's neglected to cleanse the area of sheep shit as I immediately discover when I take my position in the "magic circle" which the pagans then form on the circumference of Lisa's *al fresco* temple.

The next step is the invoking of the four elements. One person faces east and invites the spirit of air "to stand guard over our sacred space." Another faces south and extends the same invitation to the spirit of fire. The communication to water is directed to the west, and we try to get in touch with earth via the north. None of the elements choose to RSVP.

Salt and water are mixed in a tiny, oak phial. This, apparently, is symbolic of the coming together of male and female energies. "Salt to water, man to woman, god to goddess," intones Lisa as she spatters our circle with saline solution.

Mark, the priest, steps towards the west, flings his arms akimbo and calls upon the spirits of the dead to join us for the celebration. In his right hand, he holds an extremely gnarled staff with a wooden serpent coiled around its shaft and a goat's head dangling from the crook.

He recently found the skull in the woods near Tara. The goat's head is one of the most revered pagan symbols of fertility and abundant life, for everyone except the goat it originally belonged to that is.

To accommodate within our circle any resurrected phantoms who happen by, each pagan takes a step backwards. "Make room beside you for your returning ancestors and loved ones," yells Lisa over the wailing rainstorm. Mark, meanwhile, strides purposefully in figure-eight-movements around every one of us, all the while blowing on a cow horn.

It is now time for a little pageantry. Martin, the guy who had earlier welcomed me to the campsite, and an older man called Simon perform a short sketch about a traveller who meets The Grim Reaper on an isolated laneway.

The ceremony culminates with a well-known finale, the consecration of bread and wine, or, as the pagans prefer, "the consecration of the lifeblood of the Great Mother."

As in its Eucharistic counterpart, the term *consecration* is used here as a synonym for mumbo-jumbo, hocus pocus and horseflop. Strange incantations are muttered over the comestibles by Lisa and Mark. Shading the chalice and loaf behind their hands, they mime the sprinkling of some invisible powder from between their fingertips. They try to ignite a flame but soon give up, the spirit of wind-that-would-go-through-you-for-a-short-cut having gatecrashed the proceedings. A further five minutes of verbal spells are cast on the food and drink before it is finally shared out among the waiting circle.

The bizarre preparatory protocol of this sacrament is considerably undermined by the familiarity of its taste. The wine is Piat D'Or, the bread is Butterkrust Maltana.

And that's it! Pagan ritual may be every bit as idiotic as Christian ritual, but at least it's quicker. It's a crucial distinction, the difference between having a bullet thrown at you and being shot.

As we trudge back to the campsite and what's left of the mead stash, I ask Albert Coen if he *really* believes all this stuff.

"Oh yes," he responds, "The magic works. I tried a love spell once. There was a girl that I was quite attracted to, but she didn't seem to notice me. I worked a love spell, and I said to the Earth Mother, 'Give me this woman, I am crazy about her'.

"The spell was the love apple. On the night of a full moon, you take a nice, firm, round, ripe apple, and cut it in half. Each half is a talisman for each of the two people. You take a couple of strands of the woman's hair and a couple of strands of your own, knot them together, put them into the apple, with perhaps a sprig of wild thyme, a sprig of sage, and bind the whole thing together with a red cord or red ribbon. Then, take it out into the garden, find a nice place, dig a hole, and bury it.

"As you bury it, say to the Earth Mother, 'As this apple decays, and nourishes the Earth, let these two people come together'. You're giving something back to the Earth and you're asking for something in return

"About two months after I did this, the girl and I started gravitating towards each other. We ended up in a relationship for a couple of years. But I lost my business, I lost my home, I lost my family. A lot of personal stuff happened between me and other people over her. I ended up in a bedsit with this woman but nothing else.

"I got exactly what I asked for, but lost everything else. Sometimes, you have to be quite specific."

STOP! TEA JUNCTION AHEAD

Abandon hope, all ye who enter here – it's the annual pilgrimage of Daniel O'Donnell disciples to the czar of char's family homestead in Kincasslagh, Co. Donegal.

The teeth are capped, I'd wager. His smile is so bright and ceramic you could tile a bathroom with it. He's wearing a shirt of snowblinding whiteness, with creases sharp enough to cut the national debt. The tan is the colour of Bournville chocolate. His hair is mannequin perfect. Even his ears look like they've been affixed with the help of a confectioner's icing pipe.

"He's as pretty as a piece of pottery," declares Wendy Askill, a visitor from Grimsby in Lincolnshire. Mrs. Askill is 64 next month, and a grandmother of five. "His videos just don't do him justice," she adds. "He's like

189

a little ornamental figurine in the flesh."

Mrs. Askill may have a point. The expression of hazy bewilderment on Daniel O'Donnell's face looks relatively human but one gets the distinct impression that it goes all the way through his head, like the *Bundoran* through a stick of Bundoran rock. In the interests of journalistic research, I may yet have to pick him up and check the label beneath his feet to see whether he is genuine Belleek or simply a cheap copy from Hector Grey. Wendy Askill eagerly assures me that she would prefer to just pick him up.

"Oooh, he's the kind of man you could make love to for weeks at a time," she proclaims, ignoring my blushes and the fact that I have suddenly become totally absorbed in the contours of my toe-caps. "Sex with Daniel would be like a fairytale. He's a sweet, gentle, beautiful, young man, and I'm sure he knows how to show a girl a good time."

I could say that I'm a man out of my depth here but, before today, I didn't even know that depths came this deep. It's Thursday, August 3rd, and I'm standing in stricken awe amid the crush, with my mouth open like a speared fish, on Pier Road, Kincasslagh, County Donegal, just outside the gates of the fabled homeplace of the singing pinstripe himself, Mr. Daniel O'Donnell. Approximately 3,000 music haters have travelled to this tiny rural outpost, some from such exotic locations as Melbourne, Verona and Killybegs, to pay homage to their hero, on this his fourth annual Open Day and tea party.

Every corner of Ireland, from Monkstown to Maamtrasna, is represented among the throng. However, judging by the logos and nameplates on the myriad tour-buses which have been filing into Greater Kincasslagh since daybreak, about half of this swarming horde of O'Donnellites has journeyed from overseas, mostly from England, Scotland and Australia (we'll get back to the woman from Verona later). McPhail's Coaches of Newarthill, Scotland, and Snaith's Travel of Northumberland, have been especially busy.

The statistical breakdown of the crowd is probably about 85% female, 15% male. In certain cases, this ratio is actually accommodated within single individuals. There's one character in particular, a paragon of genteel femininity in every way (horn-rimmed spectacles, cotton knee-length skirt, lace blouse), except for the fact that she's the proud possessor of a pair of ham-shaped arms that make Mike Tyson's limbs look like wine-glass stems.

Her left forearm is tattooed with a rudimentary likeness of Jack Charlton, and the inscription, We're All Part Of Jackie's Army. Her right forearm sports, in block caps, the statement, I LOVE DANIEL O'DON-NELL. Neither proposition appears to be open for debate.

The average age of the Danielovers gathered here today is fiftysome-thing. The average weight of the Danielovers gathered here today is, well, something I'd prefer not to contemplate, if it's all the same with you. Some of these women are so fat that small groups of German backpack-ers are able to pitch tents in their flesh folds. At times, Kincasslagh resem-bles nothing so much as an open audition for the title role in the *Free Willy* movies.

The blokes too, camera-wielding husbands for the most part, are also the proprietors of rather enormous verandas above their toyshops. It is surely one of the great ironies of the modern age that the world's slimmest singer should have the world's plumpest fans. Similarly, it has to be said that Daniel's brand of spivish elegance has certainly *not* rubbed off on the gentlemen among his audience. Green anoraks, oily rainmacs, shiny suits with all the cut and style of body bags, tank-tops, even duffel coats (and on this, one of the hottest days in the history of heat!) – such is the attire of the Dannymen.

Tea is as essential to the authentic Daniel O'Donnell experience as tequila slammers are to stag parties and insulin is to diabetic attacks. The invitation to the Kincasslagh Open Day, which isn't so much advertised as communicated telepathically among the faithful, is actually framed as an invitation "to have a cup of tea with Daniel in his own kitchen." This is something of a duplicitous fiction.

Daniel O'Donnell doesn't live in Kincasslagh. His real home is a pala-tial residence in Rathcoole, County Dublin. Beneath those eaves, one can safely assume that he leads the life of your average everyday multi-mil-lionaire sex god, a life in which the consuming of tea with mad matrons and dotty dowagers plays a pretty minor role. Nevertheless, it is crucial to the down-home-wee-country-boy image that O'Donnell has assiduously nurtured that he be seen by his followers as a firm adherent to such down-home-wee-country-boy core values as drinking tea, drinking more tea and talking shite to daft auld ones.

Daniel's devotion to both his Mammy (yes, *Mammy* is what everybody appears to call her) and his native Kincasslagh are the other central bedrocks of his astonishing appeal. The Open Day is therefore an ingenious bringing together of all the elements in the bizarre O'Donnell cult. Understanding the phenomenon is like trying to chart a course through China with a map of India. Understanding how to exploit it, however, is what really counts. In that sense, Daniel O'Donnell is the Malcolm McLaren of The Rosses.

The family homestead is a modest but impeccably maintained, bright yellow bungalow which was built in 1968, just before Daniel's father died. As the adoring devotees never tire of telling you though, it was in the two-storey, whitewashed house across the road that Daniel was born. Apparently, Mary Ned, a cousin of the O'Donnell's from Glasgow, holidays there during the summer, and Daniel himself often talks about renovating it, some of these days.

Most fanatics are intrigued by what their idol is like in the bedroom. Danielovers are unique amidst the pantheon of the over-zealous in that their most obsessive desire is to discover what their icon is like in the tearoom. This was farcically borne out at last year's tea party when some of the day-trippers became so carried away by their close encounter of the domestic kind that they all but ransacked Mrs. O'Donnell's kitchen in search of keepsakes and souvenirs. Apparently, sugar bowls, cruet sets, cups, saucers, plates, even a saucepan, were among the booty that was knocked off in this orgy of utensil plunder.

The upshot of the looting is that the 1995 Open Day at Kincasslagh is not quite so open. You'll never again find Daniel in the kitchen at parties. This year, the closest any of us are going to get to his inner sanctum is the front yard.

"It's very sad," a comparatively youthful Scottish woman informs me, her red hair teased out so that it stands like a shrub on her head. "I've been here twice before and it was lovely to be able to go in and meet Daniel and his Mammy inside the house. The people who pilfered all that stuff weren't real fans. A real fan would never do anything to upset either Daniel or any of his family. We have too much respect for them."

The Rosses. Gaoth Dobhair. Glenties. The saw-toothed waves of Keadue Strand. The tumultuous sea cliffs at Sliabh Liag. As you survey the surrealistically magnificent Donegal landscape, you instinctively find yourself wondering just how it is that a panorama as primeval, as rugged and as raw as this could produce something as antiseptic, as unctuous and as blow-dried as Daniel O'Donnell and his music.

The hamlet of Kincasslagh is located amid heart-stoppingly beautiful grandeur. A bustling metropolis it ain't, comprising little more than Iggy's Pub and The Cope store – wherein, incidentally, Daniel O'Donnell had his first ever job. Yet once seen, it is never forgotten.

In the interests of an Open Day of at least orderly chaos, three teenage girls have been stationed beside Iggy's from early morning, distributing numbered tickets to arrivals at Pier Road as they make their way up the hundred yards or so to *chez* O'Donnell. However, dozens of people were already shuffling around the front gates of the house well before the ticket girls arrived, and most of them have declined to go back down and take a number, believing that their precedence in the queue is enough to guarantee, eh, their precedence in the queue.

When it is announced over a hastily erected p.a. system some hours later that Daniel will be doing his glad-handing in *strict* numerical order, many of these early birds became quite irate and boisterous. As the Good Book saith, the first shall be last and the last shall be greatly pisseth off.

At 11.17am precisely, a Barry's Tea delivery van pulls into the O'Donnell driveway, and bang go any quips I may have been planning about Daniel being thrown to the Lyons. A self-service Barry's Tea dispenser is set up in front of the house offering free paper cups of scald to the faithful after they've had their brief audience with the czar of char. Robert Roberts, meanwhile, have installed a coffee machine for those unspeakable deviants who don't like tea.

Such blatant product placement in the midst of these hallowed surroundings may seem inappropriate to some, but a degree of commercialisation is inevitable with an event of this scale. Daniel's Open Day is, after all, a catering enterprise on a par with the celebrated loaves and fishes buffet. Remember, we're talking over 3,000 tea bags here. And every single one of them is going to want a cuppa.

It's almost 1pm before Daniel returns from the funeral of a next-door neighbour, 75-year-old Mrs. Mary Boyle, at which he had sung two hymns (namely 'Lily Of The Valley' and 'Remember You The People', hymnfans!). As his dark grey 93D Volvo precariously noses its way through the moil and hum, a small group of women carrying a banner proclaiming themselves to be "Glasgow Daniel Fans" rush the driver's side of his car, their abundant bodies bloating with adrenaline at the prospect of an advance glimpse of their lord and master.

For a split second, it looks potentially nasty but then, just as quickly as it had erupted, the charge of the cellulite brigade subsides into a good-natured burst of cheers and applause. Still, if it had come down to a straight clash of brute force, the smart money was never going to be on the Volvo.

Within minutes, there is another p.a. announcement, this time by one of his brothers. Daniel will be welcoming us in groups of 50. He will *not* be signing anything (cue gale force sigh of mass disappointment). He will only shake hands and pose for photographs. At this point, Daniel takes the microphone and addresses us personally with some helpful hints about how we should do everything we can to enjoy ourselves.

"Do everything you can to enjoy yourself," counsels Daniel. "Talk to each other. Make plenty of new friends. Go home with lots of addresses. Then, no matter where in the world you go, you'll always be able to get a bit of floor space. And, most important of all, meet people who want to meet people."

Daniel O'Donnell is actually very good at this meeting and greeting business. When he meets and greets a person, they stay met and greeted for keeps. It's obviously all those years of unstinting practise after his gigs. With a display of boundless patience, he remains stoically in position for hours on end, shaking hands with all-comers, vigorously, exuberantly, with that breathless air suggesting that it is *he* who has rushed hundreds of miles expressly for this purpose, and not vice versa.

The closer one gets, however, the more one notices that there is something rather eerie about O'Donnell's bedside manner. The guy's tone of voice is very, very weird. It's not just the twee Donegal accent. Even *more* aggravating is Daniel's habit of enunciating his every utterance with the tentative, doubtful, confounded inflection that contestants on Larry Gogan's *Just A Minute Quiz* adopt when they're chancing their arm at an answer. As Larry would say, maybe it's just that the questions didn't really suit him today.

But he's got a word for everybody, or at least a couple of syllables. "Och aye," he purrs to one woman who whispers Jesus only knows what secrets into his ear. "Aaah eeeey," he assures another, her hand placed provocatively on Daniel's arm in a possible attempt to entice further confidences from his lips. "Ouuuuuu," he explains to a Scottish couple when they ask if he remembers them from last year's Open Day. "Ouuuuuu."

Indeed, so incomprehensible is much of what he says that it wouldn't in the least surprise me to hear Daniel respond to a fan's greeting with an excited 'Doo Wah Diddy Diddy', or try to comfort an emotionally overcome admirer with a few selected quotations from 'Papa Oom Mow Mow'. To my dying day, I will swear that, at one point, I did actually hear him say, 'Buzz Buzz A Diddle It'.

If fanatical idolmania is distasteful among teenyboppers, it is downright disgusting among the middle-aged. It's a harsh reality of the generation gap that the kind of behaviour that can be tolerated as a healthy release of sexual tension for the young necessitates the immediate confinement and sedation of anyone over 18. Screaming, crying, fainting, and involuntary urination may be cute when it's your nine year old niece, not quite so cute when it's your Auntie Maggie.

To be honest, the number of screeching lunatics at Kincasslagh is quite small but there are some. By and large, the delirium and dementia on show today is of a more muted and, therefore, more tragic brand. There are many, many women here who act and look like life forgot their address some considerable time ago. There are quite a few wild-eyed, hunted-looking loners who, paradoxically, seem to have teamed up with small bands of others like themselves specifically for the retreat to Kincasslagh. Maybe that's the whole point.

If one listens carefully enough, one can also hear much muttering in the cliques and clusters that clutter the area around Pier Road about dark subjects like nervous breakdowns, bereavements and terminal illnesses. Here and there, you can see knots of happy-clappy types dressed in gaudy T-shirts that declaim their allegiance to this or that Born Again strain of Christianity. Never forget that it was as a result of an encounter with evangelical jingoists Up With People during the early '80s, while he was at teaching college in Galway, that Daniel decided to pursue a career in the music industry.

The obvious cynical view is that, for Daniel O'Donnell, human vegetables are a cash crop that is well worth cultivating. Nevertheless, it is undeniable that his steadfast determination to fight fire with ice cream is something that carries a genuine emotional appeal for a frighteningly large array of people. All you have to do is count the number of worshippers who dissolve into tears when they are finally awarded their chance to embrace him in the flesh.

Solubility, however, is not something one would readily associate with those hardline, hardnosed fans for whom following Daniel is a series of tests and trials through which they can prove their loyalty. These citizens operate in groups, usually compact teams of like-minded female friends – though you do occasionally find married couples among their ranks. As a species, they are marked by the desire to impart a startlingly high quantity of trivial knowledge about Daniel, and by an unshakeable determination to immerse themselves in as many Danielevents as possible.

I position myself behind two of these abnormally committed Danielogists for a short time, a middle-aged husband and wife from Waterford, and when they aren't busy slurping seasick-green soup from a thermos, they teach me a great deal indeed, including the invaluable lesson that it would be an act of sheer insanity to ever position myself behind such people again as long as I live.

I learn, for instance, that Daniel was in a car accident recently, and that while he and his wardrobe assistant, Loretta, emerged virtually unscathed, O'Donnell's personal bodyguard, Joe, ("You know Joe, the heavy fella that has been with him for years") was unfortunate enough to break several ribs. Mr. Waterford believes that Daniel often drives too fast, especially on the way home after gigs, and that it's only a matter of time before he has another smash. One more cup of chew 'n' spew later, Mrs. Waterford thoughtfully counters with the assertion that Daniel is far too sensible to ever do anything that would endanger his own or anybody else's life.

A grey Toyota Corolla enters the O'Donnell yard. "Oh, that's Father Aodhán," explains Mr. Waterford. "Father Aodhán Cannon. He's a great friend of Daniel's going back years. He lives near here. He and Daniel are very close."

Three women from Daniel's Belfast fanclub stop by to say hello.

"Did ye get your tickets for the 18th, in Cork?," they enquire.

"We did, of course," replies Mr. Waterford. "We're in Row Three. It's being filmed for a live video, you know."

"Row Three! Feck ye anyway. We're back in 12. We won't be able to see ourselves in the video at all," grumbles one of the Belfastians, before they sulkily slope off to scoff their packed lunches while sitting on an upturned fishing boat on the roadside. Every now and again, Mr. Waterford looks across at the women and gleefully wiggles three chubby fingers at them. They fire back a few two-fingered gestures, and everyone laughs at the good of it all.

A red Renault arrives at the O'Donnell's. "That's Margo's car," declares Mrs. Waterford instantly, proving that hubby is not the only one to have been swatting up on the specialist subject of The O'Donnell Family, Their Friends, And Their Choice Of Vehicular Transport.

Margo, as you probably know, is Margaret, Daniel's older sister, a country legend in her own right whose star has been waning during the past decade in which her kid brother's has been so spectacularly in the ascendant. Despite what you may expect, she has not merely travelled today from her home in Monaghan to show moral support. Margo is here to flog her own wares too. The self-proclaimed "Queen Of Country'n'Irish" (that same fantastic monarchy of which Daniel is so often claimed to be King – go figure *that)* is attempting to stage a comeback at the moment. To that end, within the cordoned-off front yard, to the side of the tea and coffee machines, there is a special Margo merchandise stall.

To me, this seems decidedly tacky. It's a bit like turning up at Graceland to find a booth inside the front door devoted to the works and wonders of The King's little known older sibling, Betty Presley. As far as the ardent O'Donnellites are concerned, however, it's all fine and dandy. Any sister of Daniel's is clearly a sister of theirs.

A woman called Shirley Jones oversees the Margo table, which offers a dizzying array of Margobilia, including Margo tapes, Margo CDs, Margo pens, Margo bumper stickers, Margo photograph cards, Margo coasters and application forms to join the Margo fanclub (membership fee only £5 Sterling). For a paltry £2.50, I instantly became the envy of my friends by purchasing a stylish Margo keyring which features two alternate portraits of a very casually dressed Margo sitting, for reasons best known to herself, on the bank of a river.

Perhaps this is the stop where she has to wait each morning to formally board the Daniel O'Donnell bandwagon.

Throughout the day, a table peddling REMEMBER YOUR TEA WITH DANIEL wall-plaques is attracting a huge scrum just to the right of the house, on one of those combination hills and hairpin bends at which the Donegal landscape appears to be so expert.

The wooden mementoes feature a colour photograph of Desperate Dan swathed in the inevitable woollen cardigan and prissily holding aloft a china teapot with a loathsome shall-I-be-mother? smirk on his face. There is an evidently unquenchable demand for these artefacts among large swathes of the assembled mob. I didn't even know that inmates were allowed to hang pictures in their padded cells.

The plaques retail for a cool tenner. However, a sign tacked to the stall promises that the "Proceeds will go to various charities." *Various* is a disturbingly vague word. So is *proceeds,* so is *charities,* so, for that matter, are *will, go* and *to.* My request for clarity from the flour-haired, beer-bellied vendor is met with the catch-all reply, "It's for the handicapped."

Which handicapped charities precisely?

"A number of charities which were nominated locally," he says more than a little indignantly.

And all of the money will go to these organisations?

"About half of it. We have to cover our costs," he snaps, abruptly turning away to service yet another eager customer.

Aside from the plaques, everybody who meets Daniel is invited to make a contribution of "a couple of pounds or whatever you can afford" into an open bucket before they are given "a certificate commemorating your visit to the Open Day and proving to all your friends that you had tea with Daniel." Another wall-hanging for the institutionalised it may be, but 50p out of every pound collected, we are told, will go to "various charities."

Daniel O'Donnell is said to be a very generous man, and I have every reason to believe that he is. Nevertheless, the blindly trusting people who are contributing all these *proceeds* would seem to have a right to more information about exactly where their money is destined, and, today at least, that isn't always forthcoming.

However, in these parts, questioning Daniel O'Donnell's benevolence is a bit like asking the resurrected Christ if we could actually see the till receipt for the nails He claims were hammered into His feet and hands. Comparisons between the Kincasslagh tea party and a religious pilgrimage have been made before but they are damned difficult to avoid. There's the shrine (the house), the saviour (Danny boy), the mother (Mammy) and the message (the music).

There's also the oft-ignored fact that accommodation in Kincasslagh the night before Tea Day is as easy to come by as it was in Bethlehem all those years back when the Holy Family came in search of a comfortable B and B with full obstetrics facilities. This particular analogy falls apart, though, when you remember that Joseph and the pregnant Virgin were eventually permitted to crash in a stable, where they only had to withstand the sight, sound and smell of some livestock. They were spared the considerably less agreeable sight, sound and smell of a shower of drunken Australians singing rebel songs in the local pubs.

And then, there's The Viking House Hotel, O'Donnell's Vatican.

Purchased and refurbished by Daniel in 1993, and run by an assortment of his brothers and sisters, it is in this 14-room hotel, located just a mile outside Kincasslagh, that he keeps much of the swag he has accumulated over the years, such as gold and platinum discs, myriad entertainment awards, and, of course, his treasured Donegal Person Of The Year 1989 gong.

The hotel reception desk sells a full range of Daniel O'Donnell tapes, CDs, videos and cigarette lighters. For the visiting fans' convenience, it also stocks a large selection of batteries, an indispensable precaution in case the power supplies of either their cameras or, as is equally likely, their pacemakers, are exhausted by the spectacular surroundings.

In recent years, a custom has developed wherein certain supplicants who travel to Kincasslagh for spiritual nourishment feel that they have to round off their veneration by stealing some of the gold-plated letters from the name-stone on the hotel's front lawn. The Daniel O'Donnell coat of arms and the K, I, N and G from VIKING have so far proven the most popular booty with the pillagers. This is serious enough, but the fear among locals now must be that, sooner or later, some smartarse will discover a rude anagram lurking within the words The Viking House Hotel. That's when the real trouble will start.

But there is another, more questionable side to the deification of Daniel O'Donnell. Continually, during Open Day, handicapped children, disabled adults and frail old people are all led in to meet Daniel for an informal ritual that is essentially a laying on of hands in all but name. O'Donnell is gentle, considerate and kindly at all times but there is a disturbingly messianic undertow to some of these encounters with which, surely, even he cannot be comfortable. I thought he just wanted to dance with you, twirl you all around the floor. Isn't that what they invented dancing for?

Now, just how a guy who looks and dresses like a lampoon of a *Family Album* catalogue model ever came to be seen by so many as some sort of munificent guru with a charisma that amounts to powers of divinity in the first place is a question that can probably only ever be adequately answered by members of the psychological profession. But for those who subscribe to such notions, I have a simple query: if Daniel

O'Donnell can genuinely heal the wretched, the feeble and the lame, don't you think he'd have done something about his musical repertoire before now?

"Daniel is very priestly," insists Mrs. Dypmna Hayes, a 52-year-old teacher and native of Sligo who has lived and worked in Verona, in Northern Italy, for the past ten years. Mrs. Hayes has been a fan of Daniel's ever since a friend sent her a video of one of his concerts during the early '90s. This is her second time to Kincasslagh.

"He has never forgotten where he comes from," she continues. "He loves his mother. He's a great ambassador for the country. I tell my friends in Italy that all the men in Ireland are like Daniel and they're very envious. I've shown them pictures and they think he's very stylish and handsome."

Dympna introduces me to her mother, and to her aunt, Mary Regan. Both women are in their late 80s and both are wearing I Would Love A Date With Daniel O'Donnell t-shirts.

34-year-old Brigid Conroy (not her real name), originally from Mayo but now working in Glasgow, has gone one step further. Last year, she had her snap taken with Daniel after a show in Glasgow. She has since had that photograph enlarged and transferred onto the white cotton t-shirt which she is wearing today. She has come to Kincasslagh for the Open Day to have her picture taken with Daniel again, while wearing this t-shirt, so that there will effectively be two Daniels in the next shot which she also intends to have emblazoned upon a t-shirt. She wants to keep doing this, year after year, until she eventually has a t-shirt with an endless gallery of Daniels within Daniels, stretching off to infinity.

Aside from the quasi-scientific nature of this exercise, there is another, almost unbearably poignant, method to her madness. "I want to have a record of me and Daniel during the rest of our lives," Brigid confides. "I want us to grow old together."

After all that, the real question is *what is he like?* Well, like everyone else here, I get to spend something in the vicinity of 35 seconds in Daniel O'Donnell's company so I am ideally placed to offer a definitive personality profile. I can certainly tell you that he asks your name and where you come from with a passionate intensity that is rare among mere mortals. His ability to pose for photographs is truly God-like. He doesn't even blink when the flashbulbs pop.

There are limits to his merchandising potential. Nobody will ever bring out a Daniel O'Donnell doll because the truth is a plastic replica could only be *more* lifelike than the real thing. The guy is a living doll. He casts no shadow.

It takes several seconds of staring into his tanned, flawless countenance before I realise what it is that's so disconcerting about it. It's too tanned, too flawless, and, worst of all, it's staring straight back at me. Daniel's deep green eyes shimmer radiantly as he gazes deep into my soul and scours my spirit for a way to help carry my share of the burden that we all must shoulder in this vale of tears. On the other hand, maybe he's just squinting because the sun is getting in his face.

As I genuflect for the final time on Pier Road and prepare to take my leave, I witness a charming vignette. Daniel is obliging with a photocall for the press. One of the snappers points out that a butterfly has landed on the lower part of his supernaturally gleaming shirt. Daniel looks down, raises a hand as if to flick it away but then realises the potential scandal if the paparazzi were to procure a shot of this living saint busting the chops of a defenceless insect. Painstakingly, delicately, he gently enfolds the moth in his palm and returns it to the air with an almost imperceptible twitch of his wrist.

Seconds later, a woman in a blue dress splats the butterfly against the gable end of the O'Donnell house with her newspaper. "I'm going to keep it," she cheerfully trills to all and sundry. "It's the butterfly that Daniel saved."

STREET PREACHER FOR A DAY

Discover how a respected theological correspondent found himself handing out sheets of blank A4 paper to passers-by on Dublin's Grafton Street.

I had been preaching on Grafton Street for almost two hours when I was accosted by one of my competitors. For the previous 45 minutes, he had stared at me with android contempt from across the road. It was obvious that my jib was something he didn't like the cut of.

The man was in his 40s, tall, burly and stoic. His torso appeared to be hung on girders rather than bones. His face was pleasant but generic and bland. His single distinguishing physical attribute was a nose that looked like a large salmon-coloured conch. A visiting Cockney who wanted to have the proverbial word in his shell-like would have to whisper into the guy's nostrils.

In evangelist terms, he came over like a cross between the Reverend Billy Graham and the homicidal preacher played by Clint Eastwood in *Pale Rider*. He seemed to have all the gentility of Rev. Graham, but was a lot less sinister and cadaverous, and all the rigid composure of the Eastwood character, but was a lot less hat-wearing and fictional.

His routine was simple and ritualistic. He would read aloud from the Bible (usually the Beatitudes) for about ten minutes at a time and then, for a further ten minutes, distribute rectangular cards advertising meetings at a Worship Centre on the southside of the city.

From the off, he seemed to appreciate that I was up to no good and that the gospel I was spreading was not available in any know Gideon edition. The give-away may have been the hand-written sign at my feet which, at that moment, was reading, "For fuck's sake, listen to me!"

"The Lord be with you, brother," he said as he sidled up to me, his body language a faltering patois of suspicion and caution. Past experience has taught me that these zealous Christian folk like it when you talk to them in Biblical jargon. Fortunately, I had taken the trouble to prepare a few Beatitudes of my own, for just such an eventuality.

"Blessed are the sycophantic nephews," I declared, "for they shall inherit the inheritance."

He ignored this. "What brotherhood do you belong to," he enquired. A very good question. To which I did not have a very good answer, so I fell back on another of my homemade ejaculations. "Be patient and industrious, saith the Lord, and your reward shall be patience and industriousness," I affirmed.

"Could someone like me join your religion?" he probed.

I informed my inquisitor that there was always room in my movement for crackpots, dingbats, imbeciles, screwballs, whacked-out loners and sad losers of every stripe and kidney (though I didn't use those *precise* words).

"Religion is not something which should be mocked," he reprimanded sternly.

"There's religion and there's religion," I explained, anxious that the two concepts would never again be confused. Rev. Narky Trousers remained unimpressed, however. He proceeded to deliver a lengthy harangue about sacrilege, profanity and blah de blah de blah.

"On the other hand," I retorted when he finally paused for breath, first holding up one hand and then my other hand as a visual aid, "it's a free country."

He harrumphed wrathfully. Just as things were about to get really heated, we were suddenly surrounded by a group of kids, none of whom was more than ten years of age. It was evident from their smirking giddiness that they thought we were a right pair of eejits.

"That's all rubbish, what you're saying," asserted the ringleader, a blonde girl in a Smashing Pumpkins t-shirt. "You shouldn't be here preaching that religion stuff. Do you believe all that? It's silly. Rubbish."

"What do you believe in?" I asked the little child (or "li'l chile" as I felt it more appropriate for a man in my position to call her) .

"We're Catholics," she announced proudly, "we don't believe in any religion."

Sometimes, I think it would be a good idea to shoot the messenger. Such a policy would certainly make Dublin city a more pleasant and congenial place in which to amble, ramble, range, rove and roam (see, I'm even beginning to talk like a Bible basher).

The messengers I have in mind are street preachers, those envoys and emissaries who bring us all so much unsolicited and unwanted information from other worlds. They are the human equivalent of junk mail; persistent, inexhaustible, worthless and a damned nuisance.

Doomed, benighted Grafton Street is probably the worst affected area in the capital. On a bad day, this otherwise reasonably endearing thoroughfare becomes a clamorous Knesset of know-alls endlessly bellowing babble through amplifiers turned up loud enough to crumble concrete.

This pedestrianised shopping precinct has become an adventure playground for street pulpiteers of every species, all preachers great and small: Mormons, Moonies, Jehovah's Witnesses, Hare Krishnas, a plague of Born Again loolahs and a salty smattering of freelancers of indetermi-

205

nate denomination.

Until relatively recently, there was also the beardy weirdie who used to hang around outside HMV, creeping up on unsuspecting citizens and asking them in a maniacal, singsong voice, "Do you know Jesus?" The correct response to this query, of course, was to adopt an aggressive attack position, and reply, "No, but I do know ju-jitsu."

Every God-botherer has a *schtick*. All of them try to engage you in conversation, most have literature to give you. This eats up time, *your* time. Trying the polite but steadfast rebuff doesn't always work. The really determined ones won't take "Fuck off!" for an answer. If they so much as catch your eye, your ass is oatmeal.

Globally, some of these sects boast cult followings so small that they could do the actual following on the pillion of a single motor cycle. In spite of this, they flog their dogmas with an often breathtaking arrogance. They are unrestrained in their eagerness to tell you that your life is a hollow, meaningless sham and that they alone know how it can be salvaged.

The difference in quality between faith and gullibility is the difference in weight between a ton of New Testaments and a ton of *Old Moore's Almanacs*. The most cherished notion among proselytisers, however, is the certainty that they are virtuous simply because they believe what they believe, and that unbelief is, at best, pitiable.

By now, you're probably beginning to catch my drift. I'm not mad keen on evangelists. In fact, having observed the phenomenon at some length, I came to a momentous conclusion recently. I decided that being a street preacher is the dumbest, most anti-social, most pathetic excuse for a life I have ever seen. That's why I wanted in on the act.

The prototype for the kind of preacher I craved to be is the Very Reverend Cleophus James, the hollerin' and hootin' holy roller played by James Brown in *The Blues Brothers*.

Aficionados of that movie will remember that the dashing Rev. Cleophus is P.P. at the Triple Rock Church in Chicago where he leads his congregation in making a jubilant song and dance about their love for Jesus. When Joliet Jake (John Belushi) is released from the hoosegow, it is suggested that he and Elwood pop round to the Triple Rock to rekindle their spiritual flames by participating in one of Rev. Cleophus' liturgies of the mashed potato.

The experience causes Jake not only to see the light but to literally glow with Heavenly luminescence. Of course, given the quantity of speed, smack and sauce Belushi was gorging between takes on the set of *The Blues Brothers,* the luminescence captured by the camera may, in reality, have had an intestinal origin.

Nevertheless, there is something about the way Rev. Cleophus recites his creed that has long made me wish that I could follow in his Goodfoot steps. Why bother learning the dreary words to all those tedious prayers and hymns so beloved of vinegar-veined puritans when James Brown has already composed the definitive psalm of adoration: to wit *'Uggggggh!'*.

Let us proclaim the mystery of his faith!

There were several options as to how I could emulate Rev. Cleophus on the streets of Dublin. One was to go blackface; daub my kisser and hands with ebony polish in the tradition of Al Jolson. I rejected this approach, for two reasons. Firstly, blackface still has strong racist overtones. Secondly, you never know when you might need your self-respect again.

In the end, judiciousness decreed that my preacher would be 'based on' rather than a 'replica of' the original creation. The natty silk robe Rev. Cleophus wears in *The Blues Brothers* is not dissimilar to the dappled gowns that some college graduates sport on mortar-board day. Such apparel is readily available from formal dress-hire outlets.

However, while I like to think of myself as a bold, doughty, audacious reporter, prepared to go to elaborate lengths to nail down a story, there was no way on God's foul asteroid that I was swanning around the public highways in a getup that makes me look like a *student,* even a retired one. There are limits to what I'm prepared to do for a cheap chortle.

A few discretely mumbled phonecalls from the office to various fancy dress emporia was all it took to track down a more befitting garment. It was a preposterous and preposterously heavy burlap robe in a peculiarly dark shade of crimson which can be most accurately likened to the colour of David Trimble's face during the Drumcree stand-off.

To heighten the absurdity, the outfit was inlaid with rows of woollen piping in a peculiarly dark shade of sable which can be most accurately likened to the colour of David Trimble's *soul* during the Drumcree stand-off.

In order to complete this resplendent ensemble, I would have to contravene one of the most sacred tenets of my distinguished journalistic career and wear a tie. Ethical reservations about losing my rakish plunging-neckline aside, I knew this concession was essential to my camouflage.

There is a specific look – demented, bug-eyed, slightly woozy – that is indigenous to all preachermen. The most efficient method of securing this demeanour is to keep yourself in an all-day state of near asphyxiation, with the aid of a tie knotted as tight as a Presbyterian.

Ultimately, I realised that hairstyle was going to be the key to my transformation into a credible hot-gospeller. As you know, James Brown has a lavishly baroque pompadour permed as stiff as chicken wire. In my guise as a pavement proselytiser, I felt that this sort of flamboyant coiffure would be indispensable.

It would help attract crowds. It would protect me from the worst excesses of diarrhoetic birds. I could use it as a symbol, in my sermons, for the crushing weight under which every human must struggle in this vale of tears. It would also come in handy as a loft for stashing my preaching materials during tea-breaks.

If I could get my hands on a decent James Brown wig, I'd be laughing. Well, if not exactly laughing, at least grinning heartily. Unfortunately, my features were to remain untroubled by triumphant mirth of any kind.

"We only have an Elvis Presley wig but that would do for James Brown," the owner of one theatrical outfitters assured me. My sweet Lord! By this reasoning, a sun bonnet *would do* as Sherlock Holmes' deerstalker and a tutu *would do* as a caveman's loincloth. If I expected people to use their imaginations to that extent, I'd be performing this entire piece on radio, as a mime.

My friends at Clown Around, the party costume shop, reckoned they would come closest to satisfying my needs. But it wasn't close enough. The nearest thing they had to a James Brown mane was a shiny, raven

'60s mop, receding at the front and with ridiculous curls at the back. Frankly, it made me look more like Vincent Browne.

I decided to proceed without a wig of any kind. My photographer and make-up artiste, Mick 'Estee Lauder' Quinn, suggested that salvation lay in a tub of mousse. According to him, if I saturated my thatch with an excess of this pink goo, the effect would be wonderful. Wonderfulish, anyway.

It sounded like a bullet-proof idea. I was going to put the *gel* firmly into evangelist. As it turned out, I was also going to put the *gel* firmly into gelatinous gelding which is what I resembled by the time I had completed my styling and primping.

My hair had coagulated into a gummy mess of something akin to straw and cow dung. If looks *can* kill, I was going to have to stay well away from reflective surfaces for the rest of the day.

Corrective action was called for. How could I expect anyone to invest full confidence in a scriptural scholar with a compost heap on his head?

In a humble homage to the menacing preacher played by Robert Mitchum in *Night Of The Hunter*, Mick etched the words LOVE on my right fist and HATE on my left. Perhaps, I mused optimistically, if people were diverted into reading my knuckles, they wouldn't pay so much attention to my hair.

After running a pitchfork through my tresses to dislodge what could be dislodged, and wiping enough mousse off my face to stop my shades from slipping down my nose, I was ready to go to work.

As we headed for Grafton Street, I was starting to hope desperately that what they say is true and that a prophet *is* never recognised in his own land.

Every evangelist needs a bible, a divinely-inspired manual in which reposes the fundamental source of the dogma that he or she expounds. You cannot throw the book at sinners and infidels unless you've got an actual book to throw.

The text from which I chose to preach was *What Our Grandmothers Knew – Hints, Recipes & Remedies Of A Bygone Age*. This is a slim, 32-page Reader's Digest publication, dating from the 1960s. It was one of those

free bonus booklets that the munificent Reader's Digest company spontaneously post to people. All the recipient has to do in return is agree to
order 9,700 issues of *Reader's Digest*.

I found a copy in my parents' attic. Even after a cursory browse, it
struck me that here was an abundant treasury of genuinely invaluable
advice and information, a teeming wealth of practical tips, pointers, wrin-
kles and, yes, commandments for life.

*What Our Grandmothers Knew – Hints, Recipes & Remedies Of A
Bygone Age* is what the Bible is supposed to be but demonstrably isn't.
The two Epistles from Saint Paul to the Thessalonians may be full of florid
imagery and sonorous prose but they're both shag all use when it comes
to teaching you how to soothe chapped hands, keep white hair at bay or
make an economical bath oil with left-over soaps and perfume.

The Devil can cite scripture for his own purpose. But no matter who
quotes from *What Our Grandmothers Knew,* the integrity and truth of the
message it contains remains inviolate.

Between the modest covers of this extraordinary tome lie the hints, the
whole hints and nothing but the hints. Its every recipe is a homily, its
every remedy a benediction. Upon this rock of sense, I would found a
brand new religion, for one day only: The Church Of The Immaculately
Groomed and Devoutly Houseproud.

On the morning of my mission, I made dozens of photocopies of the
most important, apt and instructional passages. Each sheet of A4 paper
bore nothing but the extract and its relevant chapter and verse. On the
traffic island across from the Saint Stephen's Green shopping centre, I
began to sow the precious seed of the Good News.

The first quotation I distributed was, with ingenious simplicity, entitled
TREATMENT FOR SWOLLEN ANKLES. It goes as follows:

> "This simple measure will greatly help ankles that have
> become swollen after tramping about all day. Wrap them sep-
> arately in towels wrung out in very hot water. Lie down with
> your legs slightly raised and covered with a light, warm rug."
>
> Ch. 1: Vs. 17

The reaction was stupendous. I handed out 30 SWOLLEN ANKLES leaflets in less than ten minutes. Passers-by snapped them from me as though they had been waiting for them to come off the presses all morning. I could tell by their reluctance to meet my eyes and the speed with which they scurried past that they were uncontrollably eager to get away from the madding throng so that they could peruse the document in peace and quiet.

Flushed with success, I moved on to another theme, SUNBURN RELIEF:

> "A potato poultice will give rapid relief from sunburn. Grate raw potato and spread between two layers of gauze. Apply this to the face or other affected parts. For severe sunburn, a doctor's advice is necessary."
>
> Ch 1: Vs. 8

Amen. This too was a jackpot winner. The handbills disappeared like sods in a flood. Confirming my confidence in the instantaneously helpful nature of the words on these pieces of paper, I saw men and women discard them after only a scant glance. They clearly wanted to waste no time in getting to the potatoes and gauze store.

To my immense delight, one young girl came up with a pleasingly post-modern response to the tract, deploying the text itself as an instrument of sunburn prevention. She made an attractive cap out of it and plonked it on her head.

A guy who looked like he had been trying to tan himself with a waffle-iron approached, his cherry-red forehead and meaty forearms peeling like wet toilet tissue in the breeze. An ideal candidate, I thought to myself.

"Hark to the *real* truth about sunburn relief, sir," I exclaimed, proffering him a pamphlet.

"Ask me hole," he replied.

It was time for a more complex and challenging doctrine, something that would attract the sophisticated convert. I opted for a personal favourite, CARE OF YOUR SHOES:

"Rub patent leather shoes with a soft rag dipped in olive oil – after you have removed any dust and mud with a soft brush. Leave for about half an hour, then polish with a clean, soft cloth. This treatment will prevent the patent from cracking and is also good for patent leather handbags."

Ch. 5: Vs. 5

Naturally, I didn't expect the entire populace of Grafton Street to promptly drop to its knees chanting, 'You speak the truth, Messiah, tell us again how we should maintain our footwear!'. I realise that this is a difficult passage which requires contemplation and study before it yields up its true sum and substance.

There are many such troublesome and perplexing sections in *What Our Grandmothers Knew*. Trendy modernisers might have you believe that some of the instructions in this book are old-fashioned, out of date and of no practical application to the contemporary man and woman.

Pay such heresy no heed. The teachings on how to clean pewter snuff boxes, how to scour the bronze fittings on musket handles, and how to care for ivory tusks brought back from safari, are as relevant today as they ever were.

In the early hours of my ministry, my preaching style was based almost exclusively on the techniques pioneered by the great Morris Cerullo, the megastar Pentecostal evangelist based in San Diego. As those who have seen Morris in action on TV will understand, this meant that, essentially and without wanting to be too technical about it, I had to do my nut.

The problem with freaking out on Grafton Street is that it's not exactly an original idea. Pedestrians in these parts have become jaded with extravagant displays of unbridled lunacy. They assume you're just another poet reciting his own work.

I resolved to try a more subtle strategy. The lesson I was preaching orally was CURES FOR HICCUPS, a sequence of precepts which, if faithfully followed, promise eternal happiness for those who suffer from embarrassing gas.

My arms outstretched like Big Jim Larkin, I enunciated this litany temperately but distinctly, with closed eyes and quavering voice, bowing my head reverently on certain key phrases such as "tickle your nose with a feather," "breathe in and out of a paper bag 20 times," and "drink from the opposite side of the glass." I desisted only when all that voice-quavering brought on a bout of the hiccups.

As the hours passed, the single most vexatious obstacle to my preaching proved not to be the apathy of adults but the enthusiasm of children. With knit-purl regularity, knots of snotty little monsters would gather around my feet, gawping up at me with the kind of milk-white, saucer-sized eyes you see blinking amid the darkness in cartoons.

For the first time, I wished I was one of those preachers who taught directly from the pages of a Bible. I could have done with a nice, fat, bulky book to beat them off with.

The main attraction may not have been my charismatic personality but the blackboard on which I would alternately scribble pertinent slogans ("You cannot serve cod and gammon") and more detailed invocations ("To prevent pasta from sticking, add a teaspoon of cooking oil to the boiling water before dropping in the pasta").

Having been unable to procure one of those large easels and pads that other evangelists use, I had been reduced to purchasing a two-and-a-half-foot tall kiddies' mini chalkboard, which came complete with a teach-the-time clock, an alphabet primer and a non-spill beaker. Something about this seemed to undermine my authority in the eyes of passing children.

On a walkabout (it is important that a preacher be seen as accessible and down-to-Earth, and I deem that possession of these traits is most ably conveyed by strolling around aimlessly nodding and winking at all and sundry), I encountered a group of adolescent buskers in an alleyway.

These beleaguered youths were wearily and fruitlessly trying to locate the melody in a Blur number when I happened by, and so were grateful for the chance to take five.

"Let's have some gospel music," I exhorted their frontman. He squinted pensively at me for about a minute and then started to croon, *"I am just a poor boy and my story's seldom told . . ."*

"No, no, no," I interjected, ordering the playing to cease with a thunderbolt-like wave of my arm. "Not Simon And bollocky Garfunkel. Who do you think I am? A member of the Church of Ireland? How about some *real* soul."

The kid didn't seem to know his Aretha from his urethra. After a few moments of indecisive muttering, he led his troupe into something called 'He Is Here', one of those interminable, you-got-a-friend songs they teach in religion class instead of proper hymns these days.

As I vigorously sang along (the lyrics were depressingly easy to pick up), I noticed three feeble old ladies in wheelchairs at the other end of the alley. They were clearly incensed by the racket and were frantically remonstrating with their helpers, demanding to be evacuated from here immediately. We had inadvertently invented a new sacrament: The Annoying of the Sick.

Back on Grafton Street, I came upon a brood of punks. One of them, a chap with a formidable coxcomb, stopped glowering for a split-second when he saw me. He was obviously extremely moved by my selfless and inspirational attempts to brighten the day of others. "Do you feel stupid, do you?," he asked solicitously.

We chatted amiably for a while. Actually, I chatted and he turned his back to me and scowled but, hey, he's a punk and that's his job. As I took my leave, I presented him with a memento for his breviary, from which I trusted he and his mates would derive some spiritual solace. It was HINTS FOR EGGS:

> "If you need the white of an egg but want to keep the yolk for later use, proceed as follows: Pierce a hole in both ends of the shell with a fine knitting needle or sharp, pointed knife. Gently shake out the white. Then wrap the egg in greaseproof and store it in a cool place."
>
> Ch 6: Vs. 11

For the last half-hour of my career as a preacher, I decided to change tack. Abandoning my dedication to *What Our Grandmothers Knew*, I began to hand out blank sheets of A4. These were leaflets bearing messages which were of considerable less value than the paper they weren't printed on.

As I anticipated, these expanses of white nothingness went like hot cakes. "Thank you, I'll read it later," said a jaunty old man in a crombie overcoat, carefully folding the pamphlet into his inside pocket for safe keeping.

"I haven't got my glasses with me today, I'm afraid," apologised a blue-blooded dowager type. "Give one to my son instead. He'll be along in a few minutes."

Far fewer people threw the null and void circulars away than had jettisoned my other handbills. Even those who copped onto the fact that they were blank held on to them in case there was something more to it than they could see. There is, undoubtedly, a moral to all this. In religious terms, everybody wants *carte blanche* nowadays.

Towards mid-afternoon, I noticed a strikingly attractive woman watching me from a few feet away. She was the mother of two infernal, middle class, spoiled brats who had been messing about with my blackboard for almost an hour.

I pitied the poor lady. To support such a family, she would have to work outside the home 18 hours a day. To love such a family, she would have to work outside the home 24 hours a day.

The woman was holding one of my tracts, one of those with writing on them. She read it and looked in my direction again. Her pupils rummaged about in mine; desperately, imploringly attempting to make contact.

She obviously wanted to ask me a question, something important and urgent. A good street preacher must always be ready to assist people in moments of spiritual and emotional crisis.

Eventually, she plucked up enough courage to walk over. "Excuse me, I wonder if you could help me," she said, in a pleading tone. "Can you tell me where Habitat is?"

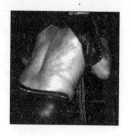

HOT UNDER THE COLLAR

"Masturbation is an integral part of every celibate's life," says Father Pat Buckley. "Most priests would masturbate regularly, as would most bishops and, I'm sure, even the Pope."

They called it wankers' corner.

Every day at 7.15am, just before morning mass, the spiritual director of Clonliffe College would hold special confessions in a small, dim oratory off the campus chapel.

The sole purpose of these confessions was to allow seminarians an opportunity to beg God's forgiveness for any acts of masturbation they might have committed during the previous night. Each individual wank had to be separately renounced. The standard penance proscribed was one Our Father and three Hail Marys.

For most of the penitents, it would take longer to recite one Our Father and three Hail Marys than it had to squeeze the cream from the flesh eclair in the first place.

By design, this was a very public ritual. Humiliation was its primary intent. The young men waiting their turn in wankers' corner were plainly visible to the entire college population. Confessional confidentiality was not a courtesy extended to these one-palm performance artists.

This tradition continued well into the 1970s. Among the current generation of clergy, most priests above the age of 40 will have prepared for ordination in either this or a very similar environment. One cleric with especially vivid memories of the Clonliffe College regime is Father Pat Buckley. During the early 1970s, he spent three years studying at the Dublin seminary. He was no stranger to wankers' corner.

"Not only was it a private confession between yourself and God and the priest but you had to announce to the entire campus that you had fallen during the previous night," he recalls. "Naturally, we were all in the same boat – but to have to admit to having just masturbated was to announce publicly that one was losing the ongoing battle with the Devil."

One of the central textbooks on the Clonliffe syllabus at the time was *The Priest And Mental Health*. This was a grimly didactic tome, appetisingly described on its flyleaf as "a hard-headed presentation by Catholic psychiatrists of newly-discovered but firmly-established facts together with discussions by competent psychologists and theologians of the significance of these facts for the clergy." It was first published in 1962, and was edited by a Professor of Logic and Psychology at University College, Dublin, the Reverend Fechian O'Doherty.

Reverend O'Doherty held that masturbation was "a sexual deviation." His thesis was that the practice is most common among youths with a "history of bedwetting, night fears and learning problems," as well as "a poor capacity for making stable relationships." The kind of boys who might be prone to hearing calls from God, urging them to the priesthood, for instance.

Most of those afflicted by the "masturbatory disorder," O'Doherty argued, were the sons of women who were "possessive and perfectionistic," and who tended to "dominate" their "passive, dependent husbands." In other words, if Junior pounds more meat than a Kepak production line, it's basically Mammy's fault.

Reverend O'Doherty drew a distinction between "habitual masturbation" and "compulsive masturbation." An habitual masturbator, in his book, was someone who churned the butter once a week or thereabouts. Anyone who indulged with greater regularity was in the compulsive category. Neither level of expertise was acceptable in a worthy seminarian.

"The more experience I have in psychiatry and the more cases of sexual disorder that I see amongst priests," wrote Fr. O'Doherty, "the more rigid I have become in advising the rejection of any student who has any manifestation of sexual disorder, such as compulsive or habitual masturbation, or any suggestion of homosexuality."

And when Reverend O'Doherty became rigid, the Clonliffe College authorities got stiff. "If you continued to attend wankers' corner, you could eventually be thrown out of the seminary altogether," says Pat Buckley. "It hasn't been unknown for that to happen. The aptly named Fechian O'Doherty believed that if you were still masturbating after your second or third year in the seminary then you weren't suited for the priesthood. That was that.

"It was a ridiculous set up. Masturbation is, of course, an integral part of every celibate's life. It's a part of everybody's life. Most men and women engage in it whether they're married or not. Certainly, most priests would masturbate regularly, as would most bishops and, I'm sure, even the Pope. But you weren't supposed to say that or even think it.

"Again, it's part of the Catholic Church's hypocrisy. Everybody's doing it but everybody pretends that they're not. The only ones who are punished are those that are found out."

Dissident priest, Fr. Pat Buckley, is in a unique position to speak about clerical celibacy, and all its empty works and promises.

As the blackest sheep in the Irish ecclesiastical flock, he now finds himself ministering to others who have been marginalised from the fold. In his tiny presbytery and church in Larne, Country Antrim, Buckley regularly receives visits from priests (the vast majority of them from the Republic) who are in relationships with women.

As a result of the current Pope's refusal to allow men who leave the priesthood to marry within the church (unless they go to court to establish that they were either "mentally unstable" or "sexually perverted" when they were ordained), Buckley is the only Catholic pastor in the country who performs wedding ceremonies for ex-clerics and their partners.

He also co-ordinates a support group for some of the hundreds (his figure) of Irish women who have become entangled in love affairs with men of the cloth. Though he has fallen most grievously foul of the Irish hierarchy, he is still a *bona fide* priest and a man with intimate knowledge of the grotesque stratagems with which the Catholic Church prepares its frontline footsoldiers for the celibate life.

Born in Tullamore, County Offaly, in 1952, Pat Buckley had wanted to become a priest since he was about three years of age. A deeply committed Christian, he was inspired by all the noble aims of the priesthood. He wanted to work among the poor and deprived, and hoped he would be appointed to a parish in an area such as Dublin's inner city.

However, Buckley was always too intelligent and too strong-willed to ever become just another cassockful of Canon Law fodder. It wasn't long before he started to rebel. When he entered Clonliffe College in 1970, the seminary was still under the aegis of the notoriously hardline Archbishop of Dublin and Primate of All Ireland, John Charles McQuaid.

"Rule 18 in the Clonliffe rulebook said that the role of the training was to take away a person's individuality," Buckley explains. "We all had to wear the same clothes, get up at the same time, speak the same way, even have the same furniture in all our rooms. They were only interested in creating robots.

"The nearest thing to it I ever saw in the real world was when I was a curate in Kilkeel, County Down. One of my parishioners there had a fish factory. The herring used to come in on an assembly line. They removed their heads first, then their guts and then their backbones. That's what happened in the seminary. They manufactured filleted priests."

Buckley's first act of revolt in Clonliffe was to stay in bed most mornings rather than attend the lectures which he felt were absurd in the extreme.

"We were supposed to study things like 'Angelology'," he states. "We'd discuss for hours how many angels you could fit on top of a pin. Literally! We also had a lecture one time on what would happen if an angel fell into some water. Apparently, an angel can fall in but it can't get out. I never really understood that theological point.

"Another time, we spent an entire week discussing what would happen if a fly got into the chalice during mass and drowned in the precious blood. What would you do? You were supposed to take out the fly, wipe every drop off it, burn the fly and then wash the cloth. I always thought that a few extra hours in bed would be more useful than any of this sort of stuff."

A Dublin seminarian's sex education customarily began with a private two hour audience with Archbishop McQuaid, in the darkened study of his Drumcondra palace.

"It was a terrifying experience," Buckley maintains. "Every first-year student had to go through this ritual. You went in quietly and sat at the corner of his desk, with your two feet firmly on the floor. He then put his right foot directly on top of your right foot – why, I don't know – and pulled his chair right up beside yours.

"He'd ask you, 'My son, do you know the facts of life?'. You were always told to answer 'No'. If you said "Yes', he'd say, 'Right, tell me them!'. So, you'd say 'No', and he'd start to tell you the facts of life in great detail.

"He'd show you the different parts of the body by drawing diagrams. He'd demonstrate how a penis would enter a vagina by using his fingers. He'd also go on at great length about the evils of sex, and masturbation, or 'pollution' as he called it. He was very, very anti-pollution. Spilling the seed is a terrible sin, he'd say, especially for a priest.

"After your two hours were over, and only then, he'd take his foot off your foot. He'd go to his desk, from which he would take a wee wooden cross. He'd give you this cross and tell you that whenever you were tempted to do anything impure with yourself, you were to tightly grasp the cross rather than your body. If you ever see such a cross beside a priest's bed, you'll know what it's there for."

✝ ✝ ✝ ✝ ✝ ✝ ✝

During this era, many seminarians were routinely issued with small, knout-like whips in the early stages of their training. They were instructed to go to their rooms at least once or twice every day, strip to their waists and flagellate themselves for ten or 15 minutes. The objective was to beat their sullied, evil flesh into righteous submission.

"However," insists Fr. Buckley, "as is often the case with human nature, there were many men who learned how to derive sexual pleasure from that sort of thing. The whipping became their sexual outlet. That's also why you had, and have, so many priests and nuns who seem to derive so much relief from beating the tripe out of children in school. It's a form of perverted sexual release."

Those being drilled for Holy Orders are repeatedly told that they must always avoid "occasions of sin," a vast category of stimuli encompassing everything from individuals to books, films or anything likely to arouse lascivious thoughts in a callow celibate's head. A seminarian's private fantasy life, therefore, tends to be unusually rich, not to say richly unusual.

"If the normal erotic world is denied to you, you start to look elsewhere for your erotica," Buckley avers. "Many priests have wonderful imaginations and can find arousal in ways that other people would never dream of. I knew one young seminarian who, it was rumoured, used to masturbate to a tape of ribald rugby songs.

"I'd imagine it's a case of beggars can't be choosers. Even religious imagery probably has its erotic side if you try hard enough. A repressed mind can be very resourceful."

Fr. Pat Buckley says that he leads a celibate life, but that this is out of personal choice rather than any sense of fidelity to church dictum. He is convinced that enforced celibacy is "both immoral and patently unworkable." He argues that priests should have the same freedom in this matter as everybody else.

He is adamant that if he were to meet and fall in love with a woman at some future point, he would marry her and continue to live and work openly as a priest. "Running away only removes the challenge and lets the church off the hook," he avows.

At the moment, he has no burning desire to father any offspring. "I was the oldest of 17 children so I had to virtually raise my 16 brothers and sisters," he affirms. "I think the family genes need a rest. But who knows? If we are to believe what we are told, Bishop Casey didn't get *his* burning desire until he was 47. I have a few years to go."

Buckley remains steadfast in his claim that there is at least one current Irish bishop who is in a long-term relationship with a woman. "It's been going on for years and is fairly widely known in Church circles," he attests.

Fr. Buckley also repeats his assertion that there is "a very large number of priests" in this country involved in ongoing affairs.

"There are somewhere between 6,000 and 7,000 priests in Ireland and I know of several dozen who are in relationships," he proclaims. "And if I, as one priest, know so many, that will give you an idea of the scale of the situation. And, I'm only talking about priests in *relationships*.

"I know of others, both north and south, who put on the snazzy clothes during the week and go to nightclubs or dances to meet women. A lot of these priests would just be looking for one night stands. And most of these guys would be smarter than Bishop Casey, in the sense that they'd use contraception. The girls involved would probably never know that they'd been involved with priests. The stuff about contraception being sinful is strictly for the pulpit, and for the public pronouncement.

"There is an idea around that, in these cases, it's always the woman's fault, that the woman steals the priest from God's altar. This is nonsense. It's obvious from the Bishop Casey business that he was at least 50% responsible, and that's usually the case. Indeed, in many of the cases that I'm personally aware of, the relationships began at times when the women were extremely vulnerable.

"I know of a couple of priests in Dublin who began relationships with young widows while they were comforting them after bereavement. The priests are usually well aware of what's happening and it's the women who are swept off their feet."

Pat Buckley confirms that there have been consistent whispers in the clerical world about a sex scandal in the past involving a senior Irish bishop which, were it to be publicly revealed, would make Bishop Casey's high jinx seem like "nothing more than a chaste kiss in the back seat of the cinema."

In this context, Buckley wonders just how far into the heart of the Catholic Church the tentacles of sexual hypocrisy and depravity extend.

"The Vatican is a very wicked city," he contends. "Practises like paedophilia and the procuring of rent boys are said to be quite popular among bishops and monsignors. There are many people in The Vatican who are in no position to criticise anybody for their sexual behaviour. That's why the first inclination in the Catholic Church is to cover things up.

"Bishops who get involved in scandals are often moved sideways to some quite backwater, much like someone is kicked up to the House Of Lords. There are a lot of glass houses and not very many stones in The Vatican."

Fr. Buckley's allegations about priests and bishops have been consistently dismissed by the Irish Catholic establishment. He has been denounced in vitriolic terms, by the former cardinal, Cahal Daly, among many others.

Each clerical sexual scandal uncovered is, in the shortsighted eyes of the hierarchy, an isolated, singular incident. A flash in the pan. It forms no part of any trend. It points to no underlying cause. Love the sinner, hate the sin. Condemn the churchman, absolve the church.

"I think that the ostrich was invented by the Catholic Church," declares Fr. Pat Buckley. "Its head in the sand and its ass in the air. Now, however, it's ass-kicking time."

TO HELL AND BACK

Lough Derg has a fearsome reputation. The island purgatory has been infamous throughout Europe as a centre of torturous penitential pilgrimage since at least the 12th century. It is said to have inspired Dante in the writing of his *Inferno.*

One Our Father, one Hail Mary, one Creed. Three Our Fathers, three Hail Marys, one Creed. Seven decades of the Rosary, one Creed. Six Our Fathers, six Hail Marys, one Creed. Five Our Fathers, five Hail Marys, one Creed.

Think of the time and effort that could be saved by Catholics every-where if someone would only let them in on the secret of the word *ditto*. Say something once, why say it again? Especially when we've got this clever little labour-saving device to help us avoid repetition. One Our Father, one Hail Mary, one Creed. Ditto, ditto, ditto. Game over. Thank you, and goodnight.

Such are the thoughts which meander through the mind during the interminable waking hours of a Lough Derg pilgrimage. When you're stranded, starved and sleep-deprived on a Gulag Archipelago for the worst part of three days, rumination tends to be a limitless resource.

For this pilgrim, the lowest point of the entire experience was the all-night vigil. I was limp with exhaustion throughout, and my belly was groaning like a porn queen. I had not yet reached the halfway stage of my three-day fast but I was already hungry enough to eat the logo off the Fruit Of The Loom sweatshirt on the girl in front of me.

And that was the thin end of my anguish. The real torment was the ceaseless praying and walking, neither of which were made any easier by being barefoot. After nightfall, the Lough Derg carnival goes indoors. The stations which, by day, are made outside on the rutted, stone penitential beds are undertaken beneath the eaves of Saint Patrick's basilica between dusk and dawn.

Each of these circular routines takes about an hour to complete, and is punctuated only by short intervals for fresh air and nicotine hits. They begin with the clanging of a bell shooing the pilgrims through the wooden chapel doors, which are then bolted by a sexton. Until you've been locked inside an isolated Donegal island church at 3.30am, you have no idea of the true meaning of *despair*.

By this point, even the priests had gone to bed. The basilica stations were led by lay men and women who had asked for the privilege. It was a big deal for these folk. Some of them blushed and fidgeted with nervousness when they stood behind the lectern. Others strode up bristling with self-assurance, as though to the pulpit born. All of them were beaming by the time they finished.

The quality of the deliveries varied wildly. I remember thinking that one guy in particular had a voice like a stainless steel spoon scraping congealed minestrone noodles off the bottom of a soup bowl. But, in truth, this may have had more to do with my famished reveries about minestrone soup than with the discordance of his locution.

In the night shelters, during the breaks, the merits of the various stations leaders were analysed over paper cups of 'Lough Derg soup': pepper and salt mixed with tap water. "That last one was a good man to give out the litany," proclaimed a smiling old woman with white hair as neat as pastry crust. "At least he was smart about it."

Saint Patrick's Purgatory is extremely popular among Catholics from Northern Ireland. Tyrone in particular, they say, is a great county for supporting Lough Derg. There are certainly a lot of people within earshot who refer to the Republic as "south Ireland."

The pilgrims on my watch were a mixed bunch, mostly of rural extraction. Women outnumbered men at least five to one. There were plenty of oldsters but a good fifth of the turnout were in their late teens and early 20s.

The most conspicuous sociological group were mother and daughter twosomes. One got the distinct impression that the daughters thought they were here for the benefit of the mothers, and vice versa.

The loudest element among the pilgrims was a wittering coven of middle-aged, Northern Irish ladies, whom I like to think of as the Vigil Aunties. These were seasoned habitués of the pilgrimage and keen that everyone should know it. One of them, it was whispered, made the pilgrimage every single week during the season.

Inveterate buttinskis and nosenheimers, they proffered unwanted advice to anyone who'd listen, and gleefully informed passers-by of their mistakes, in terms of clothing, attitude, pace, you name it.

There wasn't one of them that didn't belong to the species so memorably characterised by Patrick Kavanagh, in his fine poem *Lough Derg*, as the "Holy Biddy with a rat-trap on her diddy."

Even for a Saint Patrick's Purgatory virgin like myself, the stations ritual rapidly became rote. First, we stood with arms outstretched in the shape of a cross and said three times, "I renounce the World, the Flesh and the Devil." Then, we embarked on the Long March; trooping around and around and around the aisles of the basilica, reciting that endless catalogue of prayers so beloved of the unenlightened who have not heard the gospel according to *ditto*.

Individuals faltered and stopped for breathers but the procession continued uninterrupted. There were brief respites. Those moments when we all halted for our flapping renunciation of the World, the Flesh and the Devil. And the periodic Creeds, when we got to kneel down.

The knee is a much-overworked joint on Lough Derg, however, and often too sore to derive any relief from resting on hard wood or concrete. When each Creed is imminent, there is a subtle jostling for space at the altar rails where the kneeling-pad is cushioned. As the night progresses, the jostling becomes increasingly less subtle.

Some of us circumvented the soreness problem with Virtual Kneeling, that deft old trick whereby your ass is wedged on the bench, your arms propped up on the back of the seat in front and your toes buttressed against the ground like a fulcrum so that your knees are free to dangle in weightless comfort.

But such reprieves were short-lived. A few seconds later, you were back on your feet again, plodding, plodding, plodding, clocking up end-less miles on the cold tile.

There were 218 pilgrims on vigil with me. Maybe a dozen did their walking in the pews, gliding forward and back like electric hares on a greyhound track. The rest of us trudged on with our grim and circuitous parade around the aisles, moving in a manner that is best described as a cross between The Hokey Cokey, The Conga and a very stupid dance which has yet to be invented.

Prayer, to me, is cerebral idling. The very word seems to curb thought. On Saint Patrick's Purgatory, however, I discovered that prayer is actually a very effective method of killing, indeed slaughtering, time. As long as you get the hang of the tune, you don't even need the lyrics.

Hours drag here like nowhere else. The brain resorts to all sorts of complicated stratagems by which the clock can be beaten or, at the very least, eluded.

You start to calculate how many hours, how many minutes, how many seconds, you have thus far spent on the island and how many more you will have to spend.

You try to figure out your own age in terms of weeks, days, episodes of *Brookside*. You play Word Association Football Crazy Horse Sense and Sensibility. When things start getting really desperate, you fall back on alphabet puzzles (I bet you didn't know that Spiro Agnew is an anagram of *Grow a penis*. Or, that Virginia Bottomley is an anagram of *I'm an evil Tory bigot*).

Eventually, morning arrived. There were oohs and aahs of wonderment from people who had obviously never seen sunlight before. "It's *the* most beautiful way to greet the daybreak," trilled a rubicund Vigil Auntie, a woman who has evidently never taken a taxi home from a Leeson Street club at 5am with a takeaway bottle and a new friend on the seat beside her.

Mass was at 6.30am, for which we were joined by the previous night's vigilants, somewhat restored by their night's sleep but still discernibly worn out. Now that the rhythm of the night had been broken and we were permitted to sit in the one spot for more than two minutes, the craving for food once again became ravenous.

The priest seemed to be taunting me with subliminal references to nosh. Every time he mentioned the blood of Christ, all I could think of was a plate of chips smothered in tomato ketchup. The faint sputtering of the water and the wine being poured into his chalice sounded like a bubbling pan of rashers and eggs. The Lamb of God was a juicy roast, with all the fixings.

Mass out of the way, our next formal engagement was an "open celebration" of the Sacrament of Reconciliation at 8.30am, wherein confessions would be heard face to face, on the floor of the basilica. I chose to skip this because of my firm theological conviction that the true sacrament of penance can only be administered in the privacy of the confessional, and also because I was dying for a snooze.

I trudged through the harsh, damp morning wind to the reading room. This was a toasty-warm, waxed-floor hideaway buried in the bowels of the main building where pilgrims could relax during recesses in their penitential schedule. I was surprised to find that someone else had beaten me to it; a rotund Friar Tuck lookalike in a bulky green pullover was already snoring his head off on a bench beneath the windowsill.

I had been awake now for over 24 hours and it would still be another 15 before I was officially allowed to sleep again. I was about ready to drop. When you get this tired, your body becomes extraordinarily sensitive to noise. A slamming door cattle-prods your synapses, the squawk of a crow plays 'Purple Haze' on your nerve endings.

I could not tolerate my companion's snorting. It seemed offensively abrasive; the abrupt zipping and unzipping of a huge metal fastener as relayed through a megaphone.

I decided to ask him, politely, if he would mind turning on his side to quell the snoring but it came out as, "SHUT THE HOLY FUCK UP, LAR-DARSE!" To my astonishment, the young man remained asleep and made no response to my outburst. He merely smacked his lips and farted loudly, a Do Not Disturb sign in Morse code.

I tried to read to distract myself. There wasn't much in the way of material, apart from a few religious magazines such as *The Little Way Association,* and a book entitled *Prayers Of An Irish Mother.* Newspapers are not sold on the island. The only publications available are those brought in by the most recent batch of pilgrims.

Single copies of yesterday's *Belfast Telegraph* and the day before's *Irish Independent* had been sundered into dozens of double-page spreads to feed demand for the printed word, loaves and fishes style. I found them too disturbing to read. When you're stuck in the middle of a Lough Derg vigil, there is nothing more depressing than last night's TV listings. I started flicking through *The Sacred Heart Messenger* instead and nodded off immediately.

The next thing I knew, a fistful of knuckles were cudgelling my shoulder blade. Awaking with a start that almost snapped my spine, I found a baby-faced priest with a chinstrap beard standing over me. "Holy Moses, you shouldn't be here," he was saying, his tone one of shock as much as irritation. "Wake up. Wake up. Holy Moses!"

I glanced over at Friar Tuck. He had been roused from his slumber too, and was clutching his shoulder in obvious pain, which was something, I suppose. We had both been caught napping by one of the priests whose job it is to patrol the hidey-holes and shelters in search of shirkers. They're everywhere, these clerical snoopers, wandering about like bouncers only without the winning personalities.

"You fellas shouldn't be in here," seethed Holy Moses, holding the door ajar to hasten our exit. "You'll have to stay awake. Why aren't you at the Sacrament of Reconciliation? Off ye go, now. No sleeping!"

This wasn't Purgatory, or even Hell. It was much worse. It was a totalitarian priests' state, a clergyocracy, a sky pilot dictatorship.

The morning I left for Lough Derg was one of the most dismal of my life. At the best of times, Busaras is a dreary and desolate terminal. When you're queuing for a bus that will take you to Saint Patrick's Purgatory, it's the grimmest boneyard on the planet.

For half an hour before departure, I had stared dolefully at the locations on the electronic destination board, rolling their romantic syllables over my tongue: Ashbourne, Granard, Rooskey, Clones, Dromod, Mountmellick, Swinford, Oughterard. Oh, to be travelling to such exotic locations. Oh, to be travelling anywhere, in fact, but where I was headed.

Saint Patrick's Purgatory has a fearsome reputation. The island has been infamous throughout Europe as a centre of torturous penitential pilgrimage since at least the 12th century. It was the principal landmark on Medieval and Renaissance maps of Ireland, and was the only Irish site named on a map of the world in 1492. Rumours about the severity of its rigours are said to have inspired Dante in the writing of his *Inferno*.

Today, Lough Derg boasts a more select clientele, and has carved its devotional niche as a mystical netherworld where the most fanatical of Catholic die-hards go to suffer for their religion so that they'll feel better about making the rest of us suffer for it when they get home.

During its annual ten-week season, which stretches from June 1st to August 15th, Saint Patrick's Purgatory claims to attract an average of 30,000 pilgrims. The three-day series of penitential exercises has changed little since the 1600s and involves a perplexing pattern of prayer and motion, principally performed on and around the whorls of low stone walls known as penitential beds.

Pilgrims spend two nights on the island. From the midnight prior to arriving on Lough Derg, they are expected to observe a complete fast from all food and drink. Prescribed medication is allowed but bottles of spring water are not. "Plain" water only is specified in the leaflet outlining the pilgrimage procedure. The fast ends at midnight on the third day.

Pilgrims must arrive at the lake shore before 3pm. They must be over 15 years of age, free from illness or disability and able to walk and kneel unaided. The vigil is the chief penitential exercise of the pilgrimage, and requires denying oneself sleep, completely and continuously, for 24 hours, from 10pm on the first day. After Benediction on the second day, the pilgrim retires to bed in one of the island's hostels.

The gateway to Saint Patrick's Purgatory is situated about four miles north of Pettigo, on the Donegal/Fermanagh border. Its wrought iron arch can be approached by only one road, a glorified dirt track as narrow, crooked, cratered, warped and treacherous as a papal encyclical

Lough Derg itself is a broad stretch of water, measuring six miles by four, and girdled by short, stocky, heather-clad mountains. About 20 islands dot the lake's surface, most of them little more than rocky out-crops sustaining a few clumps of moss and two or three scrawny seagulls. Furthest from the shore, but still no more than a messiah's trot, is Station Island, the setting for the pilgrimage.

Station Island is very small, comprising two acres of natural area, but this has been augmented by reclamation at different times this century as further expansion became necessary to accommodate the pilgrimage.

Saint Patrick's Purgatory is owned lock, stock and barrel by the Catholic Church, and has been since the late 1500s. The island is their own little principality, a microcosm of how they would like the entire Irish nation to be run if only they could get rid of those pesky democrats.

Travelling across on the ferry, you are instantly struck by its miniature metropolis, the imposing granite structures which huddle together in a cramped block that almost submerges the entire island.

To the approaching visitor, these edifices exude all the welcoming warmth of Colditz Castle, combined with the frisky gaiety of Alcatraz and the soothing tranquillity of Mountjoy. When you get closer, you realise that this is a facade, and that the place is really much bleaker than that. Saint Patrick's is a maximum security Purgatory.

The fee for the pilgrimage is £15. There's no such thing as a free lunch, even when you're fasting. Cameras, radios, musical instruments, rugs and games of all sorts are prohibited . . .

On the dock, we were greeted by a nun whose overcoat and skin came in matching shades of beige. Wordlessly, she examined the new arrivals from head to toe, sizing us up as though measuring us for coffins. We were lead into the hall of the main building where a woman behind a hatch issued us with tickets the size and shape of postage stamps. I was M 113 C: a male, in bed 113, upper bunk.

"Go upstairs to your cubicles and leave your baggage," commanded the nun strictly. "Take off your shoes and socks and come back down at once."

Pillows, pillow slips, blankets and sheets were stacked in a neat pile, military fashion, on each bed, but we were told to ignore them. It was 2.30pm on Wednesday. It would be 10.15pm on Thursday before we would have permission to sleep, or even lie down.

I bade an emotional farewell to my socks and shoes. Despite my misgivings, I found that there is something immensely liberating about being in bare feet. Your toes are free to wiggle, to jiggle, to become the carefree individuals they've always yearned to be.

The breeze swirls playfully through hairs that are normally ensnared in socks, licks your anklebones and then darts up the cuffs of your trousers, whistling merrily around your shins.

Just as I was beginning to enjoy the sensation, however, I realised that I couldn't stand at the front door forever and that, sooner or later, I'd have to start walking around a bit.

To make sure that no-one is left in any doubt about who's the chicken salad and who's the chicken shit on Station Island, our clerical hosts wear shoes and stockings at all times.

While us poor secular pilgrims are pounding our plates of meat into plates of minced meat, the priests stroll around in stylish moccasins and loafers; smugly flaunting the impregnability of their soles by prancing where the rest of us fear to tread.

With so many bare feet around, the brain gradually starts to become more discerning about foot nuances. You notice the finer points of toe shape, ankle development, the elegance of an instep. You soon find yourself recognising pairs of feet belonging to faces that are black strangers.

The centrepiece of Station Island, the pilgrimage cockpit, is quite a compact area, 50 square yards at most, much of it in the sloping shade of a huge sycamore tree that is said to be 400 years old. The six penitential beds are situated just outside the doors of the basilica, adjacent to the three co-ordinates which define the frontiers of every Lough Derg station, namely the water's edge, Saint Brigid's Cross (at the basilica wall) and Saint Patrick's Cross.

There is a distinct schoolyard feel to these surroundings. Every move you make is supervised by the half dozen priests who loiter around here all day. Ostensibly, they're on hand to offer pastoral advice to the pilgrims, but they are also policing their turf.

Every now and again, one of them sidles up to a rebelliously ebullient penitent and mutters, in no uncertain terms, "Please keep your voice down."

Station Island is run by four priests: the Prior, Monsignor Dick Mohan, and three associates. They are assisted by a raft of auxiliaries and guests. Some of these are retired clerics but many are eager apprentices, grateful for the opportunity to put some of their seminarian theory into practice.

I had made the mistake of assuming that the dictat outlawing cameras on the island was just another Catholic piety not meant to be taken seriously, like the bans on artificial contraception or clerical copulation. I had smuggled in what I thought was an unobtrusive little Instamatic. I fished it out of my pocket and started taking a few warm-up snaps. Suddenly, I felt the cold hand of authority wrap its icy fingers around my wrist.

"Cameras are not permitted here," scolded the head honcho himself, Monsignor Dick Mohan, with the soft-spoken, barely restrained fury of the true disciplinarian. "We must respect the rules of the island."

I had been pointing my lens in the direction of the basilica, constantly encircling which was a steady stream of pilgrims, reciting their required seven decades of the Rosary and one Creed. Walking single file, all in the same in direction, with their beads held tautly between their hands, they resembled convicts on a chaingang, being led around in invisible shackles. A coffle of slaves, manacled to the drudgery of repentance by numbers.

A few feet away, there was an even stranger spectacle. Four women were congregated in a small circle at the shore, their raincoats tightly belted, headscarves knotted under their chins. They were discharging what's known as the "water's edge" stage of a station; now kneeling, now standing, all the time racking up more Our Fathers and Hail Marys.

When they were done, they each produced a handful of coins and tossed them into the Lough. There was a volley of violent splashes, especially from around the tufts of thick rushes in the shallows.

Intrigued, I made my way over. Hundreds of man and woman years of penitence had burnished the surface of the granite flags to a dangerous slipperiness. Timid waves splashed and gurgled against the rocks, like alternate bursts of applause and canned laughter.

On the lake bed lay a pirate's bounty of hard cash. There must have been a couple of hundred quid down there, in 20p's, 50p's, £1 coins and coppers. Beneath the pier from which the mainland boat leaves, there was a similar fortune. Station Island pilgrims float more currency than the combined finance ministries of the ERM member states.

"It's for good luck," I overheard one of the Vigil Aunties explain the next day, her feet two webs of green, blue and red veins, twin maps of the London underground. "Whatever you throw in will come back to you tenfold. I never toss in anything less than ten pounds every time I come here, and I haven't been poor a day in my life."

At around 8pm, I decided to check out the 'restaurant'. Every pilgrim is entitled to one Lough Derg meal on each of the three fast days on Station Island. These are served in a large, boisterous dining room staffed by teams of teenagers from the greater Pettigo area, among whom there is at least one world class ironist. There was a sign inside the door which read: Please Do Not Reserve Seats!

To put it mildly, I was amazed to discover that there was a choice of fare. You could have oatmeal slabs, aka 'biscuits' (that wacky ironist again, I bet), and/or slices of dry toast. Pilgrims were allowed, even encouraged, to eat plenty of both. The only drawback was that the oatmeal slabs looked and tasted like hunks of pavement, and the slices of dry toast looked and tasted like slices of dry toast.

Nevertheless, the point is that we were supposed to be fasting here.

What sort of pathetic mollycoddling was this? An actual menu with *options*. Yes, I know that both options were crap, but this is hardly the spirit that made Saint Patrick's Purgatory great, and haunted the imagination of Dante, is it?

According to Lough Derg's own literature, the Station Island pilgrimage fast used to go on for 15 days at a time back in the 1300s, relieved only by a *single mouthful* of bread and water each day.

If God is eternal and unchanging, why do we now expect Him to be placated by Johnny and Jenny Come Latelys with their poxy, little, half-arsed three-day fasts when He has already encountered generations of staunch penitents who were prepared to do the full monty?

Thankfully, at least a semblance of decency prevailed, and there was only one drink on offer in the dining room. Scalding hot, black coffee. As much as you could slurp. Without scorching your heart to a cinder, that is.

Milk was a no no, but, again, bizarrely, you could have all the sugar you fancied. Some pilgrims took this as a licence to indulge themselves. I spotted several women sprinkling sugar on their so-called 'dry' toast. One lady even went so far as to sprinkle sugar *and* oatmeal crumbs on her so-called 'dry' toast.

Sickened by such hedonism, I stormed out and returned to the penitential beds. Cooking smells soon began to tug at my attention. The aromas were heavy with spice, gastronomic ingenuity and flavour, so they certainly weren't emanating from the pilgrims' dining room. Sniffing on the air like an avid police hound on its first day at work, I traced the scintillating scent to its source, the priests' residence.

A blunt sign blared 'PRIVATE PROPERTY' from the gate, so intimate investigation was impossible. While my delirious, unfed brain was too weak to discern the identity of individual dishes, it was clear that the chieftains were having some sort of gourmet blow-out behind the ramparts of their fortress.

It must have been one of their feast days. Perhaps they were celebrating the harvest of some of those liquid assets from the bottom of the lake.

It is not only the ruling junta that dines well off the penitents who shrive themselves on Station Island. Winged parasites also get to stuff themselves at our expense.

Saint Patrick's Purgatory is infested with an infinitude of gluttonous, relentless and vicious insects. Cockroaches, wasps, bees, black flies, horseflies, bluebottles: all the bigwigs of the Irish bug world are so ubiquitous here that they constitute the very weather.

Spiders and moths fall from the sky like flurries of sleet. The glinting dew crunches beneath your soles in a massacre of gnats and daddy long legs. Those sooty clouds on the horizon? Enormous swarms of midges.

Midges be beside me. Midges be before me. Midges on my right hand. Midges on my left hand. Turn a corner, and they're all over your head like an itchy balaclava. You have to snort them out of your nose, stutter them off your tongue, pull faces to get them out of your eyes. You can almost hear their larvae and eggs popping in the seams of your clothes.

Judging by the novelty and diversity of the stabs, scratches and scars on show among those incarcerated on the Derg, there are unfamiliar plagues of creepy-crawlies around too. Holiday-makers, probably. Fat, noisy, back-packing foreigners who must fly here on package tours for pilgrim-tasting weekends.

I am obviously particularly delicious. Within hours, my ankles and lower legs were pocked like teabags with munches and bites. It was as if my arrival had been monitored by a reconnaissance party of bloodsuckers who had mis-heard my first name as *Lean* and my surname as *Buffet*.

Inevitably, cans of bug repellent spray are the most popular fashion accessory at Lough Derg. By the end of a second day of dousing ourselves with this liquid smog, most of us reeked like cubes of bathroom air-freshener.

The fragrance is complemented by the island's indigenous birdsong: a faint but persistent *tsch tsch tsch*, the gentle rattling of a snare drum. It's the sound of people making their stations in creaky plastic raingear. Everywhere you look, they're sloshing about, these hot water bottles with legs.

The link between Station Island and the historical Saint Patrick seems

236

tenuous at best. What we do know is that the focal point of the original 12th and 13th century pilgrimage vigils was a cave or 'purgatory'; a three feet wide, nine feet long burrow, high enough for an adult to kneel but not to stand upright.

This cave remained in use until 1780 when it was sealed over for fear of the danger it posed to the increasing number of pilgrims who wished to make the vigil.

The six penitential beds which today jut out of the earth like giant wisdom teeth have an even more ancient origin. They are the reconstructed remains of beehive monastic cells, or oratories, which date back to the island's Celtic monastic period in the first century AD. The tradition of making stations on the beds is said to be well over half a millennium old.

At each bed, the pilgrims repeat their mantra of Our Fathers, Hail Marys and Creeds while walking three times around the outside, then kneeling at the entrance, then walking around the inside and then kneeling at the metal cross in the centre.

On average, there's maybe 20 individuals on every bed at any given moment, a clumsy snarl-up of humanity stumbling, bumbling, lurching and toppling all over itself. Just writing about it makes me light-headed.

The distinction between kneeling and standing soon becomes misty. The full shin-span required for even a single comprehensive genuflection is a luxury unavailable in this mosh-pit. Most people therefore complete the entire circuit in a tottery crouch, a posture which I believe may not have full canonical validity. The Church has always invited its flock to kneel and pray; not to hunch over, stagger about, teeter and pray.

The less than nimble penitents end up semi-prostrate, supporting themselves with hands, knees, elbows, shoulders and by the skin of their teeth. It's the kind of unpleasant, neck-wrenching position most commonly associated with the more adventurous end of the oral sex spectrum.

Imagine the havoc that would ensue in an old folks home if the pensioners decided to play Twister. Okay, now imagine that they each downed an entire bottle of Harvey's Bristol Cream before the game began. That gives you a flavour of what's going on here.

The holy hour preparing us for our night vigil was a hoot. The lights in the basilica were dimmed and a paschal candle was lit while a New Age tape plink-plinked in the background. "Become aware of the flickering light," oozed the slick celebrant, in a fruity parody of a mesmerising voice.

Better still was the homily. We were treated to a sermon about the evils of wanking. At first, I thought it was too good to be true. We were not going to be asked to sit here in the dark and listen to a Bible-bashing discourse on wire-pulling, were we? Yep.

Like a pier-end conjuror trying vainly to bedazzle his audience with a tired old three card trick, the priest began by pretending he was picking a trio of sins at random to illustrate the problems with which we may have come to Lough Derg to wrestle. "It could be aggression," he mused. "Alcoholism. Or *(meaningful pause to suggest spontaneity)* masturbation!"

Here was a celibate man, who leads a celibate life in the company of at least a half dozen other celibate men, and *he* was lecturing *us* about the evils of pumping your gas at the self-service island. The term I'm searching for, I believe, is Ha! Ha! Ha!

The standard of sermons in general on Saint Patrick's Purgatory was abysmal. None failed to sink to the occasion. Here was a captive audience of hundreds, the majority undergoing the most concentrated religious experience of their lives, and the best the preachers could manage were bland banalities expressed with the most ludicrous grandiloquence.

Among the more folksy dissertations, there were a couple of gems. There was the young Enniskillen cleric who told us about Spot, his family's dog. Every evening when Dad was having dinner, he would sling the rind of his rasher under the table and laugh as the voracious Spot dived to catch and devour it. "I often wish that I was as hungry for God as Spot is for scraps," announced the priest, with a flourish of oratorical pride.

The same guy, malevolently warming to his culinary theme while his congregation salivated to death in the pews, later told us about how much he hates picky eaters, especially those pernickety fusspots who push their vegetables to one side. "Some of us do that with the word of God," he boom boomed. "We should all clean our plates."

When Monsignor Dick Mohan took to the stage for the 6.30am masses, there was no such messing about. He got straight down to business, informing us that recent refurbishments on the island had cost £900,000. Financial contributions from pilgrims were essential if Saint Patrick's Purgatory was to survive into the next century. Those of us who had benefited from its rites had a responsibility, a duty, to give generously.

Then, came the sweetener, the swab after the jab. "But remember," he affirmed, "giving money is an act of faith, a prayer in its own way." Donors and benefactors would be remembered at Lough Derg masses, *ad infinitum*.

The day after the vigil is dubbed a rest day. Pilgrims have only one station to make on the penitential beds during this period. The remainder of the time is our own, apart from the Renewal of Baptismal Promises at noon, the Way of the Cross at 3pm, and evening mass at 6.20pm.

There are a lot of hours to be passed before we finally get to sleep at 10pm. Our instructions are to use the day for contemplation, and, at all costs, to avoid lying down.

In the reading room, women sit around with inspirational texts by Danielle Steel and Joanna Trollope but barely get beyond a page before nodding off. Heads droop slowly, and then jerk back up a moment later. In the smokers' shelter, a quintet of auld fellas puff on pipes and experiment with new and exciting ways to use the syllable 'Ah'.

Me, I resumed my time computations, my word games and my reflection on the big philosophical dilemmas of out time: When Ronan Collins is doing the Lotto draw on TV, why *does* he always remind viewers to look out for their chosen numbers? Whose bloody numbers does he think people are looking out for?

At 2pm, the next shipment of pilgrims was delivered, 195 in total (it beats counting sheep). Today's flock look much like yesterday's. There's the bottle blonde mother-and-daughter double acts, the congenital bachelors in black overcoats, the elderly pietists of both sexes, the Tyrone people. Oh, and, eh, Frank McNamara.

Yes, it's him, *the* Frank McNamara, RTE's most revered musical maestro, Gaybo's favourite tinkler of the ivories, Mr. Theresa Lowe. Frank is, apparently, a regular devotee of the Derg and has been known to do it twice in the one year.

He certainly attacked the penitential beds with the assurance of a virtuoso, accomplishing his stations *con brio*. For the record, Frank McNamara's feet are large, sallow and shapely. He has long, tapered, pianist's toes.

Once again, a good fifth of the pilgrim contingent were what could be technically termed young people; poorly-groomed, bespectacled students with too much hair, for the most part. There is a tradition among Ulster Catholics, on both sides of the border, that those who have sat important examinations should round off their summer with a sojourn on Lough Derg, bartering penance for high marks.

There are two points to be made about this practice. If it works, all students who intercede for good results on Station Island should be automatically disqualified and forced to re-sit. The Ministers for Education in both the U.K. and Ireland should resign and admit that they have been administering corrupt, fraudulent and profoundly unfair examination systems. The possibility of criminal charges should also be investigated.

Lough Derg is a very literal pilgrimage. We are told that every welt and weal endured will pay tangible dividends. This can only mean that those who do the pilgrimage in mediation for exam success will earn an advantage; an advantage, by definition, denied to those who do not. There's a charming, old-fashioned word for this: *cheating*.

If, however, Saint Patrick's Purgatory is an elaborate sham then scholars gullible enough to believe that such a palaver will enhance their results cannot have done very well in the first place.

Ponder the venality though of an operation that so grossly exploits the credulity of naive teenage dolts. The poor saps are going to fail anyway. Now, they'll have raw feet as well as bruised egos when they go to enquire about their repeats.

Unlike the lily-livered dry toast/oatmeal slabs compromise, this is a meal that you cannot eat both ways.

Doing Lough Derg is like being on a three-day booze binge, but without the booze. When it's all over, you feel shattered, physically unwell, intellectually impaired and extremely regretful. There is guilt about the time squandered and the work in arrears. You are sure of nothing but your determination that you will never do it again.

And yet, there are Saint Patrick's Purgatory junkies. On the island, they bitch and whinge about the insanity of it all – but they know that they'll back again next year, or next week in the aforementioned case of one Vigil Auntie. These people cannot understand why everybody else doesn't love the Derg the way they do.

During breaks in the night vigil, I got talking to a pretty and loquacious thirtysomething nurse with dainty but sturdy feet whom we will call 'Martha'. A native of Sligo, Martha currently works in a Dublin hospital. This was her 11th stint on Station Island. The previous ten times were 'petitions', this latest was in 'thanksgiving'.

Martha was good company, lively and intelligent. Surprised to find a *Hot Press* scribe interested in writing about Lough Derg, she wondered what I made of the place.

"It's an adventure playground for fucking maniacs," I opined.

"Oh, you're gas," she laughed, wiping tears of mirth off the bridge of her nose.

"I'm serious," I insisted. "In the States, this place would be run by the Michigan Militia."

"You're *gas,* you really are," she persevered, clamping my arm with her hand as if she were groping for a valve that might terminate the gaseous flow.

No matter how much malign abuse I rained down on Station Island and all who sail in her, Martha refused to accept that I wasn't joking. She couldn't conceive of anyone feeling the kind of antipathy I was exhibiting towards the place. She was convinced that, if I would only follow the prayers more reverently, I'd see the value of it.

'Jack' adopted a similar attitude. He was an alcoholic from Omagh, in his late 30s. Lough Derg is a haven for the whiskey-wounded and the beer-ruptured. Jack had been here five times before. On this occasion, he had just discharged himself from a drying-out clinic in Belfast.

"I love it here," he told me. "It's awful hard, but I never think of drink when I'm here. The minute I get back home, I know I'm going to start drinking again. I'll be back next year."

241

Bare feet don't get as filthy as you might expect. They become almost marbled, resistant to dirt and mud. After a while, you simply develop a thin border of black grime around the perimeter of your soles, like a felt-tipped margin.

The Foot Baths therefore are more for relief than cleansing. While preparing to take my eagerly awaited leave of the island, I made a visit to the male baths, a large damp room where big porcelain tubs with tarnished brass taps stood on a discoloured lino floor.

The room was full of men. Most of them were from Donegal and seemed to know each other of old. It was early August, not too long after the Drumcree siege, and the Unionist marching season soon became the topic of general conversation.

"It's fierce triumphalist all the same, those lads marching up and down in front of your house," said a man in a blue woollen cardigan, lathering his shins with a bar of soap the size and colour of luggage.

"Shhh," quipped his friend. "There could be Protestants in here."

Everybody laughed. "Ah, they're a stupid crowd of eejits," asserted a voice from the corner.

"Now you're talking," agreed another. "With their silly bowler hats and their daft sashes. Isn't it about time they grew up?"

"It's bigotry," professed the man in the cardigan. "Their religion has them like that, off their rockers."

With that, he stood erect and stretched, having rolled up his trouser legs to identical folds beneath his knees. He doubled over his towel and briskly wrapped it in a Londis shopping bag. He was in a hurry.

There was one more station to do on the penitential beds before the boat came to take us back to the mainland.

THE MANIC STREET PREACHER

Though she is familiar to Dubliners as the eccentric
old lady in the middle of O'Connell Street, armed with
crucifixes and quoting scripture, few people know the
true, sad story behind Mary Margaret Doyle Dunne's
religious mission.

Using only a smidgen of poetic latitude,
it would be possible to persuade a credulous tourist that she is the country's chief power plant: a human windmill and solar generator lighting up
the national grid from her station smack-bang in the centre of the capital
city's principal thoroughfare.

It is an appealing idea. Every wave of her arms producing enough
energy to illuminate a small town. Each hop, skip and jump running its

243

own industrial estate. And the little flick of the wrist? That keeps the neon glowing in her personal talisman which shines down like a beacon upon her workplace: MCDOWELL'S, THE HAPPY RING HOUSE.

O'Connell Street after 6pm on a January evening is one of the most desolate boneyards on the planet. Respectable society has washed its hands of the district and relinquished tenure to the waifs and strays until sunrise. It's as dark as the black hole of Mother Teresa of Calcutta.

Sequins of frost wink on the pavements. Empty Tayto packets shudder in the gutters. Shattered glass crunches under foot. An icy wind blows off the Liffey, and takes piercing short cuts through the flesh of anyone sufficiently foolhardy to be still in the vicinity.

Impervious to it all is Mary Margaret Doyle Dunne, Ireland's most distinguished middle-of-the-road Catholic. Since 1pm today, she has patrolled her beat on the pedestrian pathway which bisects this boulevard of broken bottles, at the point where, during daylight, thousands of shoppers per hour cross between Henry Street and North Earl Street. Here, she prays, preaches and prances on a moral plinth she has stubbornly claimed for herself in the heart of Dublin's greasy till.

For the past 18 years, her presence at this spot six days a week has transformed an unremarkable promenade into a sacred precinct. One traffic island under God.

"I do not feel the cold and I never get tired," announces Mary Margaret. "I am a daily communicant. I have the body and blood of Christ in me. Only for that, I don't know where I'd be. God feeds me so I can speak up for the truth. God gives me all the heat and vitality I need. I come here to Daniel O'Connell Street every day to get the message across to people, the message of Almighty God and the Holy Trinity. I enjoy it. I quote scripture and I bring out salient points. I do actions with it so that the young people can understand it more.

"I ask people questions when they come up to me. I ask people if they say The Creed, and do they know who said that prayer first. People say The Creed but they do not know where it comes from. I ask them if they listen to the scripture at mass every day. They're supposed to be intelligent people but they haven't been taught their catechism properly. I tell them to go away and read their scripture and come back and let me know who said what and why.

"Almost everybody passes through Daniel O'Connell Street at some point. It is the best platform in the country for me to address the Roman Catholic laity. That is why God has lead me here to spread His message."

Mary Margaret Doyle Dunne will be 68 next April. Her ankles are swollen like bulging gunny sacks but, even in court shoes, she can still heel-to-heel and toe-to-toe with the best of them. An Irish dancing champion in her childhood, she moves with the kind of easy grace and elegance for which Michael Flatley would gladly trade his favourite set of Braun Independent cordless styling tongs.

As well as the choreographed re-enactments of scripture, Mary Margaret writes and performs her own original hymns while on O'Connell Street, usually *as Gaeilge*. "I sing songs in Irish which I compose myself as I go along," she avers. "I like to emphasise the Irish language and a return to the Irish alphabet, the pure Irish alphabet." If you get real close, you can sometimes hear her wish passers-by "sláinte, sláinte," or urge them to join her in a "bualadh bós."

She is an instantly recognisable Dublin landmark. A couple of years ago, Bord Fáilte even featured a photograph of her in one of their international brochures. No more than any other cultural icon therefore, Mary Margaret attends to her physical appearance with assiduous thoroughness.

She never ventures out without a complete fanfare of make-up and lipstick. Her smart overcoats (usually either green or red) are always neatly accessorised with expensive-looking scarves, shawls and mufflers. Then, there's the tools of her trade: the rosaries entwined like ropes of ivy around the fingers of both gloved hands, the exotic scapulars and, last but not least, the rainforest of wooden crucifixes which sprout from every pocket and pleat.

The effect is crowned with her distinctive French Roll of pale golden hair which radiates a curious greenish sheen under the fluorescent shopfronts and street lamps. Mary Margaret is a plutonium, rather than platinum, blonde.

Beneath her coat, she carries what seems at first glance to be a small hubcap. It's actually an armour-clad shield made up of holy medals – the heavy, metallic, old-fashioned kind. As with her preferred brand of faith, Mary Margaret requires her symbols of religious devotion to be austere and difficult to carry. She has no time for the gimcrack charms of store-bought, contemporary Catholicism.

Like a caged bird, Mary Margaret never ventures far from her perch. Her territory extends only a few feet either side of the Latimer Florists' kiosk which has been located at the same site on O'Connell Street since the days of Queen Victoria. Ann Stanley, the current proprietor, is a third-generation descendant of the woman who set up the original stall.

"We're at the foot of where Nelson's Pillar used to be, and we used to be called the Pillar Stall," explains Ann Stanley. "Two men killed them-selves by jumping off the Pillar. One fell on top of my grandmother's stall, the second one fell on top of my mother's."

Though they see and exchange pleasantries with her virtually every day, the flowersellers say they know almost nothing about Mary Margaret and her unusual vocation. "She keeps herself to herself," maintains Marian Kavanagh, wrapping a bunch of white carnations. "Some days she talks sensible enough but other days it's very hard to understand what she's talking about. She rambles.

"She seems like a very nice woman. She's always very well-dressed and polite. She just turns up around lunchtime, leaves her shopping bag behind the stall for safe-keeping and then starts dancing and singing around the place."

It isn't always as simple as that, however. Over the years, Mary Margaret has become a prime target for torment and persecution, invari-ably inflicted upon her with medieval relish.

At first, the big problem was theft. "I used to have a lovely framed photograph of myself with Pope Paul VI, taken at a private audience in the Vatican," she recalls. "I would set it up on the street for everybody to see. One day, a man came along and said, 'This is very nice' and just picked it up and walked away with it. My daughter painted a beautiful big picture of Matt Talbot for me, and that was stolen too."

More recently, familiarity with Mary Margaret has bred a much uglier species of contempt. Liquid lunchers with greying hair and flushed faces regularly halt their taxis to scream obscenities at her. Broad-hipped, head-scarfed women scold and upbraid her from a safe distance and then scurry away amid a blizzard of expletives and vituperative gestures. Parents cackle, and goad their children into sneering and calling her names.

What with the wind, the passing buses and the incessant cop sirens, Mary Margaret often doesn't hear the abuse or even notice that she's being abused. She likes to lose herself in her acts of worship, totally aloof from the glare, clutter and nagging pettiness of her surroundings. Nevertheless, she has developed a honed instinct for scenting serious trouble in the air.

Like a wildebeest sensing the imminence of rain, she intuitively knows when to retreat and when to stand firm. A flicker of baleful eye-contact might be the sole prologue to an eruption of random violence, but any kind of warning is better than none

"If I get someone who's inclined to be aggressive, I'm usually able to communicate with them," she asserts confidently. "If you cannot communicate with them then you might be attacked. Christ communicated. I say to them, 'Look, Christ is not violent. There is Hell and Heaven. If you want to be violent, you will end up in Hell'."

More than frequently, such entreaties fall on dumb ears. Kids are the worst. They slip beneath her radar and stage shock assaults of extreme viciousness. Teenage couples who spend entire afternoons on the banks of the Floosie In The Jacuzzi ravenously grazing on each others' faces can't go home happy unless they've tried, at least once, to blitz her with water bombs or beercan missiles. A swift kick to the back of her legs is another popular offensive.

Gobbed upon by punks, jeered by Goths, menaced once by a female suedehead with a broken milk bottle, Mary Margaret is exhaustively well-versed in the diverse guises favoured by our marvellous young people.

"She has a terrible time," attests Ann Stanley at the flower stall. "The younger kids seem to be the most spiteful. They shout awful things at her, really rude and disgusting things. Young mothers also treat her very badly. I've seen lots of them just standing there laughing and getting their kids to run up to her and insult her. They seem to think it's great fun."

And that's only the half of it. Mary Margaret has learned the hard way

247

to be very careful out there. O'Connell Street is crawling with all manner of religious nutjobs and weirdoes. You might expect that one of the few benefits that go with being a howling Jesus freak yourself is that you don't get pestered by other ranting, raving Godballs. No such luck.

In Mary Margaret's experience, the really dangerous crazies are the holy ones. "They come up and start quoting scripture at me," she scoffs contemptuously. "They think there's something they can tell *me* about scripture. One man even pulled the rosary from around my neck."

Mary Margaret speaks with a unique accent, a lock-jawed blend of *Clunturf poshese*, Dubbalin argot and Scandinavian inflection. She has a rich, deep, polished-bronze tone of voice. On her lips, the word 'Catholic', for instance, is a multi-syllabled mouthful which can be most approximately rendered as *Caw-aw-thaw-lick.*

During our various encounters, she made repeated reference to a priestly brotherhood which I heard as the 'Up Late Fathers'. I took this to be an obscure order which allows its membership to defer bedtime until way after midnight. It was only on painstakingly scrutinising my tape and notes that I realised she was talking about the Oblate Fathers.

Anyone who spends appreciable time in Mary Margaret's company cannot but be struck by the fact that she is a woman in considerable emotional pain. Her worldview is coloured entirely by her Catholic devotion and her sense of grievance at the catastrophes which have befallen her. The agony and the ecstasy.

Mary Margaret's life has undoubtedly been warped by great tragedy. Between cavities in the bricklike babble, certain clear facts emerge, that can be related here:

She was born Mary Margaret Doyle in April 1928, and was raised in Bagnallstown, County Carlow. In the late '50s/early '60s, she had her own hairdressing business in Dublin. She married a man called Dunne, an engineer with the Department of Posts & Telegraphs. They had six children, two daughters and four sons. In 1968, the family moved to Geneva, in Switzerland, where her husband was engaged in research work for the P&T.

"We were four years in Geneva, Switzerland," elaborates Mary Margaret. "When I went to Switzerland, I became secretary of the Catholic Women's Club whose aim was to promote fellowship with God and the Holy Trinity. This was 1968, the year after Queen Elizabeth signed the abortion bill in England. I went to the coffee mornings in Geneva, and I asked a question about why they were taking Protestant books into the Catholic library. The American president asked me to become Secretary of the club. Then, I began to realise that they were not upholding womanhood, especially Mary's place in the scriptures, as the Mother of God who upheld marriage. I began to ask more questions about my faith and to look more deeply into things.

"While I was in Switzerland, the then Pope, Pope Paul VI, gave me three blessings: one at the United Nations when he came to address the International Labour Organisation, one at a mass overlooking Lake Geneva, and the third in his Vatican palace when I had a private audience with him during Christian Unity week in 1972. I asked him to promote devotion to Mary because Mary was the Queen of Ireland and I could see her position was under threat."

Returning to Dublin in 1972, Mary Margaret joined the ranks of the Catholic stormtroopers who were up in arms about what they saw as the rising tide of Godless liberalism. She became an especially ardent crusader in the battle against the introduction of contraception. "When I came back to Ireland, I found that a lot of girls were unmarried, at least that's what they were telling us. I spoke out very strongly against contraception. I then began to examine why the young men did not know scripture. It's in the Bible that a man must take care of his wife. Who's teaching scripture? This was the big question."

Meanwhile, her husband was embarking on similar religious explorations. "He began to ask questions like how could God have a mother?" professes Mary Margaret. "He did theology. He realised that the true Catholic teaching had not been given to us. Then, my husband, a post office engineer, started to investigate telecommunications and found that they were not upholding true Christian communication values. He also began to examine the educational system, for his boys in particular. The Holy Spirit teachings of Saint Patrick who brought the Mother of God to

Ireland were not being taught in the schools. He stopped the children going to school."

At this point, the clarity of the narrative begins to diminish sharply. Mary Margaret says her husband's refusal to allow their children to attend school attracted the attentions of the law, and that her three youngest boys "were taken away by social workers advocating contraception, divorce and abortion information, and put into a Protestant school." She further alleges that both she and her husband were then immediately committed to Saint Brendan's Mental Hospital. "The Eastern Heath Board said there was something wrong with my husband and that we were both mad," she seethes, her eyes glassy with fury. "Our children were made wards of court. I wanted to go to the courts but they would not let me go down to the courts from Brendan's. Eventually, they let me go but not my husband."

According to a spokesperson for The Eastern Health Board, the broad strokes of Mary Margaret's story are substantially correct but, while they inevitably refuse to go into the details of a specific case, they stoutly maintain that proper and *fully-justified* procedures were followed in terms of their intervention.

"The committal procedure is very stringent," insists Maureen Browne, media relations officer with the EHB. "You wouldn't be committed to a hospital for not sending your children to school. That's just not one of the criteria for committal to hospital. Children in these cases are put into residential care, and only if there is very good reason. If the Health Board had taken a child who was a Catholic by upbringing into residential care, it certainly wouldn't go and look for a Protestant school for that child. There aren't even that many Protestant schools in the country.

"As a client of ours, she is deserving of confidentiality. If this unfortunate woman was committed to hospital for a psychiatric illness, and if her children were taken off her for a particular reason, she is still entitled to that protection 20 years down the road, whether she wants it or not."

In 1978, Mary Margaret's husband died. Shortly before his death, he was released from Saint Brendan's, his body, according to Mary Margaret, "reduced to a frail skeleton."

It is now an accepted fact that, during this era for the most part, Saint Brendan's was indeed a grim and miserable asylum where little of genuine therapeutic value was done for the patients. Apart from everything else, Mary Margaret's experience of this institution, both at first hand and through her husband, has left her with a burning hatred of the authorities in general and of psychiatric hospitals in particular.

"The law destroyed everything," she exclaims plaintively. "My uncle was an Oblate Father who married me on the feast of the Holy Spirit in the Oblate Church of Mary Immaculate, Inchicore. I had another relation an Oblate beside him on the altar and a parish priest beside him. What did the State do? They trampled on my Catholic marriage, put my three boys into Protestant schools, and reduced my husband to five stone weight, almost dead, before they handed him back to me after five years.

"They're talking about quick deaths in the North of Ireland. My husband got a slow death. He was reduced to bones. So, until all the Catholics in this country say it was wrong, I'll be out on Daniel O'Connell Street exposing the truth. Until the Catholics apologise for what they have done to my Catholic marriage and until I see the Holy Father's teaching of 2,000 years implemented, I will be out there."

One would expect that the Catholic establishment would be very proud of Mary Margaret and her campaign to bring Christ's scriptural message to the world and its estranged wife. Far from it, however. Her only allies have come from the extreme fringes of the Irish Christian fellowship.

After her husband's demise in 1978, Mary Margaret launched a frantic offensive of public protests, and letter-writing to TDs, the President, the newspapers, anyone she could think of. "I stood outside the General Post Office one Christmas Day with my six children to show my utter disgust at telecommunications for not speaking up for my Catholic rights," she recounts. "I picketed Saint Brendan's but they would not listen to me. Everybody just dismissed me and shrugged off what I was saying. Then, this gentleman called Gerard O'Mahony saw one of my letters in the papers and contacted me. He got me to speak up for the faith at the General Post Office. The police arrested me and accused me of a breach of the peace. But, at the court, they were unable to say that I had used threatening, abusive or insulting language, because I had not. The judge threw out the case. He did not even say, 'This is wrong what you've done, Mrs. Dunne'.

"I started going to the centre of Daniel O'Connell Street. Mr. O'Mahony brought a statue of the immaculate conception to Daniel O'Connell Street, and I would go there every day upholding that. He was taken away by the guards but I'm still there. He brought his car and they said he could not have his car in the middle of the island yet they allow motorcycles and everything to be parked there now. I have been on Daniel O'Connell Street almost every day since 1978."

Gerard O'Mahony, whom Mary Margaret cites as such a major champion and supporter, is a solicitor by profession and director of the Christian Community Centre by inclination. His quest is to "promote the power of prayer harnessed to Christian action." He's also a sometime pirate broadcaster and man-who-says-the-Rosary-on-the-street-quite-a-lot.

I spoke to Mr. O'Mahony, but it wasn't easy. Before he would deign to answer any questions, I first had to endure a rigorous interrogation about whether or not I was "working to develop and advance the law of God and the broad benefit of Christian ideals."

O'Mahony's memories of life on the pedestrian island with Mary Margaret are not entirely fond. "We had a white Sicilian marble statue of Our Lady on O'Connell Street from May '78 until August '83," he says. "The statue was very much admired by artists and those with artistic ideas from all around the world. While it was there, we frequently had lunchtime Rosaries and played songs of praise, by the likes of John McCormack, on tape and amplification. Mary Margaret would frequently come along and her contribution was nil.

"It wasn't prayerful. Whatever illness she had at that stage, and probably still has, was affecting her. To try and restrain her from interrupting loudly would take three or four able men."

Eventually, O'Mahony abandoned his *al fresco* basilica on O'Connell Street altogether. He was defeated not by Mary Margaret but by the infinitely more sinister figure of Garret FitzGerald.

"When Garret FitzGerald came along as Taoiseach, he didn't like the

Rosary being said on O'Connell Street," testifies Gerard O'Mahony. "It was giving a bad impression to people up North that he wanted to ingratiate himself with. That's what I feel. We felt that he thought it was not nice to see people praying so close to the Bord Fáilte information kiosk on O'Connell Street. Then came his abortion referendum. We announced that we would have a novena of prayer for the successful outcome of that referendum about 14 days before the vote. The following morning, our temporary shelter was gone. The following week, the statue was gone, taken away, we understand, by Dublin Corporation although they deny it."

Mary Margaret is a busy woman. She lives in Kill-o-The Grange, Dun Laoghaire, with two of her sons. Her morning begins with pen and paper. Every week, she hand-writes about a dozen tracts, outlining her religious beliefs, which she photocopies in Saint Paul's Catholic Book Club, in Clonkeen Crescent, Dun Laoghaire. Some of these are mailed to politicians and journalists. Most are distributed to what she calls "the Irish people" on O'Connell Street.

Then, it's off to mass, usually at either her local Holy Family Church, or the Star Of The Sea Church in Sandymount. It would be fair to say that she takes an *active* participation in the celebration of the Eucharist.

"At mass, I often confront the priests," she asserts defiantly. "When I feel that things they are saying are wrong, I'll stand up in the church and speak. I never interrupt the consecration or the main part of the mass. But when the priest has finished his scripture reading, I might indicate something. If he hadn't put the right interpretation on something, I would inform him of this and say so.

"On the altar recently, they had this literature on Christian Unity in which there was a lot of stuff about human communities. Saint Paul said, 'You cannot look at a child from a human viewpoint anymore'. When the child is baptised, he's divine. So, I said to the priest, 'What are you talking about human communities for?'. That's not the true message of the scriptures. We are divine after our baptism. Women are holy as well as men."

Mary Margaret is not impressed by the quality of education and training given to modern day priests. "I feel that they have to go back to scripture. They have to start teaching The Creed properly. They also have to teach the place of woman. In other words, why did they allow what happened to me happen in my parish? I was taken away to a mental home by social workers that were anti-Catholic. Why did the priests allow it? They had nothing to say. I do blame the priests. Why did they not convert the guards in my parish to the right way of thinking? They seem to be lacking in perception."

Mary Margaret's sole source of income is a pension she receives from her late husband's former employers. She appears to live comfortably, taking taxis everywhere for instance. However, she is also a generous woman, and is sometimes to be seen taking down-and-outs into cafés for cups of tea and sandwiches.

A Bewley's regular, she and I agreed to meet in their Westmoreland Street branch one morning. Arriving early, I had chosen an isolated table near the back where I'd hoped we would be inconspicuous, even if she decided to vault into an impromptu song and dance adaptation of the stations of the cross, or somesuch. It was a futile manoeuvre. As I was slowly coming to realise, Mary Margaret will not be stage-managed.

Barrelling into the café, she noisily summons me over to the serving counter and brusquely insists that I hold her shopping bags and obtain cutlery while she buys her breakfast: a pot of lemon tea, two slices of toast and some butter. "I will only drink tea made from real tea leaves," she declares. "I don't approve of those bags at all. They're just rubbish. And I only eat real Irish creamery butter. *Not* that other stuff – it's just not up to Catholic standards."

Cashier paid, she leads the way to an already occupied booth with about as much spare room as a Japanese commuter train at rush hour. We squeeze in, shopping bags first, forcing one customer to get up and leave in a paroxysm of pique. Our remaining companion, a short yet portly young woman, attempts to reclaim some lost territory by extending to full span her arms and her Patricia Cornwell hardback, but to little avail.

Slathering a triangle of toast with a pat of tasty Cathospread, Mary Margaret gets straight down to business.

"We are a country with 95% Catholic people but we are being denied the power of our faith," she maintains. "The government has sanctioned contraception, divorce and abortion information. Mary Robinson has signed for these things. The government are not educating people about their scripture. This is why the country is in the state it's in. There are no Catholic standards anymore.

"There are no Catholic standards in banking. A good economy begins with stability of the family. They have not brought about stability of the family with their contraception, divorce and abortion information. The Catholic family is under attack. The EEC should uphold the true scripture. All these high interest rates! Children leaving the educational system unable to go right into work. That's not Catholic standards."

"What exactly *are* Catholic standards?" I enquire.

"Good linen tablecloths, and serviettes," she replies emphatically. "We've the best agricultural land, the best fishing waters, the best tourist industry, the best forestry and the highest calling is the priesthood. So, why are we not all employed? Because there's no proper catering standards. There's no-one preparing food properly anymore. There's no proper cloths on the tables or linen serviettes or linen cloths. All that would promote employment.

"You go into these catering places nowadays and they're all dark. The same with public houses. You should not have to go into public houses for a meal. It's a bad atmosphere for children. We should have bright restaurants, proper standards. People should be taught to cook and prepare food properly instead of handing us out turkey vol-au-vents with only a tiny bit of turkey in the middle of them, and you're paying about seven pounds for that in a hotel. Proper lamb chops, steak – this is what my mother used to feed me on when I was in Bagnallstown.

"Food is not what it should be. It's not Irish Catholic standards. Go down to Clery's, or any of them. It's not Irish catering anymore. We used to have good restaurants before we joined the EEC. Now, they're all fast food. That's not upholding our Catholic standards."

Mary Margaret has written lengthy letters on this theme, to the Irish Department of Agriculture and to the bureaucrats in Brussels. Neither body has chosen to respond. Undaunted, she believes that only by becoming a politician herself will she be able to stimulate genuine action.

In the 1992 General Election, Mary Margaret stood as an independent candidate in the constituency of Dublin North-Central (she gave her address and place of work to the electoral registrar as "Dublin's inner city"). She insists that she paid all of her election expenses out of her own purse. For her efforts, she received 143 first preference votes.

"It was my first time ever and I got no help from anyone," she protests. "I would like to stand again. I do believe that the people in Ireland must start using their intelligence. We were known as the island of saints and scholars. Now, we are the island of prisons, psychiatric hospitals and disability pensions. Christ said He came so that we might have life. It all stands on scripture. Mary Robinson does not stand on scripture. The Devil is the father of lies, destruction."

Our conversation is abruptly interrupted by the arrival of an interloper who we shall call 'Declan'. Like most peace-loving Christians who approach Mary Margaret, he is here to cause trouble.

Anoraked up to the chin, shoulders snowy with dandruff and lint, Declan's most striking sartorial statements are a slack noose of grey woollen scarf and a pair of glasses with huge, square lenses which magnify his eyes to billboard-size.

At a guess, he's somewhere in his late 20s but seems to wear his youth like it was an affliction. His wearily pious demeanour and slithery gait suggest that he longs to be swathed in the crepe of a saintly old age. Declan is a real Charlie Church, a veritable Vinny Veneration, with a zealous mission to inform others of the error of their ways. He has obviously clashed with Mary Margaret before.

"How's the hypocrite?" he taunts loudly over my shoulder. A tremor of aggression immediately passes between Mary Margaret and Declan. One can almost hear her internal gears mesh and grind as she prepares for battle.

"This is part of what I have to put up with," she tells me with obvious self-restraint. "I would call Declan 'Declan' but he calls me a hypocrite."

This comparative equanimity is soon undermined, however, as her normal pallor is blasted with a rush of puce. "Go away from me now, Declan," she chides. "You think I'm supposed to listen to you because you were in the Legion Of Mary at one time. I have a meeting with this gentleman from the press. I can't talk to you today."

Within a heartbeat, our corner of Bewley's Oriental Café is transformed into a Biblical temple of furious diatribe and bitter denunciation: Ye serpents! Ye vipers! Woe to you, scribes and Pharisees! Okay, they didn't use those precise words but the tone of virulence is stark and unmistakable.

"You don't practise what you preach," charges Declan bluntly. "You're up there preaching the gospel every day and yet you don't forgive your enemies."

"Who have I to forgive?" snaps Mary Margaret, craning her neck to face her accuser and promptly forgetting all about the gentleman from the press. "Who are my enemies?"

"The ones who broke up your marriage."

"Exactly!" bellows Mary Margaret thunderously, causing the Patricia Cornwell fan to hiccup with fright. "And God said don't break up marriage: 'What God has joined together, let no man pull asunder'. God said uphold marriage. Do you uphold marriage? You are a man, and you've sanctioned contraception, divorce and abortion information. You are a man. God said take care of your wife."

"I'm not married," counters Declan.

"I *am* married."

"No, you're not married."

"I am married."

"Your husband is dead,."

"I have six children."

"You *were* married."

"Yes! And who broke up my marriage, my Catholic marriage? The men, the government, broke up my Catholic marriage."

"Oh dear God" sighs Declan with mock exasperation. "Christ is all gentleness, you are far from gentle."

"Christ was not all gentleness," refutes Mary Margaret vehemently. "He took up the whips in the temple, and called people hypocrites, those who were not upholding marriage."

"You'll have no peace."

"I have wonderful peace, Declan."

"You don't impart it to others. You impart dissipation to others. You're gaining peace from me."

"And you're calling me a hypocrite," she laughs caustically, a laugh which seems to frighten children in the vicinity even more than her yells did.

"You're like a whitewashed tomb," proclaims Declan. "All clean on the outside and dead man's rottenness and dead man's bones on the inside."

The girl with the book gets up and scurries away, casting fearful glances over her shoulder.

"Go and do something with your life, Declan! Go and become a priest. I am speaking out for the Catholic faith."

"No, you're not," spits Declan derisively. He's leaning across the table now, his right thumb and forefinger joined to form a pointed spear of reproach. "Standing up at mass every morning and annoying the priest! You don't just stand up and cause havoc at mass. That's disobedience. The priests have a very tough job, you know. Tougher than you have."

"Then why aren't you obeying the priests?" storms Mary Margaret. "Because if you've sanctioned contraception, divorce and abortion information, you are not obeying the priests."

"Who says I've sanctioned those things?"

"All of your country has. So, go out and do something about it. I'm out in the middle of Daniel O'Connell Street every day. I've written my letters to the politicians."

"You're laughable. *(He laughs)* I'm laughing at you."

A waitress approaches and meekly asks Mary Margaret to keep her voice down.

"I won't be a bit quiet," shrieks Mary Margaret. "I'm exposing the truth to everyone. I won't stop until the men do their duty, and stop the prisons, the psychiatric hospitals and the disability pensions, the lot. Christ is all beauty, all knowledge, all wisdom. Go along and learn about Christ. He cured the sick, gave sight to the blind, made the lame walk, raised the dead. He didn't go along with all your nonsense and disability pensions."

"Women are to blame as well, you know," asserts Declan. "Behind every man, there's a woman."

Suddenly, a middle-aged man with tragically red hair and a stillborn moustache taps me on the shoulder, a swimming pool of saliva cascading down over his chin. "You shouldn't be talking to that woman, you know," he burbles through spittle bubbles. "She has a Protestant interpretation of scripture. She's annoying me."

"You should not be annoyed," shouts Mary Margaret, now losing interest in Declan. "I am Roman Catholic! I'm upholding the immaculate conception. Go and learn about scripture and you won't be annoyed. Go and learn about how it should be in Ireland."

Declan, however, will not be ignored. "You're psychotic," he barks. "You're not rooted in reality, Mary Margaret."

"You have a Protestant interpretation," adds the ginge.

"Our baptism proves that we are divine," trills Mary Margaret. "We are not rooted in humanism but divinity."

I make my excuses, and run like Hell.

In another age, Mary Margaret Doyle Dunne would be hailed as an important prophet and preacher. Fired by a devotion to scripture that has taken root in her psyche like a wild and uncontrollable vine, Mary Margaret believes that her mission has been predetermined by fate. She views her life in the Cinemascope of divine destiny. Every day, she is propelled to O'Connell Street by nothing less than the tide of history.

"I grew up in County Carlow, in Bagnallstown," states Mary Margaret. "My grandfather built two family homes. So why is there such bad housing in Catholic Ireland? My grandfather could have two family homes, with four bedrooms, over a hundred years ago? This is where history comes in. The Vatican II Council said that God speaks through history.

"Lord Bagnall was a great British leader who founded Bagnallstown. He was a great military leader but Hugh O'Neill defeated him at the Battle Of The Yellow Ford in Armagh. My mother's name was Brigid, after the 5th century saint. She was born in Kilkenny and I was baptised Mary in Kilkenny. At the 1641 confederation, in Kilkenny, Mary was made Queen of Ireland by Eoin O'Neill. We have divorce now and abortion information. Mary is not the Queen of contraception, divorce and abortion information. We are letting down the Confederation of Kilkenny.

"My mother's surname was Hogan. She was a descendant of High King Brian Boru. I lived in Clontarf for a while and Brian Boru defeated the Danes at Clontarf. She married into an English family called Doyle but they became more Irish than the Irish themselves. A Doyle built the first bridge over the Liffey, which is Daniel O'Connell bridge.

"My late husband was born in the Liberties in Dublin, and was born on the feast of Our Lady of Lourdes. He was a descendant of the Normans. They brought devotion to Saint Anne, the mother of Mary, to The Liberties where he was born. Therefore, he was upholding devotion to Saint Anne."

And what about Mary Margaret Doyle Dunne? How does she think history will look back on her life in 100 years time?

"That is up to Almighty God," she smiles. "He might let me live forever."

WHEN IN ROME

... do as the Oirish do. 5,000 Irish pilgrims descended on Vatican City for the Beatification of Edmund Ignatius Rice, founder of the Christian Brothers. When they got there, they organised a céilí.

It is not long after ten o'clock on the glorious morning of October 6th, in the year of grace nineteen hundred and ninety-six. I am sitting in Saint Peter's Square, Rome, among an estimated crowd of 60,000 pilgrims, 5,000 of whom are Irish, and 7,000 of whom are wearing the green polyester scarf that identifies them as members of the international Edmund Ignatius Rice family.

As high white clouds move in stately caravan across the domes of The Vatican, a banner featuring a likeness of the Kilkenny-born founder of the Christian Brothers is unveiled from an upper window of Saint Peter's Basilica, thus marking the moment of his Beatification.

Henceforth, he is Blessed, only one step away from being a saint. More than that though, Edmund Ignatius now joins Uncle Ben on that slim roll call of the most widely revered Rice men of all time . . .

At the centre of the gigantic altar on the steps of the Basilica sits 76-year-old Pope John Paul on his gilded throne. Through a colleague's binoculars, I can see that, though the mass is now in full swing, his eyes are closed tightly; whether he is in prayer, gripped by a stab of severe pain or merely enjoying a post-breakfast snooze, it is impossible to tell. His left hand is trembling uncontrollably. When he stands to approach his lectern, he moves with slow, painful, stiff deliberation.

The Holy Father is swathed from the shoulders down in glistening vestments of brilliant green, a lofty white mitre poised on his head. He resembles nothing so much as a can of ice-cold Heineken with a paper cup on its lid. As he turns to resume his seat, the can appears to wobble and teeter. I find this an unbearably moving spectacle. The ice-cold can of Heineken which I had tried to bring into the Square with me was confiscated by a security man and unceremoniously dropped into a plastic bin.

Attempting to regain my composure, I strive to concentrate on the ceremony. The Pope is having a furious spluttering and coughing fit. He sounds as if he's choking violently. Oh no, sorry, he's just speaking in Ukrainian. The distinction between this language and a furious spluttering and coughing fit is extremely subtle. The Ukrainian for the word 'Rome', for instance, is *Rzym*. The Ukrainian for 'everything' is *wszystkm*.

John Paul is endeavouring to get his frail tonsils around Ukrainian because Marcelina Darowska, a 19th century nun from Szulaki, in the Ukraine, is being Beatified this morning alongside Edmund Rice. Through her intercession, it is eventually hoped that the people of her country will one day be bestowed with more vowels.

The glossy, lavishly-produced souvenir missal for today's service comes not only with brief passages of Ukrainian and English, but also of Spanish and Polish, there being a Spanish sister (María Ana Mogas Fontcuberta) and 13 Polish martyrs (forget it!) also on the list of Beatees. But the body of the missal, like the mass itself, is in Italian.

In preparation for my trip to Rome, I had only managed to learn the Italian for a single expression, *to wit:* 'Take me home and I'll show you a good time' *(Portami a casa, e ti far ó vedere come divertirci)*. Unfortunately, it's a phrase which no longer occurs very often in the modern liturgy.

Nevertheless, as always with the monolingual when abroad, I refuse to allow my own ignorance dampen my innate optimism. Throughout the mass, I keep sneaking regular glances at the prayer book, in anticipation of the miraculous moment when I will suddenly, without realising it, acquire the ability to read the Italian bits.

The Beatification mass was concelebrated with the Pope by over 40 priests, monsignors and bishops. 150 others helped out as Ministers of the Eucharist, with dozens more chipping in on duties like the readings, leading the prayers of the faithful and generally mincing about beside the Pope.

Behind the scenes, there were obviously several highly-mobile, assault teams armed with flame-throwers, riot guns and heat-seeking rifles, under strict orders to 'mop up' any female that gets within 150 metres of the altar. What else could explain the virtual obliteration of all evidence from the official platform that there even exists another gender?

At either side of the Pontiff, there was amassed a veritable Gideon's Army of bishops (in rich purple) and cardinals (in bright red) lowing into their breviaries like herds of flamboyantly dressed cattle who use breviaries. In his scarlet bonnet and matching scarlet gown, Cardinal Daly looked positively beautiful. So too did the 21 Irish bishops present (Brendan Comiskey cried off at the last moment), some of them perhaps too beautiful. Rome is, after all, a notoriously dangerous city for the pert and the nubile. The stereotypical Roman Casanova is a grope-happy lech who won't take no, or indeed a swift kick in the apostolics, for an answer.

What if one of our Episcopal divines had been attacked on the street by an Italian stallion driven wild by such enchanting visions? Imagine the scandal. Imagine too the smug moralists who would inevitably say that it was the bishops' own fault. "All that silk, all that gaudy jewellery, all those come-and-get-me frills, all those lacy frocks," the finger-pointers would cruelly bleat. "They were just feckin' askin' for it, weren't they?"

Adding a touch of sombre black at the back were the Vatican officials, various Curia dignitaries and the papal nuncios (who, given their characteristically impenetrable, bad-hand-at-Scrabble names, should really be called the papal *unpronuncios*).

Then, came the Irish politicians (10 or 11 TDs and Senators, and several sweaty tons of Mayors and Alderpersons), led by the Minister for Education, Niamh Breathnach. One or two out of this predominantly male delegation thoughtfully brought their wives along, possibly so that they could personally worship later at the shrine of one of the greatest of the Roman saints, Yves Saint Laurent.

The gang was well and truly all here. A total of 18 chartered planes had been required to fly out the Irish pilgrims. There were delegates from every one of the 26 countries in which the Christian Brothers are now based, including war-torn Sudan, their latest conquest.

This was another of those designated Great Days To Be Irish, and nobody wanted to miss out. As if to emphasise the point, there were more RTE people in Rome for the weekend than members of the Swiss Guard.

Among the congregation, you could see Edmund Rice T-shirts, banners, hats, bags and scarves. Though contemporaneous portraits show him as a beady-eyed, weak-chinned individual, today's artists apparently prefer to see him as a dead ringer for Patrick Swayze in his youth and for Spencer Tracy in middle-age.

Meanwhile, up onstage, the Pope struggled to stay awake, his weak voice piping like a thin whistle amid the booming baritones of his concelebrants.

Perhaps taking his cue from Gary Glitter, Pope John Paul had an ambulance waiting by the Basilica throughout the Beatification mass, driver at the ready. After he had recited the midday Angelus, he announced that he would be entering the Gemelli Polyclinic that evening for an operation to remove an inflamed appendix. Nobody, especially not the reporters who informed you of the assertion as fact in doleful tones on TV and radio, believed that this is the whole truth.

As long as there is a single breath left in the Holy Father's body, he's going to use it to tell a lie.

There were an estimated 700 Christian Brothers, over one third of the fraternity's total global population, assembled in Saint Peter's Square. Most wore their collars. Many had name tags and Edmund Rice badges. All of their necks were lassoed with loose nooses of the ubiquitous green scarves.

But those of us who were confined to a C.B.S. during our formative years do not need to see such external plumage to recognise a Christian Brother. We can spot them ten miles away, which happens to be the minimum distance at which we feel comfortable in their company these days.

Most Christian Brothers carry a heavy freight of ego. In many ways, their dogged crusade for the Canonisation of their founder is an extravagant manifestation of nothing but ego. The unconfirmed word is that the campaign to have Edmund declared a saint will ultimately cost them in the region of £2 million.

An order like the Brothers could do a mighty amount of worthwhile service with 2,000,000 lids if they chose to spend it in the real world. It would come in very handy, for instance, if they were interested in paying decent, equitable compensation to some of the people whose lives they have destroyed.

Never in the history of classroom warfare has so much damage been done by so few to so many. I know that corporal punishment is now, technically, outlawed. But the Brothers are still steadfastly refusing to decommission their leathers. Or to even mumble the tritest of apologies for their crimes against humanity.

More ominously, the rumblings in the outgrowth suggest that, in terms of child sexual abuse committed by Christian Brothers, we ain't heard nothin' yet. The Newfoundland outrages are merely the tip of a very nasty iceberg.

Before we go any further then, it would probably be a good idea to scan the Beatification day crowd and shoot a few word-pictures of the folks who have followed in the footsteps of Edmund Ignatius, the legions of the snapped, the cracked and the popped who make up the modern day community of Rice krispies.

Dotted throughout Saint Peter's, there were men with names like Benedict, Augustine, Boniface, Malachy, Regis, Aloysius, Pius and Columba. Back home, in their classrooms, these same guys are known more informally to their pupils as Skippy, Ducky, Fuckiface, Brother Blobby, Waddler, Mutt, Hal (the universal schoolboy diminutive for people with Halitosis), The Incredible Hulk, Pepe Le Pew or, simply, The Bollox.

Dismiss this lack of respect as adolescent ingratitude if you wish, but it is the pupils, past and present, who know the Brothers best and who see them at their worst. Down through the decades, our overwhelming experience has been that the order is crawling with men so maniacally brutish, so irrationally full of cold fury, so profoundly messed up, that they could have made it as Colosseum Gladiators or maybe even have played senior football for County Meath.

There are three principal categories of Christian Brother, all of which were amply represented in The Vatican. There's the really terrifying ones, the Doctor Caligari doppelgängers; their lidded eyes, reptilian features and cindered bodies belying the fact that many of them are still only in their 40s.

Indeed, the smattering of fresh, youthful recruits discernible in Rome could easily out-Caligari their predecessors any night of the week. These guys are often borderline psychotics with the borders being forced further back every minute that passes. They'd have your guts for garters and your lungs for lingerie as soon as they'd look at you. And some of them are extremely fond of garters and lingerie.

At the other extreme, there's the creepy, cellulite-jowled, happy-clappy types who want to be everybody's friend. Colossally pleased with themselves on account of the 'sacrifice' they are making for their faith, they constantly look as though they're about to take a bow. In the presence of a woman, they usually become frisky and flighty, strutting around as though their underpants were The Home Of The Whopper, but secretly terrified in case they actually have to make eye-contact with a female.

In Saint Peter's Square, it was these schmucks who most demonstrably relished every moment of the service. You could see them swaying slightly on their feet during the hymns, a handsomely bound leather missal clutched in one hand and a plastic Irish tricolour in the other. When the congregation was invited to exchange the sign of peace, they left their seats and *cruised,* shaking every hand, left and right, within a half mile radius.

Then, there's the guys who can no longer tell pork from chicken. The ones who live in a permanent fog and whose eyes flood habitually, not from unhappy memories or sudden surges of melancholia but because their catheters are full.

I sat across the aisle from precisely such a befuddled gentleman on the flight to Rome. When he was served his airline lunch, he commenced his repast by eating sugar straight from the sachet.

In almost every C.B.S. in Ireland, there has traditionally been two or three Brothers who continue teaching long after the last bead has fallen off their abacus. Dwindling vocations and the lust to keep control of schools by dint of their sheer presence clearly have something to do with this phenomenon. But, there is also a rather distasteful cult of the bewildered among the Christian Brothers.

One of the myriad booklet biographies of Blessed Edmund circulated to the media tells us that, in his later years, Rice "needed full-time nursing and had few lucid intervals." However, this particular account goes on to state that, during those confused, concluding days, he would frequently cry out, "Praise be to you, O Lord Jesus Christ."

This titbit is adduced as yet further proof of Edmund's peerless sanctity, which merely goes to show that these reprobates will stop at nothing. Poor old Edmund was clearly ga-ga by that stage. The odds are that, five minutes later, he would also frequently cry out, "Joe Lane, Londis, here, to tell you all about our Autumn bargains."

The Vatican is, basically, The Kremlin with better paintings. It is an immense, centralised, secretive, Machiavellian bureaucracy surrounded literally on all sides by 30ft high walls. Because of its dark history and the sheer volume of (mostly ill-gotten) swag harboured within its confines, this 108.5 acre independent republic exerts an irresistible pull on the public imagination. The public, however, are the last people who will ever be allowed a glimpse of the reality beneath the domes.

Purely by chance, on the morning after Pope John Paul had gone into hospital, I found myself wandering aimlessly and unchecked through corridors not all that far from the papal apartments. These are located above the barracks of the Swiss Guard, in a building next to Saint Peter's Gate on the Via del Pellagrino.

Though now augmented by armed security forces, the Swiss Guard are the Pope's private army. They still wear the original blue, yellow and red, 16th century, Medici dynasty outfits designed by Michelangelo.

The Guard's main contemporary purpose is to serve as an elaborate joke at the expense of women and homosexuals who say they find men in uniform attractive. They are experts at remaining stoney-faced no matter what, but that's only because they can't see themselves.

The Swiss Guard evidently don't go in for very much taboo-taboo-tabollicky-boo type roistering during off-duty hours in their quarters because, apparently, the Pontiff's boudoir is *directly above* their bunkhouse. For all we know, *he* may keep them awake at night.

Anyway, on the morning in question, I was genuinely lost, having taken a wrong turn on the way back from a rather desultory museum tour. As I was wearing my Città del Vaticano *press accreditamento,* most of the officials I passed seemed to think I was on some sort of important journalistic business. Which, of course, I was.

Around every corner, there was another member of the Swiss Guard. Perhaps it was because the Pope wasn't actually in the building at the time, but they paid me scant attention.

There was the ever-present possibility that, at any moment, I would be shot dead as a dangerous intruder but my attitude was that I'd cross that *ponti* when I came to it. As it happened, after about half an hour, I found my own way out into the Piazza del Popolo.

To my disappointment, all of the internal doors I had encountered were locked, but I found the corridors and colonnades fascinating in themselves. Despite the omnipresence of what were undoubtedly invaluable vases and tapestries, the place felt like a very large, rural-Irish parochial house.

The carpets and curtains, all in shades of violet and puce, are obviously quality duds but they looked filthy and worn. At the risk of sounding like Lloyd Grossman, the net curtains were little cleaner than motorcycle mud flaps. I also spotted a couple of cobwebs above some of the (naked) light bulbs.

In one murky alcove, off a corridor, there sat a battered, leaking horsehair armchair, and beside it a candle haphazardly stuck in frozen rapids of cold wax. Maybe this is where naughty boys like Brendan Comiskey have to sit when they're summoned to The Vatican to have their wrists slapped.

Best of all though, was the silt of dust on many of the windowsills. I wrote my name and a short message with my forefinger in one such deposit of grime. It will probably be there for the next 600 years. Eventually, it will be incorporated into tours of The Vatican: "This is the miraculous inscription of LIAMFAYWOZHERE. They say that it is a sign from above, that it was writ here by the moving finger of the Almighty Himself. It is one of the great mysteries of the church's third millennium. The secret of what it means is said to be handed in a sealed envelope to each new Pope on his election but it is too shocking to be released to the general public."

The organised tours of The Vatican are essentially worthless. To my philistine eye, all the glories of The Vatican (the art, the architecture, the knick knacks and geegaws) look better in the brochures than they do in real life. The curators and guides, meanwhile, are usually priests, Holy See lickspittles, full of chutzpah and chitchat certainly, but still adamant toers of the party line.

Now, I don't expect the tour guides to dish the dirt on The Pole's collaboration with the CIA, to read aloud juicy extracts from the Vatican register of paedophile bishops or to name the people who murdered Pope John Paul I. But they aren't even remotely upfront about the shenanigans of those Vicars of Christ who are safely dead, buried and condemned to Hellfire. The instinctual lies and revision of history extends to The Vatican's galleries and museums.

The Borgia Popes, the prime pastas of papal debauchery, are completely written out of the story. They are not even alluded to in the official, and very expensive, souvenir Vatican tour book. This despite the fact that the Borgias were the principal patrons of Renaissance artists such as Michelangelo. They were the men responsible for initiating much of the artistic resplendence that The Holy See now holds so dear.

Similarly, the truth about the assertively gay Popes, such as Sixtus IV, is also unashamedly brushed aside. And yet, the walls of The Vatican are ablaze with more images of vigorous homosexual horseplay than you'd find thumbing through a whole year's subscription of *Big Boys, Tool Box* or *Hot Buttered Buns*.

Adjacent to the building which now houses the Gallery Of Modern Religious Art (inaugurated by Pope Paul VI in 1973), there are the Borgia Apartments. These are the chambers in which, among other highlights, Pope Alexander VI (Rodrigo Borgia, 1431 – 1503) held his notorious nightly banquets. Unfortunately, the apartments are not open to visitors.

Pope Alexander VI was the Elvis Presley of his day. Thoroughly depraved, he spent his days eating, drinking and making merry, and dedicated his nights to enjoying himself. He delighted in sponsoring orgies, and was not beyond staging naked entertainments in the churches of Rome.

He was also profoundly corrupt in financial matters, and was a foremost practitioner of simony, the buying and selling of religious favours. For 24,000 gold pieces, he once sold a nobleman Vatican permission to commit incest with his sister.

Fortunately for the sake of posterity, an average evening *chez* Alexander was chronicled by his regular master of ceremonies – Buchard, the Bishop of Austria – who wrote in his *Diary Romanum:*

"50 reputable whores, not common but the kind called courtesans, supped at the Vatican and after supper they danced about with servants and others in that place, first in their clothes and then nude . . . Candelabra with lighted candles were set on the floor and chestnuts were strewn about and the naked courtesans on hands and feet gathered them up in their mouths, wriggling in and out among the candelabra . . . Then, all those present in the hall were carnally treated in public."

With a yell of, "Let the whores be mounted!," the Pope would lead his guests in a frenzied gangbang that invariably lasted well into the next day.

His Holiness would then give prizes to the men who copulated the highest number of times with prostitutes.

For Pope John Paul II, just *knowing* that this kind of carousal once took place under his own roof must be enough to slice his heart to coleslaw. Contemplate his feelings of shame, remorse, sorrow, anger. Why *couldn't* he have been born 500 years earlier? No wonder the old boy looks so shook.

It is one of the great ironies of history that an organisation as malevolent, as furtive, as remorselessly expansionist and as paranoid as The Catholic Church should have its seat of power in the centre of the capital of a country such as Italy.

In Italy, a rule is a proposition. The first national language is the shrug. The Italians are so relaxed, gregarious and carefree, they make the Irish seem like a nation of stockbrokers.

In my hotel room, the English translation of the emergency fire warning read as follows: "The general fire warning is given by a loudly siren. If a warning signal comes working, a fire is in progress. Leave the room soon!" That *soon* is not just a slip of the inter-lingual tongue, it's a perfect summary of an entire people's attitude to life. They genuinely don't give a fuck.

The comparison between the breezy insouciance with which the Roman in the street views his or her political past and the obsessional defensiveness with which the Vatican lackeys guard theirs is instructive. Take the case of Mussolini, Il Duce.

Benito was a formidable nutjob. He was not only clinically bonkers but also in thrall to superstition, a *bona fide* sex beast, and, eventually, a syphlitically brain-damaged megalomaniac. However, all of these pesky details were ignored because he was strong on law 'n' order, and because he had a freakish knack for tapping into the prejudice, vanity and idiocy of the peasantry.

Talk to the old (and some not so old) geezers in the *trattoria* or the *osteria* today and you'll hear Il Duce's name mentioned warmly. They speak about how Italy's economy prospered under his dictatorship.

They'll refer to his legendarily punctual train time-table. They'll insist that while his attempt to remake Rome in his own imperial image ruined much of the city, he was also responsible for some archaeological excavations and building refurbishments that are the envy of the world today. But then, pretty soon, they'll start cackling and chuckling at what an absurd charlatan he was. They'll recount how he had a mortal fear of hunchbacks, cripples and open umbrellas, and how he never ventured anywhere without a small statue of Saint Anthony, the patron saint of healing, in his pocket.

They'll recall the time he forbade any public laughing at the Marx Brothers' film *Duck Soup,* because he believed that such laughter undermined respect for authority. They'll imitate the way he used to flap his arms when he delivered speeches.

They'll really start to chortle when they inform you that, in later life, Mussolini developed a penchant for Irish lucky charms. He painted shamrocks on the hood of his red Alfa-Romeo, for instance, and believed that they protected him from car crashes.

If you (well, I) weren't already too smashed on Chianti to move a muscle let alone a limb, they'd take you to the Piazzale Loreto, a meeting place for destitute prostitutes, where Mussolini and his long-time mistress Clara Petacci were hung by their heels after their executions in April, 1945. The old geezers think that this is especially funny.

Rome is, by its very nature, an extremely tourist-friendly city, until after dark that is, when the friendliness extended towards female tourists in particular grows extraordinarily lukewarm. You see very few women on the streets from 11pm onwards for the simple reason that a stroll through late night Rome is an arduous hike through a menacing obstacle-course of pimps, hookers and aggressive come-ons.

Every few hundred yards, yet another gravel-voiced, middle-aged sleazoid with a cigarette dangling from his lips emerges from the shadows. "Normal bar, normal bar," he drones, crooking his arm and leading the way down a darkened alley towards what you just know is a very *abnormal* bar where drinks will cost the price of a Leonardo Da Vinci original and from where your corpse could well end up in the Tiber before daybreak.

A burly, blonde woman with bullet-hole beauty marks appears at a junction on the Via Veneto (the most famous and widest street in Rome) while I'm walking back to my hotel at around 4am, her fur coat clasped tightly at the neck. Glance at her once and she smiles. Glance a second time and she flicks open the coat, and starts rolling her pallid, suspendered hips in time to some wanton backbeat that only she can hear.

Stare for longer than five seconds and she's down on her knees, thrusting her left middle finger in and out of her mouth and sucking it like it was a particularly delicious swizzle stick. In retrospect, I'm sure she was trying to tell me something but, for the life of me, I couldn't grasp what it was. I really will have to learn some Italian before I go back.

On the day before the Beatification, the 40-plus Irish media contingent visiting Rome were invited to a press conference and lunch at a villa on the outskirts of Rome known as the Generalate de Fratelli Cristiani, the world headquarters of the Christian Brothers since 1967.

It is some gaff. Reposing amid landscaped splendour atop a forested hillside, the site of the Generalate affords a remarkable, panoramic view of Rome. The multi-winged building (which incorporates offices, Christian Brothers training facilities and accommodation quarters) is an enormous shrine to several competing schools of ornate architecture, its roof constructed from what looks like a variety of giant, coffee-coloured U-bends.

The grounds are an Irish head teacher's wildest fantasy. A lush quilt of impeccably-tended playing fields, fringed with pathways, running tracks, and park benches, and cross-stitched with over 2,000 strapping trees. Next time you hear Christian Brothers expounding on what a humble organisation they are, mention the words 'Via della Maglianella' (the address of the Generalate), and watch them gag on their own special pleading.

Our host was Brother Big, the Superior General of the global congregation. His name is Brother Edmund Garvey, an authoritarian man in his 50s with bat's wing eyebrows and a quiff of sleek black hair. Most of the other Brothers at the Generalate are either Australian or from Europe, though several Irish pairs of hands were drafted in for the weekend that was in it.

The buffet was as refined as you'd expect, with plenty of caviar and champagne. As I munched and swilled and rambled about, I was struck by how flagrantly camp many of the foreign brothers were. There were plenty of *louche* cravats, cigarette-holders, dayglo shirts, permed hair-dos, open-toed Roman sandals and comfortable slacks on view. There was much talk about wine and opera and clothes, all set against a constant sorority gala of whispers and giggling.

There was certainly none of the taciturn desperation for manliness-at-all-times that has been the traditional hallmark of Christian Brothers in Ireland. Some of these guys were, to paraphrase *Blackadder,* as effeminate as Effeminate Jacqueline McEffeminate, Professor of Effeminacy at Queen's University.

One man in particular took the cake. He wasn't a Christian Brother as such but worked closely with the Generalate, especially on matters relating to travel arrangements. "Delighted to meet you, I'm Noel of Rome," he proclaimed, extending a heavily bejewelled hand of greeting in my direction.

"Eh, hiya. I'm Liam of Trim," I replied.

Noel of Rome (via Waterford) was a hoot, very theatrical but eminently knowledgeable about all things Roman. He was appalled by the scruffiness of the Irish hacks, and offered to bring some of us shopping "for some real garb" later in the day. He took a particular shine to a guy from Radio Limerick for whom he promised to "buy shoes in the Latin quarter, and then cook a delicious meal."

The 'press conference' was a farce. The spin para-medics from Fleishmann-Hillard Saunders, the Christian Brothers' personal PR firm, were on emergency stand-by in case of accidents, but their services were not required. The journalists did a more than adequate job of policing themselves. There were no embarrassing questions from the floor, no references to the scandals in which Christian Brothers have been involved in a variety of countries, no whiff of controversy whatsoever.

Edmund Garvey simply read out the press release reiterating how fab Edmund Rice was and what swell guys the Brothers are, and his adoring audience (because that's what we had become) took notes, occasionally interrupting his flow of thought to pose incisive queries the tone and content of which basically amounted to, 'Are there two *l*'s in swell?'. This, apparently, is how it usually goes at the coalface of religious correspondence.

Outside on planet Earth, however, the Christian Brothers are now an organisation so deep in the crapper that only a miracle could save them. For our convenience, he was wheeled out too; the miracle man, Kevin Ellison, whose incredible claim to have been brought back from beyond the threshold of death's door by an Edmund Rice relic provided the final piece in the Beatification campaign jigsaw.

Ellison is a 39-year-old father of three from Newry, who works as a Health and Safety Officer with Armagh County Council. When he was 19, he was stricken with a volvulus (spontaneous twisting and strangulation) of the bowel which had lacerated itself. In hospital, after the performance of a laparotomy (abdominal surgery), his condition deteriorated alarmingly. A subsequent operation found that his bowel had turned to "a mass of gangrenous material with no viable bowel in sight."

Ellison was expected to die within 48 hours. As he tells it, he was given a relic containing a minute fragment of Edmund Rice's bone by a family friend, a Brother Laserian O'Donnell. Having prayed with this relic, Ellison says he made a full recovery, to the astonishment of his doctors.

One doctor in particular took an X-ray of Ellison and allegedly found that he has only three feet of viable bowel, a fraction of what is normally thought necessary to sustain life. Ellison declines to name this doctor. Edmund Garvey also refused point blank to provide this name or the names of any of the doctors who had treated Ellison in Newry and in Belfast.

Ellison's was a singularly unimpressive testimony. He spoke as if by rote and was exceptionally defensive when, eh, interrogated by the press corps. "How soon after you started to pray with the relic, did you feel a sense of peace?" probed Joe Power, religious affairs correspondent of the *Irish Independent*. "Has your devotion to Edmund Rice continued?" cross-examined that fearless searcher for truth, Clem Loscher, here on behalf of something called *The Irish Family Newspaper*.

After the press conference, one journalist, Bernard Phelan of *The Star*, had the temerity to express his dissatisfaction with the so-called medical evidence. As Phelan was preparing to leave, he was informed by the head of the PR delegation, Michael Parker, that he alone would be given an opportunity to peruse the Brothers' book of documents relating to the case and the sworn statements by witnesses, but only for a couple of minutes and without taking any notes.

In the corridor, Edmund Garvey handed Phelan an A-4 sized, hard-bound, red-covered book containing 280 pages of tightly-typed text. This was, ostensibly, the Brothers' only copy of the Ellison file, the other three existing copies having been salted away in The Vatican.

Phelan was not permitted to read the file in private or even while sitting down but had to content himself with lying against a radiator in the corridor while Edmund Garvey stood over him. Phelan had barely time to flick through it once when it was taken back from him by Garvey who said sharply, "I think you've had that book for long enough now and you really shouldn't have had it all."

This is what is known, in Christian Brothers terms, as transparency.

When in Rome, do as the Oirish do. This was clearly the motto of the backroom perpetrators of the Edmund Rice weekend. The highlight of the Sunday festivities was "The Hooley In The Hall." A fucking *céilí*.

Here we were in one of the most historic, diverse, lively and culturally rich cities on the planet and the infernal Paddies decide to spend a whole afternoon out of their brief sojourn leppin' around to naff diddley aye, and bellowing along to the kind of barbarous come-all-ye's which would have provided the perfect mood music for the *vomitoria* of ancient Rome. I suppose I should be grateful that they didn't bring Liam O'Murchú along to act as *fear an tí*.

The Hall in which we were to Hooley was the Fiera di Roma, an enormous suburban exhibition centre. It is, essentially, a hangar, as unsightly, vast and drafty as Silvio Berlusconi's ego. Inside were a couple of thousand Brothers, their family members, friends and pupils as well as assorted other Rice heads of indeterminate origin.

The ambience in the Hall was one of grim determination to have fun at all costs. The fun-having was intense. The competition among the fun-havers fierce. Grown adults, many in their twilight or at least drivetime years, vaulted around the place clapping, grinning, gurgling, shrieking and generally exhibiting all the major symptoms of fun, except pleasure.

It is truly astounding how a chummy gathering of the scrubbed-faced, cow's-licked, devoutly pious attempting to whoop it up in a wholesome manner is a more nauseating sight than one you will ever see in any cat house, drug den, speakeasy or desperado's lair. Personally, I blame the balloons.

There is surely no more potent symbol of bogus joviality than the balloon, especially the pink balloon. Balloons are the reason that God gave us the pin. They are not multi-coloured bags of festive atmosphere, they are sacks of stale, tepid air. They are an aid to high jinx only in the minds of people who use terms such as *high jinx*.

The Fiera di Roma was bursting at the seams with balloons, especially pink balloons. In my experience of revelry, which is considerable, a party held in a room bedecked with small, swollen, rubber pouches is either a party for five year olds or a party hosted by medical students who have spent all afternoon inflating condoms. Neither of these fall into the category of soiree at which the sane among us want to be seen.

At least half the guests were perched in the rows upon rows of single-seater schooldesks facing stageward. Neatly arrayed before them were the packed lunches that were parcelled out on entry to the Hall, comprising salad baps, cartons of fruit juice and sticky jam tarts.

Mumsy, matronly women in cardigans and sensible shoes fussed about in their tiny desks and tried to get comfy. From their expressions of agony, it was clear that cramp had already set in, but they weren't going to let a little thing like that hinder their enjoyment.

The stage was cleverly located directly below a giant industrial fan which devoured at least 65% of the volume of each performers' offering, and drowned out a further 25%. Lamentably, 65% + 25% only comes to 90%.

The musical presentations were similar to what you'd hear during senior citizens' days on *Live At 3*, but not as raucous or erotically-charged. The bands and choirs were all Irish, their sets and patters all too Irish.

"Okay, everybody stand up, and repeat after me," exhorted one band leader, his Edmund Rice scarf wittily tied in an elaborate reef knot around his left arm. "HIGH HO DIDDLEY O! That's the chorus of the next song. Every time we get to it, I'll wave and you stand up and sing out loud. HIGH HO DIDDLEY O!"

The chorus duly arrived. A mere third of the crowd sprang to their feet. "High Ho Diddley O!" they chirped unconvincingly.

"It's okay if you don't feel like getting up," counselled the band leader. "Hold hands with the person next to you instead, but do sing along. HIGH HO DIDDLEY O!"

This time, they all joined in with gusto: "HIGH HO DIDDLEY O!"

"Okay, now you have it!" responded the band leader. "Here we go! Brother Edmund Rice keepin' us on the move! HIGH HO DIDDLEY O!"

It was time to get the high ho diddley fuck away. I went next door to a somewhat smaller but nonetheless cavernous shed where the Brothers were staging their youth event, aimed at the dozens of schoolchildren and adolescents among the Edmund Rice family. It was dubbed the "Rice Rave."

This I had to see. The prospect of the Christian Brothers meeting the Chemical Brothers was intriguing. Had they secretly decided to honour the life of Blessed Ed by encouraging their students to neck some commemorative tabs of blessed E? Was I about to witness the birth of a whole new genre? Vatican Trance, for instance? Or, Holy See Hop?

Well, not exactly. Aesthetic monstrosities invariably ensue when musty sorts like the Christian Brothers endeavour to get all trendy and hip to the modern groove, and this was to be no exception. Conclusive proof that we were headed for yet another cultural mutation could be found on the official itinerary of events in which the Rice Rave was described as being especially for "heavy metal lovers."

I left after five minutes, my hastily scribbled notes reading: "Barely six people here . . . kids playing 'Purple Haze' . . . badly . . . Brothers with fingers in their ears . . . Aaaaargh!!!"

By early evening, back inside the main hangar, The Hooley In The Hall was hitting warp drive. The call-and-response audience participation routine had been abandoned in favour of no-holds-barred Hooley-ganism. Onstage, an accordion-happy combo of Christian Brothers belted out such classic masterpieces of understatement as 'An Puc Ar Buile' and 'Come Down The Mountain, Katie Daly'. This ain't no party, this ain't no disco, this ain't no fooling around. But they sure as Hell gave me the C. B. Jeebies.

The older Brothers went absolutely apeshit when they hit the dance-floor. They jigged, they reeled, they hornpiped, they savoured the humours of Bandon, they wandered through the whinny hills of Leitrim, they rustled the mason's apron, they brought down the walls of Limerick and they re-built them again.

Most of these guys acted and moved like men who had spent the past 20 years chained to radiators in gloomy monastery attics. Their unbridled excitement at being free again was palpable, and it even had its own sound. It went, "Yeeooow!" 30 seconds later, it would go, "Yeeooow!" once more. Their dander was up and there was no stopping them now.

There was an experimental bearing to their steps and gestures. They'd lift a knee chest high just to see what it felt like, and then they'd lift it higher and wiggle it about a bit. While they danced, emotions shifted across their faces like wind on water; delight, joy, exhilaration, bliss, rapture, chronic craziness.

I moved to the far side of the Hall. Here, there was a waist-level, white-clothed table which ran the full length of a gable wall. It was the Edmund Rice Memorabilia stand, purveying not only desirable but useful merchandise such as Edmund Rice key rings, rosary cases, relic medals, relic cases, medal clips, picture frames (both silver and magnetic) and stickers (both white and transparent). Stills of the Beatification mass we had endured only hours before were already on sale at 7000 Lire (£3 approx.) a shot.

People were snapping up this tat in bulk, literally taking possession of box-loads of the stuff. Order forms on which the quantities of each item required could be indicated were distributed among the horde of customers. Fistfuls of Lire were being handed over. As cash trays overflowed, they were upended, with typical Italian nonchalance, into a master heap on a cankered woodwork bench behind the table.

Every half hour or so, a silver-templed Brother with a pugnacious jaw would sweep part of this Carrauntoohil of currency into a leather satchel and take it to a van outside. He whistled while he worked.

ALSO AVAILABLE FROM HOT PRESS BOOKS

U2: THREE CHORDS AND THE TRUTH
Edited by Niall Stokes
Critical, entertaining, comprehensive and revealing, *U2: Three Chords And The Truth* never misses a beat as it brings you, in words and pictures, a complete portrait of U2 in the process of becoming a legend.
Price: £8.95

THEY ARE OF IRELAND
by Declan Lynch
They Are Of Ireland is a hilarious who's who of famous Irish characters – and chancers – from the worlds of politics, sport, religion, the Arts, entertainment and the media. Written by Declan Lynch, one of the major new Irish literary talents of the '90s, this is one of those rare events – a book of comic writing that actually makes you laugh out loud.
Price: £7.99

MY BOY: THE PHILIP LYNOTT STORY
by Philomena Lynott (with Jackie Hayden)
The story of Philip Lynott as told by the woman who brought him into the world and who was at his side during the final days of his life, *My Boy* is not only an intimate and revealing portrait of an Irish rock legend, but an immensely moving account of a mother's devotion to her beloved son through the good times and the bad. A No.1 best-seller.
Price: £7.99

U2: Three Chords And The Truth, They Are Of Ireland and *My Boy: The Philip Lynott Story* are available from Hot Press, 13 Trinity St., Dublin 2. Trade enquiries Tel: (01) 6795077 or Fax: (01) 6795097. Mail order, send cheques/POs or credit card details for £8.95 *(U2)* and £7.99 *(They Are Of Ireland* and *My Boy)*, incl. p&p, to the above address.